Plays in Time

Plays in Time
The Beekeeper's Daughter
Prophecy
Another Life
Extreme Whether

By Karen Malpede

With commentaries by Marvin Carlson, Christen Clifford, Rebecca Gordon,
Karen Malpede, Cindy Rosenthal, Najla Said and Alexander M. Schlutz
Production Photographs by Beatriz Tiche Schiller and Ari Mintz

intellect Bristol, UK / Chicago, USA

First published in the UK in 2017 by
Intellect, The Mill, Parnall Road, Fishponds, Bristol, BS16 3JG, UK

First published in the USA in 2017 by
Intellect, The University of Chicago Press, 1427 E. 60th Street,
Chicago, IL 60637, USA

A catalogue record for this book is available from the
British Library.

Series: Playtext
Series editor: Patrick Duggan
Series ISSN: 1754-0933
Electronic ISSN: 1754-0941

Copy-editor: MPS Technologies
Cover designer: Luba Lukova
Production manager: Katie Evans
Typesetting: Contentra Technologies

Print ISBN: 978-1-78320-815-9
ePDF ISBN: 978-1-78320-816-6
ePUB ISBN: 978-1-78320-889-0

Printed and bound by Bell & Bain, UK

For, and with, George

Contents

Acknowledgments

Special thanks to The Raymond & Irene Wilborn Charitable Foundation, The Puffin Foundation, Henning Hoesch, the late Saul Reichbach and Julie Rizzoto for sustained support; to Patrick Duggan, series editor, and Katie Evans, production editor, Intellect Press; David Lynn and the Kenyon Review for rescuing *Another Life* and for providing a home for my writing; Erika Duncan and Lise Weil for their notes on my introduction; and to Erika, again, and Martha Bragin, Ynestra King and Jan Clausen for conversations over years.

Foreword

Marvin Carlson

The British theater has had the good fortune of possessing a strong tradition of politically-engaged drama all through the past half century, a half century when the creation of such theater has never been more urgently needed. Unfortunately, the United States, despite its significant (and often negative) contribution to many of the major political events all over the globe during this half century, has developed no comparable tradition, and only a handful of important dramatists seriously concerned with global and national political issues. Prominent among these has been Karen Malpede, four of whose powerful works are presented in the present collection.

The first of these, *The Beekeeper's Daughter,* was first produced in Italy at the Dionysia Festival of World Drama in 1994, the year before the bloody and prolonged Bosnian War finally came to an end, and it is set in 1993 at the height of that conflict. Although the shadow of Bosnia hovers over the action, this is not, strictly speaking, a 'war play,' but is set on an idyllic Adriatic island only three hundred miles from the conflict whose inhabitants Robert, his beekeeping sister Sybil and his bisexual lover Jamie seem quite oblivious of that horror until Robert's daughter Rachel, a human rights worker, arrives seeking asylum for Admira, one of the thousands of women degraded and raped in the ongoing war.

Their arrival forces all of the characters to confront their largely repressed and often conflicted feelings about their sexuality, their present and past relationships, and their convictions and assumptions about male and female roles, violence and passion. As befits a work set on an island in the classic Adriatic, the play moves easily between contemporary and classic reference, weaving a rich poetic tapestry of human relationships and of negotiations with the extremes of human love and hate. Today, two decades later, with not only the Adriatic but the entire European continent attempting to deal with the political, social and psychological challenges of countless abused and damaged Muslim women like Admira, the play strikes a disturbingly contemporary note.

Prophecy, the next play in the collection, comes from more than a decade later, premiered in London in 2008 and in New York in 2010. Between the two plays came the almost unimaginable events of 9/11 and the resulting plunging of American society into an ongoing paranoia, justifying almost continuous foreign military engagements. Here none of the play's characters enjoy even an illusory isolation from the corrupting and corrosive powers of war. It is woven into the most intimate parts of their lives, poisoning love relationships, aborting unborn children, and placing almost unbearable burdens of memory and responsibility on those who do somehow survive. The ghosts that hover over the play are predominantly those of the Vietnam War, which left a mark on an entire generation, killing many and leading others to kill or to participate in actions that left them with permanent wounds, some physical and others mental. As in *The Beekeeper's Daughter,* the spirit of Greek tragedy also hangs over the play, reminding us of the unexorcised spirits of aggression and cruelty that were already a subject of fear and fascination in classic times. Even more directly this play utilizes the trope of the theater and the power of the theater to break through the wall of denial that both individuals and societies must erect to protect themselves from confronting the evils they commit. In the words of the seer Tiresias in *Antigone,* the young protagonist finds both release and unbearable pain for what he has done, and his experience and self-confrontation spins out into the lives of all those who surround him, each of whom suffers in one way or another from the web of fear, suspicion and destruction woven about them by a society committed to violence and conflict.

Like the victims of wartime trauma, the married couple at the center of the play, Alan and Sarah, have flashbacks to fateful moments in their relationship, to the late 1960s, when protests at home and a brutal escalating conflict abroad placed almost intolerable burdens and inhuman choices upon young Americans like Sarah and her lover Lukas, a protester who would later die from mortal wounds received in Vietnam, and to 1982 when Hala, the young woman with whom Alan has become infatuated, returns to her native Lebanon and to the conflicts then raging in that country. In 2006 when the main action of the play occurs, the personal and political conflicts and betrayals of four decades come back to exact their toll, both psychic and physical. The illegitimate child of Hala and Alan returns from Lebanon, a potential suicide bomber and a literal representation of the American exportation of violence and injustice coming back in the form of new threats. Echoes of the Greek warnings about the connection between hubris and suffering reverberate through the play, with the dark words of the seer Tiresias and the troubled chorus in *Antigone* serving as powerful and ominous intertexts. The play is by no means totally pessimistic, but like the Greek tragedies it echoes, it looks unflinchingly at the terrible price that must be paid for human arrogance and intolerance. The final lines come as close in mood and tonality to those tragedies as anything I know in the contemporary theater. Beginning with a citation from the famous conflicted ode to man in *Antigone,* the speech moves to a contemporary context: 'We have all done this thing. Not one / Young man with a gun / or a bomb strapped to a chest. / These things are in the hands of men.' Sorrow and tears are a proper response to this situation, but through the tears there is a hint of something better than can be anticipated: 'Let / Mourning come, dawn will break' (in the theater, of course, the second word can be heard as either 'mourning' or 'morning' picking up an earlier exchange about the coming of morning). The words not only sum up the overall tone of the play, but gain particular resonance from their echoing the chorus's repeated appeal in *Agamememnon,* an appeal central to Greek tragedy: 'Cry sorrow, sorrow, but let good prevail.'

Another Life, created in 2011, deals directly with the most traumatic event in the United States in the early twenty-first century, the attack on the World Trade Center on September 11, 2001. The play is remarkable among recent American drama on several accounts, First, it is one of the very few plays yet created in the United States that deals directly either with the events of that day or with the many abuses of civil and human rights that were carried out in reaction to it, most notoriously the system of secret prisons for torture encouraged, supported, and in many cases staffed by United States agents around the world. Although both subjects have been widely treated on European stages, few American dramatists have been willing to confront them, partly one might imagine, due to the tradition already mentioned of avoiding directly political drama on the modern mainstream American stage, and, more disturbingly, out of a desire on the part of many Americans, encouraged by political leaders all the way up to President Barack Obama, to put such matters behind them and look forward to a more moral future. One is unhappily reminded of the post-war years in Germany, when a similar attempt to forget the Nazi period was widespread, a willful denial and blindness that has since been happily in large part overcome. Whether America is ever able to forget its often deplorable actions, nationally and internationally, in the wake of 9/11 remains to be seen, but so far attempts to deal with those actions, as Malpede has done, have been few indeed, either in the American theater or on the American political stage.

In addition to its political boldness, the play also challenges the traditional presentational style of the American stage. Both *The Beekeeper's Daughter* and *Prophecy,* despite their echoes of Greek tragedy, can be considered within the general mode of realism, often with heightened or symbolic elements, that characterizes much of the more ambitious work of this national tradition. *Another Life* moves us into another dramatic realm, closer perhaps to a modern allegorical drama or the dream/nightmare plays of late Strindberg, but with a political rather than a psychological underpinning. It also moves from figures suffering from, and in some measure consciously or unconsciously contributing to, the global system of fear, injustice and inhumanity that seems impossible today to escape, even on the most idyllic Greek island. Here we move to the center of this cruel and inhuman system, to focus on a figure who, if not the creator of the system, represents the desires and the drives that power it. This monstrous figure Handel stands at the center of the play like a dark star around which the others revolve and all of whom he seeks to dominate, humiliate and crush. It is that evil power, in its personal, national and international operations, that the play darkly demonstrates. Handel, in some respects an all-too-familiar example of contemporary humanity, has at the same time distanced himself physically and emotionally from the rest of humanity, establishing a hermetic world around himself in which he can torture, dominate and enslave with impunity. The isolation of this world and its separation from humanity at large is powerfully suggested from the very opening monologue, which shows this self-centered monster speaking his own language, its distortions suggesting linguistically the distortions of his own humanity. This strange self-referential and quasi-human speech is in certain ways reminiscent of the monstrous Skriker, in Caryl Churchill's play of that same name. Her linguistic distortions are distinctly different from those of Handel, but in both cases they suggest an uncanny, inhuman mode of thought that befits these nightmarish creatures who have made their way so disruptively into contemporary society.

Despite this intense self-occupation, or indeed as one of the manifestations of it, Handel must reach outside of himself to find others upon which he may feed, like the spider in the center of a gigantic web. In the tradition of allegory, but with distinct human touches, Malpede selects Handel's prey with the clear intention of suggesting how his devastating influence has circled the globe and contributed to most of the darkest moments in modern international history. His trophy wife Tess is from Chechnya, the continuing festering wound in the Russian imaginary as Iraq and Afghanistan have become in the American, and creating a nexus in those ongoing struggles. Lucia, Handel's adopted daughter, is from mysterious and still-resistant China. She is most closely emotionally connected with a union organizer whom Handel sees as representing everything that seeks to restrict his power, but who ironically appears in this play only as a ghost, a victim of the terrorist attacks on the World Trade Center, attacks clearly brought about by Handel's overweening lust for power.

Perhaps the most tragic figure in the play is Abdul, an Egyptian cab driver who suffers most grievously from Handel's desire for power. Entering the play as an innocent, even noble figure unselfishly attempting to help others, he is drawn into Handel's web and eventually becomes essentially an abused slave. In the process we see him tortured in one of Handel' s black sites, under the supervision of one of Handel's agent/minions, significantly a half-Syrian, half-US interrogator. One of the most powerful and most appalling elements of the play is its graphic descriptions of the interrogations in such black sites, where Malpede leaves the rather abstract and allegorical self-musings of Handel to present material drawn directly from real-life reports of these atrocities.

Extreme Whether, Malpede's most recent work (as of this writing), continues to address the most important issues of our time, precisely the sort of topic that despite or perhaps because of its enormous political and social ramifications, remains surprisingly absent from the dramatic concerns of the vast majority of United States playwrights. With this work, Malpede seems to be moving into an area of concern different from that of the other plays in this collection, but the slightest reflection will reveal that this is not so. Malpede's works make clear the inter-relatedness of most of the world's most pressing problems – profound economic inequality, racial and ethnic injustice, incessant wars and, most threatening and pressing of all, the steady deterioration of our natural environment, with the threat of the extinction of ourselves and most of our fellow inhabitants of this suffering planet. The actions of a figure like Handel in *Another Life* underlie the crises in *Extreme Whether,* just as the actions of Frank in *Extreme Whether* enable the depredations of the Handels of this world.

In her introductory notes to this play, Malpede notes that it juxtaposes the styles of what might be called psychological realism and magical realism, and that through 'juxtaposition of lyric and realistic modes, I try to create a poetry of the theater that frees the imagination and allows us quite literally to come to our senses.' Although that description provides an excellent way into this powerful play, it also suggests a quality of each of these four works, all of which, in varying degrees, blend the lyric and the realistic modes to create a poetry of the theater that is not only uplifting spiritually but inspiring politically. Malpede ingeniously sums up this double perspective in her search for a theater that 'frees the imagination and allows us quite literally to come to our senses.' Indeed, quite literally that is its aim, but also quite figuratively, since it seeks to bring us to our senses intellectually, morally and socially, it seeks to do that, as all great theater does, by deeply involving us sensually as well.

An introduction to these four pieces would be incomplete without an acknowledgment of at least some of the artists who have worked closely with Malpede over the years and who have become closely associated with her contributions both artistically and politically. Chief among these is George Bartenieff, who co-founded with Karen Malpede and the late Lee Negran Theater Three Collaborative in 1995 to produce Malpede's *The Beekeeper's Daughter*. All three had distinguished individual theater careers before that time, but since 1995 Malpede and Bartenieff have continued to work together on the highly regarded Theater Three Collaborative, which in addition to Malpede's own work has created Festivals of Conscience and talks and talkbacks with public intellectuals, activists and specialists in the areas of controversy explored by individual plays.

Another important theater artist whose career, especially in recent years, has been often intertwined with Malpede's is the actress Kathleen Chalfant, for whom Malpede wrote the central role of Sarah (Bartenieff played her husband, Alan). Although Chalfant has not been so consistently connected artistically to Malpede as has Bartenieff, they have often been connected during the past two decades by a mutual commitment to the major social and political issues of the time, including resistance to the nation's ongoing militarism, the penal system, economic inequality and, more recently, climate change. Indeed it would be difficult to name any more prominent socially engaged artists in the New York theater today than Malpede, Bartenieff and Chalfant. The four plays in this collection indicate clearly how movingly and theatrically effectively Malpede, the only playwright in this trio, continues to carry out this important and regrettably still rather lonely mission within the New York theater community. In a generally rather conservative and traditional theater scene, her work and that of her actors and other co-workers continue to provide a very special and extremely important voice.

The Drama of the Thinking Heart

Karen Malpede

Increasingly, I think of my theater as post-tragic, written in the most dangerous times known to sentient creatures, when the tragic reversal from good fortune to bad is perhaps already the inescapable trajectory. Written on the precipice of climate and perhaps also nuclear disaster; written with the intent of pulling us away from blind obedience to this ominous fate. Written to allow a glimmer of clear sight in which we grasp the inevitability of the crisis even as we act to shake it off.

As a playwright, I am keenly aware of the ritual source of ancient drama. Gilbert Murray, the great classicist, relates a 'tale from Pausanias, that when Aeschylus, as a child, was put in a field to watch the grapes and fell asleep, Dionysus appeared to him and commanded him to write tragedy. When he woke up he tried and found it quite easy' (1940: 147). From which we may conclude not that writing tragedy is simple, but that there is an inviolable connection between nature and creativity, between human nature and *biophilia*, our love of World (Wilson 1986).[1] Wishing to retain connection to that same earth-centered impetus, I begin by asking, what sorts of actions can I put on stage that might allow contemporary people to engage in experiences that would help us face our dangerous reality? How might the intensity of the ritual passage be reinvented so that modern participants are brought to conscious reassessment of our role as protectors of the web of life?[2]

In the back-and-forth exchanges between characters facing the extremes of modernity, an intensity of thought and feeling might be reached that allows expulsion from the collective mind of wearying numbness, a breaking-through to a vision, momentary, fragmentary, nevertheless real and embodied, of a dance of life, a returned embrace – a connectedness to others and to natural forces. This, then, is an imagistic, ritual language theater whose purpose is to address the violence of the now and to bond us more securely to the endless round of life.

The Beekeeper's Daughter written and performed during the Bosnian war, 1993–95, was revived in a June 2016 production in recognition of the plight of current refugees. The play is structured as a ritual in which the celebrants (here I include the author/director, actor/characters and audience) enter more deeply into the reaches of their unconscious minds as the story progresses scene by scene into wilder nature, moving from the House, to the Beehives, deep into the Forest and finally to a cliff at the edge of a stormy Sea. In this play, the antagonist is traumatic memory; each character has their own. Robert and his daughter, Rachel, bear separate memories of the suicide of Dora, his wife, her mother; Sybil of her role in her own daughter's death and Admira of her imprisonment with multiple rapes and impregnation. Only Jamie, the Dionysian bisexual tempter/liberator of them all, is free of a traumatic past; his disruptive presence releases the creative force. The play is a paean to creativity as the antidote to violence. Its central character, Robert Blaze, was inspired by two passionate creators – Robert Graves and my friend, Julian Beck – and the character's speeches articulate the sentiments, sometimes the actual words, of both.[3]

Fear of refugees is a fire being stoked across the world, but what is really at stake here is not so much fear of the other as fear of what openness to the suffering of others will awaken within the self. *The Beekeeper's Daughter* is built from the concerns of the ecofeminist movement of the 1980s and 1990s in which I was deeply involved; reviving it in 2016, it felt contemporary. I wanted a play in which nature, tamed and wild, stood for the unconscious, driven by a language that cut through gender roles, showed men as nurturers of infants and explored the possibilities of healing the self by reaching out to others.[4]

Extreme Whether (2014) is largely an *agon*, a verbal contest or debate, between two climate scientists and two representatives of the fossil fuel industry. Theirs is a battle between the accretion of terrifying knowledge, as the scientists measure the extent of the quickly melting polar ice and try to predict the climate system's tipping points, and the extractive representatives' amassing of ever more money and power. As is usual in drama, the chief antagonists are related by bonds of blood; in this case, they are fraternal twins, as am I, and each twin's need to prove oneself separate and distinct gives added force to their battles over scientific truth, fracking and the family land. Writing this play about the censorship of science during the Bush Administration, I had no idea that now, in 2017, denial of science was going to become an ever-more securely entrenched and potentially lethal part of the US political system.

But the verbal dueling is interrupted and counterbalanced in ritual ways – just as the agon sections in a Greek tragedy periodically give way to contemplative choral odes or charged speeches of the messengers or prophets. The forward movement of the play, its bitter conflict of truth versus profit, is halted periodically by collective moments of *biophilia*, moments in which the beauty of nature asserts itself so powerfully that the characters have no choice but to suspend conflict in order to wonder at their love of world.

The aged steward of the inherited estate whom everyone calls Uncle and the young self-defined intersex Annie serve as oracular voices, one of the past, the other for the future; it is they who call the hyper-rational, intellectual adults out into the natural world. And it is Annie who gives voice to the voiceless creatures, all of whom are dependent upon human choices now. *Extreme Whether* ends with an epilogue in which the choice confronting the human race is starkly posed. Uncle reappears from the netherworld (as a god might do at the end of a Greek tragedy) to offer, not a curse, but an inclusive vision of biological life ever-lasting here for the grasping.

Between these two plays – both reliant upon connection to the natural world – come the plays about the wars. After *Beekeeper*, in despair, I had given up writing original drama, and turned to short fiction, much of it based on interviews I'd done with close survivors of the September 11, 2001 attacks in New York City, a stage adaptation with George Bartenieff of the Holocaust diaries of Victor Klemperer, *I Will Bear Witness*,[5] a public participatory ritual, a docu-drama and the essay. But the crisis of the invasion of Iraq roused my wish to be heard in a dialogue of my own making and I returned to dramatic fiction. I began a play, *Prophecy*, loosely based on my earlier short story of the same name,[6] which would expand to bear echoes of the Sarah, Abraham, Hagar monotheistic story of origin. I was writing with actors in mind, George Bartenieff, of course, but also Kathleen Chalfant and Najla Said. I had met the two women when they came to read names in our *Iraq: Naming the Dead* ritual in the seventeenth-century graveyard of St. Mark's Church-in-the-Bowery in the East Village during the Republican Convention of 2004, and then they joined the cast of the docu-drama I put together that marked the second anniversary of the invasion, *Iraq: Speaking of War.*[7]

In the United States, more, perhaps, than in the United Kingdom, we have blinded and numbed ourselves to our own crimes, much to the detriment of our common life. It is precisely here that theater has a role to play, where there has been no justice there might yet be drama that bears witness to the manifold costs of doing war and torture.

Those whose young adult years (university years in my case on two of the most radical US campuses[8]) were marked by the war in Vietnam, with friends drafted and dead (or fleeing the draft), body counts, images of children burnt by napalm and by young people shot on college campuses, most readily grasped the horrors that would inevitably follow the invasion of Iraq. Just as we had opposed the war in Vietnam, we opposed Gulf War I and, obviously, the full-scale illegal invasion of Iraq when it came in 2003.[9]

A marriage haunted by memories of Vietnam sits at the center of *Prophecy*. Past and present collide when the couple's lives are intruded upon by two young people, his half-Muslim, half-Jewish daughter from an extra-marital affair and her acting student, an Iraq war veteran, both of whom are victims of current wars in the Middle East.

In 2006, as I was writing *Prophecy* during a retreat in Macedonia, Najla Said was being evacuated from the bombing of Beirut, and sending emails out. The suicide rate of Iraq war veterans was on the rise, though largely unremarked upon at that time. In *Prophecy*, the young will suffer most. The absolution craved by the young man who has killed cannot come from the aggrieved young woman from the Middle East.

Another Life began by reading Beckett. The layered language of *All that Fall* intrigued and I began a long monologue – the words of the private contractor and mogul Handel. But my previous work co-adapting the diaries of Victor Klemperer was even more influential. Klemperer, a philologist, wrote about the corruption of language under fascism. We were victims of a similar descent from reason as the nation 'ramped up' for 'shock and awe.'

Handel's story is invented but it shows what happened to the population as the terrible events of September 11 unleashed a vindictive and terrified urge for revenge from which the United States and the world have yet to recover. The mercenary empire Handel founds, Deepwater, is modeled on Eric Prince's Blackwater. George Bartenieff, who created the role, took physical cues from Rupert Murdoch, Dick Cheney and Omar Gaddafi. Lately, Handel's increasingly unhinged bellicosity brings to mind Donald Trump.

Handel, who profits off of torture, is the most purely immoral character I've concocted – though Dean Charles Muffler in *Prophecy* must be a close second causing almost directly the death of Lukas in Vietnam and the suicide of Iraq-war veteran, Jeremy. Rage at war was a dominant driver of both plays, yet *Prophecy* is full of domestic humor, between husband and wife, teacher and students, father and daughter, and *Another Life* is as close to satirical comedy as anything I've written. There is more humor in each of these four plays than their topics might suggest, a discovery that often surprises actors and audiences – who need to become nimble to adapt to the quick back-and-forth whip of the comic cutting through.

The four plays in this volume are linked by being born from contemporary crises, hence *Plays in Time*. And in each of these crises, language has been used by power to distort and debase: stirring up ethnic hatreds and fears, telling lies about so-called 'intelligence' condoning an illegal invasion and war, justifying torture 'to keep us safe,' calling scientific truth 'a hoax.' Fighting escalating wars for oil while the planet is literally burning up because of burning oil represents insanity of the highest order. But the plays, written in response to this tragic reality, are intended to come *in time* in other more significant ways as well: in each play characters dig deep to share their sorrows and to speak their truths. By saying what they've never felt safe or compelled enough to say, old hurts and hatreds are rectified, violence challenged, knowledge shared and visions of other ways of living together on this planet are expressed and through expression lived, at least for significant moments, in public before an audience. These plays are meant to speak to human potentiality as much as they decry human history.

A poetic, ritual drama enhances our ability to take in the unbearable, see through lies and dogma, understand the truths of our own times and be fully present in the moment. Intellect without feeling is often deadly; emotion without thought renders us weak and easily manipulated. Poetic drama provides the opportunity to *think feelingly*. We are enriched when we do so with others, in rehearsal and in community with an audience. A poetic theater is necessarily a physical one. The language that enters the bodies of the actors moves through them and moves them to express themselves corporally. These expressions of the body and of bodies in relationship also provide visceral images of possibility to the audience, enlivening them as they breathe with the actors on the stage.

In *Extreme Whether*, Uncle explains, 'There's a wilding inside that connects with a wilding up there,' and that *is* what it feels like when creation takes hold of one. Something stirs that can no longer be contained. Necessity flaps madly in the gut like a free-flying bird that will dash itself to death or find release. This is why poetry is wild nature produced by human nature, a song between a living cosmos and an ever-emergent self. This is why preservation of life in all its sentient forms is the work of the dramatic poet and why the poet must be fiercely engaged in the exploration, creation and manifestation of justice on this earth and for earth's creatures.

I hope that as these plays age, they lose none of their original bite – but come to stand as records of modernity gone terribly wrong – but also terribly right, for each play has its heroes – or, rather, each play is made up in the majority of characters who refuse to partake in the violence swirling around, who insist that the only struggle worth entering is the one for sentient thought. This capacity to think and feel at the same time, to feel the impact of our thoughts and think about the truth of our feelings, is what will finally make us completely human – for we are not yet whole. These plays look forward and back; they envision and remember. Their plots sear into consciousness our crimes and present acts of reconciliation. Their stories tell of what was and might yet be. In each play, characters surprise themselves by acting in empathic ways. They love across boundaries. They forgive. They gain wisdom from protecting others. They truth tell. As their connections and commitments deepen, they discover determination and strength they did not know they had. The actions of these characters alter the narratives; they turn the trajectory from disaster toward sustaining life.

I am remiss if I do not acknowledge the core artists who have made these plays reality over the past 22 years; their talents may be glimpsed in the photos. Without these collaborators, I would not and could not have written and directed these plays – for Theater Three Collaborative exists on a shoestring, at the very edge of the American theater where it is mainly ignored if not reviled by the establishment. Primarily, since 1987, when our mutual friend Judith Malina cast him in my play *Us*, I have been inspired, taught and goaded by the amazing shape-changing talents of producer/actor George Bartenieff, classically trained in dance by his parents, in Shakespeare at RADA and the Guild Hall, yet dedicated to the avant-garde's merging of the physical with poetry and its urge to transform. I have written a major role in every play for him and cannot write until I understand what his role will be. Luckily for me, he can act any and every thing. We go over every word and action together, many times, before and during rehearsal, and after the play is done. When we founded our theater in 1995, to produce *The Beekeeper's Daughter*, the late Lee Nagrin, an absolutely singular, multi-creative voice, for whom I had written the role of Sybil, just as I wrote Robert Blaze for George, brought with her two design geniuses: lighting designer Tony Giovannetti and costume designer Sally Ann Parsons, and I've had the privilege of working with them ever since. Artist Luba Lukova came to us at that same time, and she has designed all our graphics plus video projections for several plays. Composer Arthur Rosen has written scores for each of these four plays; Michaelangelo DeSerio has designed two of them and overseen production on one other and Carisa Kelly has become Sally Ann's co-designer. Beatriz Schiller has been our main photographer. Actors who have stuck with us, acting in multiple readings and productions, and otherwise advising, include Abbas Noori Abbood, Kathleen Chalfant, Christen Clifford, Najla Said, Kathleen Purcell, Alex Tavis and Di Zhu – while many others have graced single shows. Media specialist Catherine Greninger has allowed us to function. This book is a record of 22 years of theater work done outside the mainstream by renegade artists. I am profoundly grateful to all my collaborators over all this time.

References

Graves, Robert (1948), *The White Goddess,* New York: Farrar, Straus and Giroux.
Malpede, Karen (2006), 'Prophecy', *TriQuarterly,* #123, Northwestern University Press, pp. 178–97.
Murray, Gilbert (1940), *Aeschylus and the Creation of Tragedy,* Oxford: Oxford University Press.
Wilson, Edward O. (1986), *Biophilia,* Cambridge, MA: Harvard University Press.

Notes

1 Edward O. Wilson introduced the concept that there is an instinctive bond between humans and other living systems in his book *Biophilia* (1986).

2　I take the word 'protectors' from Native American tribes who reject 'protestors' in its favor, as they make a stand against oil and gas pipelines across their native lands (and all the United States is native land, actually).

3　Robert Blaze in the play quotes Graves directly when he says to Admira in the final scene: 'poetry is rooted in love, and love in desire, and desire in the hope of continued existence' (1948: 409). Sentiments such as: 'We pushed forward the boundaries the possible. We made everyday life wildly exciting and human love heroic,' from Robert's 'Happy' speech in Scene III with Rachel, and, in fact, much that Robert says is inspired by and are certainly meant to recall the passions of my late friend, Julian Beck, co-founder with Judith Malina of The Living Theatre, who died in 1984. An earlier play, *Us,* is dedicated to Julian's memory.

4　Writing about language, politics and sentience, I realize the influence on my work of a dear friend, Dorothy Dinnerstein, author of the influential feminist book, *The Mermaid and the Minotaur* (1976), published in the United Kingdom as *The Rocking of the Cradle and the Ruling of the World* (1987). Dorothy was a passionate lover of nature, deeply concerned by the twin threats of nuclear war and environmental disaster and trying to write, at the end of her life, a book to be called *Sentience and Survival.*

5　This production won an OBIE for acting for Bartenieff and played in New York, London, Berlin and Washington DC; it toured for three years, in the United States, Germany and Austria.

6　In the short story, the war has not yet begun. The student, Jeremy, comes to say good-bye to his teacher, Sarah, before he deploys, rousing her memories of Lukas. Alan, Hala and Mariam do not yet exist.

7　*Iraq: Speaking of War* was performed on March 19, 2005 at the Proshansky Auditorium, The Graduate Center, City University of New York, to mark the second year of the invasion of Iraq, and again the following October at the Culture Project, with Iraqi music by Emar ElSafar, percussion by Johnny Faraj and an original suite, 'B-A-G-D-A-D' by Milos Raikovich. Peter Francis James, Najla Said, Kathleen Chalfant and George Bartenieff, all of whom later performed in *Prophecy* in New York, in 2010, were in the cast, along with Judith Malina, Hanon Reznikov, Dalia Basiouny and others.

8　Undergraduate years at the University of Wisconsin; graduate school at Columbia University's School of the Arts.

9　A group of artists and intellectuals gathered at Robert J. Lifton's Center on Violence and Human Survival at John Jay College and signed a full-page advert in the *New York Times* opposing George H.W. Bush's Gulf War I. Allen Ginsberg, Grace Paley, Daniel Ellsberg and I were among the signers. All of us were keenly aware that Gulf War I, the depleted uranium left on the ground in Basra and the ensuing draconian sanctions on Iraq would cause untold suffering and were but a prelude to greater coming military action – which, nevertheless, took more than a decade to unfold. Lifton had pioneered Vietnam veteran's rap groups and was one of the first to recognize the ravages of what is now called PTSD on American combat veterans. I wrote an unpublished play called *Blue Heaven: Going to Iraq,* produced at Theater for the New City, in 1992, about this 42-day war and down-and-out artists, one of whom was Muslim, in the East Village at the height of the AIDS epidemic.

Part I

The Beekeeper's Daughter

In memory of two friends,
Ned Ryerson and Dorothy Dinnerstein.

For the people of Bosnia and Herzegovina and all who are forced to become refugees.

The Beekeeper's Daughter premiered at the Dionysia World Festival of Contemporary Drama, Veroli, Italy, in 1994, directed by Karen Malpede. George Bartenieff played Robert Blaze; Lee Nagrin played Sybil Blaze; Funda Dyal played Rachel Blaze, Jared Reinmuth, Jamie Knox, Christen Clifford, Admira Ismic; The New York premiere was at the Florence Mission Project, Bleecker St. Theater, directed by Karen Malpede, assistant director, Mahayana Landowne, lighting by Tony Giovannetti, costumes by Sally Ann Parsons. George Bartenieff played Robert; Lee Nagrin, Sybil; Christen Clifford, Admira; Brendan Corbalis played Jamie; Carolyn Goelser played Rachel. Theater Three Collaborative revived the play in 2016 at Theater for the New City, directed by Karen Malpede, lights by Tony Giovannetti, costumes by Carisa Kelly and Sally Ann Parsons, set by Michaelangelo De Serio, music by Arthur Rosen. George Bartenieff reprised his role as Robert Blaze; Evangeline Johns played Sybil Blaze; Najla Said, Rachel Blaze; P.J. Brennan, Jamie Knox; Di Zhu, Admira Ismic.

Characters

Robert Blaze, an American poet living in self-chosen exile
Jamie Knox, an androgynous American literary critic
Sybil Blaze, Robert's sister, the beekeeper
Rachel Deming-Blaze, Robert's grown daughter, a human rights worker
Admira Ismic, a Bosnian Muslim war victim

Setting

The Beekeeper's Daughter takes place on an island in the Adriatic Sea, early summer to fall 1993, with an epilogue nine months later. Four settings are called for: the House, an open expanse near the Beehives, the Forest, and a cliff near the Sea. The settings should be simple in the extreme; there is no need for them to be realistic, but they should be suggestive of an austere Mediterranean beauty. It is best if each scene takes place in a different location on the stage. In the 2016 production, the stage was rectangular and each scene spilled closer toward the audience. The House, raised, was upstage, the Hives just below, the Forest mid-stage, and the cliff was played a few feet from the first row.

Scene I

The House

(The main room of a simple, stone house on a remote Adriatic island; a large window leads to the outside, two doors on either side lead to bedrooms and the kitchen. Outside the house, downstage, are Sybil's beehives. Sybil, a large woman dressed in white beekeeping smock, gloves, hat, and veil, stands by the large window, watching. Sound of a flute being played. A beautiful, young, androgynous man, Jamie Knox, dressed in shorts, tank top and flowing kimono, nearly dances into the room and stretches himself out on the chaise lounge; he is followed by Robert Blaze, the flute player. It is obvious that these two men have just made love.)

SYBIL:	The bees are cold.
JAMIE:	I feel so wonderfully hot.
SYBIL:	Rachel's coming.
ROBERT:	Rachel? Rachel who?
SYBIL:	Your child.
ROBERT:	So I'm told, though since I neglected to keep her mother under and lock and key, I can't be entirely sure.
JAMIE:	If you were speaking like that about anyone except your first wife, I would take it as a sexist remark.
ROBERT:	Dora was a rather astonishing libertine.
JAMIE:	It's the misfortune of the female poet that the knowledge that she slept with virtually every major voice of the twentieth century so far exceeds her literary reputation.
ROBERT:	Dora wrote with Sapphic passion…
JAMIE:	Quite.
ROBERT:	… for that I forgave her everything.
JAMIE:	However, you are the oracular voice for the new age.
ROBERT:	You, the light of the last chapter of my life. Why is Rachel coming here?
JAMIE:	To share paradise with us, why not?
SYBIL:	To see me.
ROBERT:	Rachel is nothing like Dora. Serious to a fault. When she found she could not save her mother she decided to save the world.
JAMIE:	Poor Rachel. *(He is quoting* ROBERT*)* 'The world continues its destructive course/so we must squander love upon the open flesh.'
ROBERT:	Rachel has always been obscenely chaste. She saw how sex destroyed her mother.
JAMIE:	Sex was Dora Deming's elixir; she had to forget the doomsday voice inside her head.

ROBERT:	Don't romanticize Dora. In many ways she was a perfectly ordinary extremely difficult woman.
JAMIE:	Forgive me, dear, I'm making you jealous.
ROBERT:	I was jealous every moment Dora was alive…
JAMIE:	Well, after all, I came here to write about Dora…
ROBERT:	It's a terrible feeling, jealousy.
JAMIE:	I didn't know you'd be waiting to suck out my heart.
ROBERT:	It's the only human emotion that also tortures the gods.
JAMIE:	Oh, coldness is worse. Coldness is worse than anything hot.
SYBIL:	The bees are cold. I can feel them shivering in their hives.
ROBERT:	I feel I should bolt.
JAMIE:	How silly you are.
ROBERT:	Silly?
JAMIE:	Stupendously silly.
ROBERT:	I've never been called silly in my life.
JAMIE:	Bizarrely, divinely, wickedly, ecstatically silly. I'll say it in print if you like.
ROBERT:	How liberating, yes. To think, I've been suffering from a surfeit of serious thought.
JAMIE:	No, my silliness, you have been a closet silly all along.
ROBERT:	Silly, of course. It makes me feel like a new man. Completely free of the past.
JAMIE:	'It'?
ROBERT:	You, you, you. You are the source of all my happiness.
SYBIL:	Dora's daughter returns to the hive.
ROBERT:	Tell me the truth, Sybil; your blasted bees are giving you an omen.
SYBIL:	Brother, don't ask for the future from bees.
ROBERT:	We should leave for the mainland. Let Rachel fend for herself.
JAMIE:	'The bee is eating at the honey jar Eating our food we stole from her The isolated queen who in her cave Fed the baby Zeus and gave the god The sting with which he poisons love.'
ROBERT:	Dora scribbled that at lunch one day.
SYBIL:	A bee was eating from her plate.
JAMIE:	Robert, play for us. (ROBERT *begins to play an ancient Greek line.* JAMIE *takes* SYBIL *up in an austere dance. The whistle of a docking ferry boat cuts through their movements.*)
SYBIL:	Rachel, my dear, sweet, Rachel.

JAMIE:	Well, I can't wait. I'm going to meet her at the dock.
ROBERT:	Nonsense, you don't know who she is.
JAMIE:	The daughter of Dora Deming and Robert Blaze. She will stand out in a crowd.
ROBERT:	She'll find her way here quite nicely.
SYBIL:	I'm going. Where's my cane?
ROBERT:	Nonsense. I'm going myself.
SYBIL:	Brother, wait. I see the whole thing through to the end. You know how that is? When a window through time is opened up.
JAMIE:	What do you see, Sybil?
SYBIL:	The view opens up, then it closes. It comes over me like the sea breeze.
ROBERT:	Sybil, please.
SYBIL:	They all ask but no one wants to know. They can't stand it.
ROBERT:	It's true, Sybil. No one wants to know the future.
JAMIE:	We've been so perfectly happy.
ROBERT:	Don't speak of our happiness.
JAMIE:	Don't be afraid. Rachel is your child as much as Dora's and while you are indisputably brilliant, you are also eminently sensible and extraordinarily kind.
ROBERT:	Rachel is the fruit of my possession by Dora Deming. One should love one's daughter purely and simply, showering her with benign paternalism, but I've always been awed by Rachel. She inherited her mother's ruthless passion without the healthy amorality of the artist.
SYBIL:	Rachel wants to fix everything.
ROBERT:	She works for a group called Witness for Human Rights.
SYBIL:	She's a child.
ROBERT:	She's been documenting war crimes.
JAMIE:	Sounds lethal and so I'm coming with you.
ROBERT:	Good, darling.
	(*They leave.* SYBIL *sits on her stool, her back to the window.*)
SYBIL:	My poor dear child. Why do you ask so much? All day long my bees have been upset. Stung me twice. Whenever I forget…
	(SYBIL *begins to hum a lullaby.*)
	(RACHEL *and a very pregnant woman dressed in worn blue denim jumper and baggy sweater appear at the window.* RACHEL *is young, beautiful and haggard; she's too thin, and obviously she has never paid any but the slightest attention to her appearance. Her face is already lined with worry. At once, one sees that* RACHEL *is an odd combination of absolute nervous passion and wily strength.* RACHEL

is completely protective of the pregnant woman, who stares with wide frightened eyes around which are large dark circles. RACHEL *steps into the house and turns to carefully help the other woman. They stand listening to the song.)*

RACHEL: We can rest here. Can't we, Aunt Sybil.

SYBIL: *(As she opens her arms)* Come here, my child. Welcome home.

RACHEL: I'd hardly call it home, except that you're here. I've never seen this place before. My father probably forgot I was coming.

SYBIL: Never mind, I will fold you in my arms.

(RACHEL drops into her aunt's ample arms; a safe haven at last.)

RACHEL: It's been years.

SYBIL: Look at you. You've grown wrinkles on your face. Your mouth already is falling down. You were too serious growing up.

RACHEL: You don't change, Aunt Sybil.

SYBIL: I'm embalmed. You will eat my honey now; it preserves the flesh. Grief needs a home.

(SYBIL and ADMIRA lock eyes.)

RACHEL: I've seen too much.

SYBIL: Anyone does who looks out past their nose.

RACHEL: I wrote down every abomination known to man. Do you think anyone cares?

SYBIL: Who have you brought the old beekeeper?

RACHEL: Admira…

(But ADMIRA has vanished out the window.)

RACHEL: Shit, she's run off.

(RACHEL follows, looking out the window, she catches sight of ADMIRA and stops impatiently.)

SYBIL: She looked at me.

RACHEL: Admira won't talk about what happened to her.

SYBIL: She's with child.

RACHEL: She was a student at the university. Of comparative religions. What a joke. She speaks five languages. Don't mention the child to her, yet.

SYBIL: You should not have brought her to me. I don't want to…

RACHEL: Her life is ruined, her city destroyed. You are my one hope.

(RACHEL is out the window, after ADMIRA.)

RACHEL: Admira. Admira, this is the safe place I've told you about.

SYBIL: The bees will keep them both away from me.

(SYBIL puts on her beekeeping bonnet and crosses the terrace to the beehives.)

(JAMIE and ROBERT enter.)

ROBERT:	Did you hear something?
JAMIE:	No. With a woman. Is Rachel gay do you think?
ROBERT:	Rachel has a Mother Teresa complex.
JAMIE:	She's brought her lover home to meet her father. An artist, no doubt. Then we could all be quite jolly.
ROBERT:	You're an incurable optimist.
JAMIE:	You're rather a fuddy-duddy; I suppose all visionary poets have a bit of fuddy-duddy at the core.
ROBERT:	Fuddy-duddy, indeed. Let me look at you. *(Pause)* What has happened to me?
JAMIE:	You fell in love with a chameleon. And I fell in love with your wisdom. The wealth of feelings written across your face. The humus of the rounded belly. It's what Michelangelo saw when he progressed from the David to the Prophets. And he couldn't finish them. Even he couldn't quite dig them out of the rock. Whereas the David is just an idealized form. Pure object with no inner life.
ROBERT:	Only the ancient Greeks truly understood the pull the young man has on the old. The bursting heart inside the firm hot stone.
JAMIE:	I came here to resurrect the lost voice of Dora Deming. Now I'm writing a book about you. 'Robert Blaze: The Feminized Male and the Future of Life on Earth.' Dora must be insanely jealous from the grave.
ROBERT:	Still, I'm very much surprised at myself.
JAMIE:	I know, you've never done this before.
ROBERT:	Once, as an undergraduate, like everyone else.
JAMIE:	Well, I already have my Ph.D.; so you are reaping all the benefits of my superior endowment.
ROBERT:	With pleasure, still I'm amazed at myself. And, now, my stern, judgmental Rachel is somewhere around.
JAMIE:	I think you have to own the fact that you are a bisexual. Not just theoretically, rhetorically, but in your belly. I certainly am. In the States we are a growing special interest group. There are bisexual support groups. Bisexual singles dances. How-to books. Lobbying efforts.
ROBERT:	In the States every profound idea is immediately trivialized. Melted down in the pot. So I fled.
JAMIE:	To the birthplace of our lovely civilization.
ROBERT:	Lunacy is everywhere. We're going to have to exact a great deal of kindness from ourselves.
JAMIE:	You mean to torture me with your adoring gaze.
ROBERT:	And brutalize you with my tongue.

JAMIE:	Now you're speaking words I understand.
	(The two men kiss, and as they do so, they see ADMIRA, *the pregnant woman standing in the doorway watching them. She runs.)*
	Rachel?
ROBERT:	She's brought death into the house.
JAMIE:	Was that Rachel?
ROBERT:	Didn't you feel it? The icy chill.
JAMIE:	Don't be ridiculous.
ROBERT:	It's not enough I have to live here with Sybil and her bees; the cold hand of Dora Deming is reaching up to spoil my late happiness from the grave.
JAMIE:	It was just a pregnant woman from the village whose horizons were suddenly broadened. Let's find Rachel.
	*(*RACHEL *appears at the door, her arms protectively around* ADMIRA's *shoulders.)*
RACHEL:	I'm Rachel.
ROBERT:	Hello, Rachel. This is Jamie Knox.
RACHEL:	Admira, this is my father, Robert Blaze. This is Admira Ismic, father. I've brought her here to stay with me.
ROBERT:	Daughter…
	(He moves to embrace her.)
RACHEL:	Don't come any closer.
ROBERT:	Rachel…
ADMIRA:	It is my pleasure to meet you.
	(She speaks clearly, but stiffly. There is tremendous pain hidden in the voice. It's difficult not to be stunned. She holds out her hand.)
JAMIE:	The pleasure is ours, I'm sure.
ROBERT:	Welcome. Welcome both of you.
RACHEL:	We had nowhere else to go.
ROBERT:	This is your home.
RACHEL:	Three hundred miles from this paradise of yours there's a living hell.
ROBERT:	So I've heard. Let me look at you Rachel. You look…
RACHEL:	Old.
ROBERT:	… just like your mother. When I met her she was…
RACHEL:	… exactly my age.
ROBERT:	You must forgive me if I seem a bit shaken.
RACHEL:	Or are you just embarrassed at being surprised with the newest in your long line of teenage Dora Deming muse replacements.
JAMIE:	Well.
	(He realizes she's mistaken him for a woman. Enjoying her misperception, he stays as far from her as he can.)

ROBERT:	Can't you give me the benefit of the doubt. I'm sincerely moved by seeing you, Rachel. I'd like to give you a hug.
RACHEL:	'Fraid not. Both Admira and I are quite leery of the male body right now.
ADMIRA:	My husband has died. Rachel offered to bring me here to rest for a while. I hope not to bother you too much.
RACHEL:	We're going to spend most of our time alone with Aunt Sybil so you need not plan group meals or excursions to Delphi or anything like that. I'm actually glad you'll be occupied going over your entire oeuvre with Miss Knox.
ROBERT:	I'm afraid there's only one extra room. We didn't expect…
RACHEL:	One room is best.
ROBERT:	Jamie has come to interview me for a book about your mother.
RACHEL:	Mother's poetry is finally being rediscovered. Even where I was, the women were reading her.
ROBERT:	Now Jamie is writing about my work, too.
RACHEL:	I thought your work had never left the mainstream. When I was a child, Ms. Knox, a steady stream of female graduate students found their way to our door in order to deepen their understanding of Robert Blaze's unique relationship to the earth goddess. I think you'd be far better off writing about my mother; she was a cynic.
ROBERT:	Rachel, perhaps you and your friend…
RACHEL:	Admira Ismic
ROBERT:	Mrs. Ismic ought to rest…
RACHEL:	We've just come from the war.
ROBERT:	Can I get you a drink?
RACHEL:	I think we should rest. Is there a bottle of water in the room?
ROBERT:	I'll get some and I'll get more towels. Would you like some fruit?
RACHEL:	Fruit. But, of course, here fruit exists. Admira, would you like some fruit?
	(ADMIRA *is silent; she stares at the floor. Suddenly:*)
ADMIRA:	Please, no, no. Don't go to any trouble for me. Thank you very much.
RACHEL:	Fruit vanished ages ago. Along with running water. Shoes. Milk. Everything but guns and cigarettes.
ROBERT:	I'll bring you some apricots, grapes and figs. I'll leave them outside your door.
JAMIE:	I'll go, dear. (*To* RACHEL *as he walks through the door to the kitchen*) You see, you were right to come here. This is the Elysian Fields, after all.
RACHEL:	When I was young, I thought it was Mt. Olympus wherever my parents were.

JAMIE:	The two of them, they must have seemed like gods.
RACHEL:	*(Staring at her father)*
	Ruthless…
ROBERT:	Let me show you the room.
RACHEL:	We'll find it ourselves.
ROBERT:	It's the last on the hall, to the left.
	(The women exit toward the bedrooms.)
	(ROBERT sits down heavily.)
ROBERT:	Dora Deming, will you never loosen your strangle hold on me?
JAMIE:	*(Enters with the bowl of fruit)* What fun, she thinks I'm a woman.
ROBERT:	How strange, when it's perfectly clear you're Dionysus.
JAMIE:	She just cannot imagine her own father with anyone else but a long line of thirsty graduate students. Were you really that tacky?
ROBERT:	I think she can't quite imagine anything at the moment but that poor woman's suffering.
JAMIE:	Her eyes are like marble.
ROBERT:	I'm completely shaken.
JAMIE:	She's quite pregnant.
ROBERT:	Here we sit, fancying ourselves to be among the most enlightened thinkers the world has ever known while across the water the savages are in ascendancy.
JAMIE:	Do you really think anyone of us is safe from his own savagery?
ROBERT:	I left the world in order to better pray for it. Poetry is savage prayer.
JAMIE:	I'll take the fruit to them.
ROBERT:	The most extreme suffering, Rachel is drawn to it like a bee to the nectar. Dora didn't have a political bone in her body but she infused her daughter with an absolute fascination for pain beyond endurance. Dora's pain which no amount of loving kindness could mitigate.
JAMIE:	That's why you've earned your Dionysian prize, you weary old man god. Come, dear. I'm just going to leave this fruit outside the women's door. Then I'm going to shower the Milky Way all over you.
	(JAMIE leads ROBERT off; SYBIL enters, tap, tap, tapping her cane. It has grown dark.)
SYBIL:	The bees are cold in their hives. The honey will be thin. It goes as it goes. We must make do with what we have.
	(RACHEL enters in a white night gown; she runs to her aunt's lap and cries.)
SYBIL:	Child, child, what are you crying for?

21

RACHEL:	I don't know. I thought I was beyond tears. I thought I would never cry again.
SYBIL:	Well, well.
RACHEL:	It must be coming here. To you.
SYBIL:	Well, that's all right then.
RACHEL:	Why do I have to come here to confront another one of my father's blissfully beautiful lovers. Why should I have to put up with that?
SYBIL:	Why indeed?
RACHEL:	It's clear my father idolizes her. He always needs someone to adore. I bet Jamie Knox will drive him mad with jealousy. *(She cries harder)* After all I've seen, why am I crying about Jamie Knox?
SYBIL:	Maybe you would like your father all to yourself for a change.
RACHEL:	I can't stand another one of my father's stupid love affairs. Not now when I have to be strong. I'm acting like a child. How absurd.
SYBIL:	They call it paradise here. It's all right for me. I have my bees.
RACHEL:	The great man living in total isolation and complete self-indulgence, endlessly pontificating about the human soul.
SYBIL:	What will she do with that child?
RACHEL:	I'm so exhausted, I can't think anymore. That's what happened. The tiniest shred of kindness. Figs and grapes left outside a door on a blue enamel plate. Oh, god, I died and woke in paradise. I would think so myself except for the latest soap opera being played in front of my nose.
SYBIL:	What can she do with it?
RACHEL:	Listen to me, Aunt Sybil, because of you I believe that it is possible to live through the worst thing anyone can imagine and become whole again.
SYBIL:	You're frightening your old aunt.
RACHEL:	It must be possible. Because if it's not possible then surely human beings are doomed.
SYBIL:	People who have lived as I have lived are not necessarily wise.
RACHEL:	You taught me everything. You and your bees. You will help me with Admira, Aunt Sybil. You must help me.
SYBIL:	And the child? The child she's carrying?
RACHEL:	She'll give birth to it. We will help her do it.
SYBIL:	She wants to kill it.
RACHEL:	She wants to kill herself. But you and I will keep her from doing that. At least we must try.
SYBIL:	You're just like your father.
RACHEL:	If I could save one, just one life; you don't know how many nights I lay awake praying for that chance.

SYBIL:	But, at least, your father knows enough to stay at home and write the whole thing out in his head. He can make it happen however he wants it to happen because they're all his people and he's their one true god. Go to sleep, now, Rachel. It's gotten dark.
	(JAMIE *comes down the hall, he is completely, beautifully naked. A loose robe draped around him.* RACHEL *bumps into him.*)
RACHEL:	Get out of my way.
JAMIE:	It's so hot. I got up to look at the stars. Would you like to come out?
RACHEL:	How can you walk around this house like that?
JAMIE:	It's so hot. And I didn't think it was fair to leave you in the dark as to my true gender.
RACHEL:	Actually, *Mr.* Knox, I was simply hoping you were a nice young androgynous woman, preferably gay, come here to write about my mother. Then there was a chance we all might have gotten along.
JAMIE:	You've nearly got it. A detail or two is not quite accurate but then that sort of thing is hardly important. I think we'll all get along famously.
RACHEL:	I don't want to be around men.
JAMIE:	I have nothing in common with my brothers in the grip of testosterone poisoning who are butchering one another for land and nation.
RACHEL:	I find you impudent and disgusting.
JAMIE:	Really?
RACHEL:	You're walking around my father's house naked.
JAMIE:	How was I supposed to know you were up? In any case, I'm afraid I can't muster up the least bit of shame when it comes to my body which by all accounts is astonishingly irresistible.
RACHEL:	I think your body is perfectly repulsive, Mr. Knox.
JAMIE:	Thank you, Ms. Deming-Blaze. Is this the nineteenth century?
RACHEL:	I'm afraid not. Actually, it's the desperately late end of the twentieth century. And I have a woman down the hall who was held in captivity for three months, tied hands and feet to a bed, repeatedly brutalized day and night by a bevy of smug, self-satisfied men just about your age.
JAMIE:	I'll bet they were terrified of themselves.
	(*Every thought and feeling pent up inside her for so long comes rushing out at this young man who is so annoying, yet so strangely empathic, even appealing.*)
RACHEL:	Oh, yes, I'm certain the thought of a trembling naked woman tied to a bed struck abject terror in their hearts and made them all

want to cry out for their mothers. But, nevertheless, to prove that they were made of heroic stuff, they took turns raping her over and over. And the act itself had an odd effect on them for it seemed to endow them with a superhuman strength. By all accounts they became even fiercer soldiers. Only in hell could such a scene be possible. How is it possible for a woman to continue to live? Is it possible? Why should she? So she can tell her story? But the women cannot speak about what was done to them; they have lost the power of speech. Then we must wonder if the birth will kill her? Then, again, how will she be able to restrain herself from murdering the child she bears? If the child survives, what will become of it? Is there any way out of this circle of suffering? Or have the monstrous actions of those young men, no doubt under orders, but how then does one command an erection, created only two choices for the survivors: madness or the turning of themselves into monsters. One can imagine a future race of heroes raised on their mothers' knees to become the avengers of their mothers' rapes. If the mother lives. I will not have you walking naked in this house, Mr. Knox, have I made myself perfectly clear. Put on your clothes.

(RACHEL *turns and exits.*)

JAMIE:	Isn't she splendid! She's everything I would have hoped for from Dora Deming's daughter.
SYBIL:	Her mother killed herself.
JAMIE:	I know.
SYBIL:	Rachel is all I have left.
JAMIE:	She's wonderful. Brilliant, arrogant, committed, more beautiful than she dares to imagine. What a family. You know, Sybil, I never had a family. I don't even know my father.
SYBIL:	The dead one. You could be with her.
JAMIE:	I love Dora's work but I think I prefer the company of Robert and Rachel, thank you very much.
SYBIL:	The dead one with the swollen belly, keep her away from me.
JAMIE:	I would be happy to help if Rachel will let me, which she won't. I'm not afraid of suffering, you see. It does seem rather odd, but I have been blessed with the gift of happiness.
SYBIL:	I'm always right but no one ever listens to a thing I say.
JAMIE:	I'm not the least bit afraid of the dead woman.
SYBIL:	I'm glad for that.
JAMIE:	I'm going outside to dance underneath the moon. Maybe Robert will wake up and take photographs.

(JAMIE exits. SYBIL remains seated in shadows.)
(ADMIRA walks down the hall, she is still fully dressed. She stands at the window, looking out. Her pregnant belly silhouetted in the moon light. ROBERT comes down the hall, bare chest, a camera around his neck. He sees ADMIRA at the window. Stops, focuses and clicks. She jumps, stands speechless, shivering.)

ROBERT: Oh, I'm very sorry. Please forgive me. I promise you, I won't come near you.
(She backs away.)

ROBERT: It was a very beautiful picture. I'll give it to you. You at the window in the moon light. Can you understand what I say?
(ADMIRA stiffens but slowly, during his speech, she relaxes.)

ROBERT: I saw a luminous light in your eyes. As if you were looking quite far away, into some other time and place. That's why I snapped the shutter. Without thinking. I am sorry. I won't do such a thing again. You truly are safe here. No one will hurt you. Maybe it was just the moon, but I don't think so. I think your eyes were sparkling for a moment. Odd, isn't it, that in Western art we have no representations at all of pregnant women until we come to the fifteenth century Pregnant Madonna of Piero della Francesca. She was a victim of Immaculate Conception. And she seems completely perplexed by her situation. Of course, we assume that in her case the whole process was fairly gentle. But we have to think that, don't we? My point is that even the Mother of Christ didn't choose her own fate. How few women actually do? Perhaps that's the real difference between women and men; men think they are free; women don't even bother to pretend. Surely, Mary didn't ask to become the mother of a god. I say 'a god' not 'god' you notice. I am what one might call a pagan. I really am a believer in multiple gods. How can one not be, after all? Look at the violence unleashed by the endless fights over which god is the best. We have to learn to accept. The divine spirit is reborn all the time to mortal women. We never know. Actually, in classical mythology, most gods were born to mortal women by an act of rape. In that sense, I suppose, Immaculate Conception was a forward step. If, indeed, the phrase is not simply a cover-up. Perhaps there's no way a truly divine presence could enter our present world except as the result of incredible force. Does this sound too much like justification? I don't intend that. It's just that for every extreme action, there's bound to be an equally extreme reaction. And for us all, the same question remains in the end: how much do we let external events create us and how much do we hold ourselves responsible for what we become? In your case, the question poses itself at the extreme edge of tolerance. Still, I would hesitate to say you don't bear some responsibility, not for what has happened to you of which you were obviously completely innocent, but for what, despite everything, you might still imagine yourself to be. *(RACHEL enters.)*

RACHEL: I'm here, Admira; he doesn't mean any harm. Father, what are you doing?

ROBERT: Babbling, I'm afraid.

RACHEL: How do you dare?

ROBERT: I don't know. Something about her set me talking.

RACHEL: She's fallen asleep on her feet. At last.

ROBERT: Let's move her over to the couch.

RACHEL: She might wake up screaming.

ROBERT: Maybe not.
(They move her to the couch; then step away, out to the terrace.)

ROBERT: We ought to undress her.

RACHEL: No, she can't bear it.

ROBERT: She smells a bit rancid.

RACHEL: She's filthy, but what can I do? She can't bear to be touched and she won't touch herself. The most important thing now is that she not be forced to do anything, so she begins to feel free to choose the simplest action. That's why you and that other person have to stay completely away from her. She really shouldn't be around men. I wouldn't have come here if I had had the slightest notion about the sex of your current lover.

ROBERT: I assure you, I'm quite surprised myself.

RACHEL: It's the last thing we needed.

ROBERT: Don't be such a prude, Rachel.

RACHEL: I'm trying to protect Admira; I'm sorry if that seems like prudishness to you. What were you saying to her?

ROBERT: Oh, nonsense I suppose. Somehow, she makes everything seem like nonsense.

RACHEL: I know.

ROBERT: Rachel, we are difficult people, you and I; above all, we must try to be kind to each other.

RACHEL: I wish you would send him away.

ROBERT: But I need him.

RACHEL: Why can't you ever be enough for yourself? Why are you always needing the most unlikely people?

ROBERT:	Why didn't you just come away from all that suffering for a while? Why did you bring it with you?
RACHEL:	Because I'm trying to do some minuscule good.
ROBERT:	I'm trying to write some poetry.
RACHEL:	We're stuck again just where we've always been.
ROBERT:	And since both our hearts may be broken, let's try to call a truce with one another.
RACHEL:	Look, I'm a professional. My heart has nothing to do with it.
ROBERT:	Perhaps. Let's go to bed.
RACHEL:	I'll sleep here on the floor. I don't want that idiot naked boy dancing through.
ROBERT:	He's climbed into the window in my room by this time. I'll see he doesn't bother you again.
RACHEL:	Good.
ROBERT:	It's not very comfortable.
RACHEL:	It's all right. I'm used to it.
ROBERT:	I'll bring the mattress.
RACHEL:	Please, don't bother.
ROBERT:	Right, well, good night.
RACHEL:	Good night. Thanks for getting Admira to sleep.
ROBERT:	Just luck.
RACHEL:	With healing it always is.
ROBERT:	With poetry, too.
RACHEL:	Well, why not trust to luck for a while and send that person away?
ROBERT:	Let's not get started again.
RACHEL:	Right.
JAMIE:	*(Calls from the bedroom)* Robert! I will come down the hall to get you if you don't come here this instant. *(ROBERT goes to him.)*
RACHEL:	Whatever possessed me to come here? To this rarefied hot house. *(SYBIL gets up and goes back into the house.)*
SYBIL:	I'll stay with her as long as she's sleeping.
RACHEL:	How do you stand it, Aunt Sybil?
SYBIL:	She's sleeping now.
RACHEL:	I meant my father and his latest paramour.
SYBIL:	If only you had someone to hold you…
RACHEL:	If only you could rock me like you used to… I'll relieve you in the morning. I'm afraid we're both on duty, now. Tomorrow, I'll find a doctor who can write me a prescription for some sedatives.
SYBIL:	The child's inside.

RACHEL:	That's why I need your help.
SYBIL:	*My help.* I'll sit here until she wakes up.

Scene II

The Beehives

(The day is hot and bright. Several basket beehives sit on stumps and stones. In the foreground a large tin bathtub in which ADMIRA *sits.* SYBIL *is singing and washing* ADMIRA's *back delicately with a natural sponge.* RACHEL *sits nearby, a novel,* The English Patient, *open on her lap, she watches them, a soft smile on her face.)*

SYBIL:	There you are, clean as the day you were born.
ADMIRA:	Don't stop.
	*(*SYBIL *picks up a tin watering can, gently showers* ADMIRA.*)*
SYBIL:	Summer rain.
ADMIRA:	Don't stop your song, Sybil, don't stop singing.
	*(*SYBIL *begins to sing again.)*
ADMIRA:	Your voice keeps me anchored here.
	*(*SYBIL *continues to sing.)*
	Otherwise, I would run. I would turn into the white cow, who was it? Chased by the big fly.
RACHEL:	Io.
ADMIRA:	I would jump off the edge of the world.
SYBIL:	Now that's nonsense, isn't it, when you are rooted right to this spot by a silken cord that runs through your mother's mother to you and on again to the end of time.
ADMIRA:	How was she like that? Io.
RACHEL:	Zeus raped her.
ADMIRA:	I see.
RACHEL:	I hate mythology.
ADMIRA:	Robert told me about Io.
RACHEL:	He would.
ADMIRA:	How the girl suddenly felt four feet under her and a thick hide. We were speaking of change. How suddenly one becomes so different from who one was.
	*(*SYBIL *holds out a pure white thick towel.)*
SYBIL:	Come, now, you won't turn into a white cow sitting there. You'll turn into a prune.
	*(*ADMIRA *steps out of the bath wrapped in the towel.* SYBIL *gently rubs her dry then slips a pure white dress over her head.* SYBIL *begins to fix her hair.)*

ADMIRA:	So much is gone.
RACHEL:	So much of you is just being silent for a time.
ADMIRA:	I don't know what became of anything.
RACHEL:	You will remember; we will help you. You will put yourself back together. I promise.
ADMIRA:	It dropped out of the sky.
SYBIL:	Listen to the bees. Eternity is in their hum.
RACHEL:	You're stronger everyday.
ADMIRA:	Whose hands are these?
SYBIL:	How pretty you look.
	(ROBERT *comes out of the house carrying the baby.*)
ADMIRA:	Robert dotes on him. That is how to say it?
ROBERT:	Not quite. Robert dotes on both of you.
ADMIRA:	Robert dotes on everyone. It's a fault.
ROBERT:	Doting too much?
ADMIRA:	Too much doting may not be good for Robert.
ROBERT:	An anti-doter in our midst, daughter.
RACHEL:	Double doting is the sole antidote for anti-doters.
ROBERT:	The soul needs no antidote for anti-doters when doting is the soul's pure delight.
RACHEL:	Groan.
ROBERT:	Or words to that effect.
	(JAMIE *enters carrying a hamper of food.* RACHEL *helps him spread the picnic cloth and pour the wine.*)
JAMIE:	Wine and fruit in the late afternoon.
RACHEL:	Great.
ROBERT:	Let's celebrate.
JAMIE:	The sheer, complete and total, wonderful boredom of daily life. Never thought I'd say that.
ROBERT:	Never.
JAMIE:	How thrilling this quiet is. Rachel's actually reading a novel. The baby only woke up once during the night. Sybil made biscuits for breakfast.
ADMIRA:	Sybil sings all the time to me.
SYBIL:	The bees have been singing all day long. They sing about where the nectar is.
JAMIE:	I have nearly finished my chapter.
ROBERT:	It does seem miraculous.
ADMIRA:	To me, very much.
ROBERT:	You've made an astonishing recovery.
SYBIL:	Well, well…

JAMIE:	Quiet, please. A toast to us all!
ROBERT:	To many more long, slow, happy days like this.
JAMIE:	To our friendship.
ROBERT:	To the rejuvenating powers of love.
	(Pause)
ROBERT:	I find you all so very beautiful.
JAMIE:	It's true. It's true.
RACHEL:	Thank you for taking us in.
ROBERT:	Of course.
RACHEL:	And for all you've done.
ADMIRA:	I am not too much of a guest.
ROBERT:	Nonsense. I'm truly happy. Happier, now, than I've been in a long while.
SYBIL:	The bees come home in the late afternoon.
RACHEL:	I love the sound of the bees coming back, drunk and dripping with pollen.
ROBERT:	Perhaps we should move?
SYBIL:	Bees only sting when fear is in the air.
ROBERT:	Really, Sybil?
ADMIRA:	One must live without war.
RACHEL:	*(Toasts)* To life without war, for everyone, everywhere.
JAMIE:	Paradise on earth.
ROBERT:	*(Murmuring to the child)* Child of paradise, that's who you are.
ADMIRA:	It's good, you two together.
ROBERT:	Suddenly, I'm writing about mothers and sons.
JAMIE:	Why not fathers and sons?
ROBERT:	I hadn't thought of my mother in a very long time.
SYBIL:	I think of her everyday.
ADMIRA:	Sons should honor their mothers. Honor and protect them.
RACHEL:	Of course, they should.
ADMIRA:	That's how the world made sense to me. But I make no sense of anything anymore. Not the kindness of all of you.
JAMIE:	Kindness is completely inexplicable.
	(SYBIL begins to sing again. ADMIRA lays her head on RACHEL's lap; RACHEL strokes her hair. RACHEL leans back to rest against SYBIL.)
	(SYBIL begins to hum softly; her sound increases as ROBERT begins his speech so that it is a jam session of words and music between brother and sister.)
	I want you to write about fathers and sons.
ROBERT:	One can't help what one writes, my dear. One really has no choice in the matter.

JAMIE:	One can't help who one loves.
ROBERT:	I'm writing a new version of the Metamorphoses, in which sons are transformed into mothers. Mothers into lovers. Lovers into the beloved priests of the eternal she-god. And the ruiners, the despoilers of earth, the money-grubbers turn into worshippers of her many moons. Warriors transform into servants of life, bearers of seed, sacred flame, and fierce with desire. I've wanted to do it for a very long time. I want to sing out to everyone 'Change form. Change form. Don't be afraid. It takes but an instant to see the world in a new way. Turn, turn.' (ROBERT's *words and* SYBIL's *song crescendo.*) These days I want to write and write. I know it's futile. But what else can I do?
SYBIL:	Bees know what they need. In one short life, bees accomplish everything; they nurse the young, make food.
JAMIE:	Just a minute please. Before signing on to Sybil's cult of the bee may we all pause for a moment to consider the fate of the poor drone bee who literally explodes in the air at the exact moment he provides the queen with all the fertilized eggs she will ever need. (*He does a deep back-bend, enacting the death of the drone bee.*) Dying instantly in the midst of his ecstasy.
SYBIL:	It happens to one drone in a thousand.
ROBERT:	Striking fear eternal into men's hearts.
SYBIL:	Most drones live quiet lives; the worker bees feed them, care for them. Clean the hive.
JAMIE:	It would happen to me. In another life, I was the drone bee.
ROBERT:	Consort to the Bee Goddess.
JAMIE:	Spilling my guts for love.
ROBERT:	Her son who is both her lover and victim.
JAMIE:	Helpless to resist her.
ROBERT:	Don't be afraid, my dear. From your ashes rises up a serpent whose egg she eats so that the son is reborn to her once more.
JAMIE:	To be sacrificed again on her alter.
RACHEL:	This conversation is insane.
ADMIRA:	Don't protect me, Rachel. You want I should tell you all kinds of things, but you don't want me to hear.
SYBIL:	Let them be.
RACHEL:	The devouring goddess. Rubbish. This is what men always think. It's just an excuse for your wars.
JAMIE:	Whose wars?

RACHEL:	Yours. Until you do something to stop them. Put your body on the line.
JAMIE:	Sure, I'll go stand between the murderous hordes. I'll chant mantras at them. 'Brothers' I'll say.
RACHEL:	Yes, if enough of us did that. If we stood shoulder to shoulder in front of the victims.
JAMIE:	Rachel is an amazing woman, Robert. She puts an intellectual to shame.
RACHEL:	We could do something if we wanted to. We, 'the enlightened ones,' something, anything but this idle chatter all the time.
JAMIE:	I think she may even be a dreamer, like her father.
RACHEL:	There are sick people in this world, who kill with impunity because we let them.
ROBERT:	Murderers become like gods in men's eyes; they seem immortal because they are so totally devoid of pity.
RACHEL:	My father's talk always sounds totally infantile to me.
ADMIRA:	Robert talks like a child always.
RACHEL:	I always thought both my parents were children.
ROBERT:	Poor Rachel shouldn't have had poets for parents.
RACHEL:	It's been difficult.
ROBERT:	I suppose so.
RACHEL:	It's all right; I stopped listening long ago.
ROBERT:	That makes it better, I'm sure.
RACHEL:	The air here is so crystal clear. Pure.
JAMIE:	Children are difficult, too, as we know. They make adults wrinkle their nose.
ROBERT:	It is that time again.
RACHEL AND JAMIE:	Not near the food.
ADMIRA:	I should do it.
ROBERT:	Nonsense, you just had your bath.
ADMIRA:	If I could.
SYBIL:	Let me.
ROBERT:	It's all right, Sybil; I'll just take him off for a minute.
SYBIL:	I delivered him.
ROBERT:	For your brilliant heroics on that night you are exempt from ever having to change a diaper. I, however, was simply pacing like a lunatic around the perimeters of the house. So, now, I must suffer.
RACHEL:	Admira did all the work.
ADMIRA:	I don't know.
SYBIL:	I just held my hands out. He came out wrinkled and pink. I gave him to Rachel.

RACHEL:	And I laid him on your chest. You remember his eyes.
ADMIRA:	I remember his eyes because I could see already they were green.
RACHEL:	Like your eyes.
ADMIRA:	Like mine.
ROBERT:	I heard you all inside crying so I knew there was a happy ending.
ADMIRA:	Sybil began to sing. Sybil sang and sang.
SYBIL:	I sang when you looked in his eyes.
RACHEL:	And you named him Robert.
ADMIRA:	Because Robert is the first kind man.
ROBERT:	Now the Roberts have serious work to do.
	(He goes into the house to change the baby.)
JAMIE:	A man who changes a diaper is a heroic man.
RACHEL:	History could be rewritten around that concept.
JAMIE:	I haven't the stomach for it myself.
SYBIL:	His poop smells so sweet.
JAMIE:	No, history.
RACHEL:	Sybil's right, until they begin to eat actual food, babies have the sweetest smelling poo.
JAMIE:	I can't say I ever noticed.
SYBIL:	Mother's milk is sweet.
RACHEL:	It tastes like vanilla ice cream. That's why the whole village lines up every night outside the gelateria.
JAMIE:	Did Dora nurse you, Rachel? I inquire as her biographer, of course.
ADMIRA:	We drank a glass of my milk.
JAMIE:	You did? Why didn't I know about that?
RACHEL:	It was a female rite.
JAMIE:	A goddess orgy without my consent?
ADMIRA:	Sybil also drank.
JAMIE:	This is the sort of thing that drives men to distraction. Breast envy. It's terrifying.
	(ROBERT with the baby returns.)
ROBERT:	What?
RACHEL:	Please, Jamie.
JAMIE:	Male envy of the female breast.
ROBERT:	I don't believe in it. Adoration, yes.
JAMIE:	Come, now, don't you wish you could nurse that child?
ROBERT:	I am nursing him.
ADMIRA:	My milk dried up.
	(JAMIE jumps up.)
JAMIE:	I am in complete envy of the female breast.

SYBIL:	*(To* ADMIRA*)* It often happens like that.
ADMIRA:	After we drank it, my milk went away.
RACHEL:	It's all right, Admira. You nursed him for a while.
ADMIRA:	I can't tell.
JAMIE:	You were beautiful with that child at your breast. I really can't stand it.
ADMIRA:	He saw me?
RACHEL:	Jamie is making fun of us. He doesn't really feel that way.
ROBERT:	I hope not. I'm feeling rather inadequate.
JAMIE:	The priests of the goddess castrated themselves to become more like women. You wrote that in one of your books.
ROBERT:	Self-castration was a form of worship.
RACHEL:	In light of current events, I think we should bring the custom back.
JAMIE:	I thought you weren't interested in goddess talk?
ADMIRA:	He put the evil eye on me.
SYBIL:	It can happen like that.
ROBERT:	Sybil, for god's sake.
SYBIL:	Men are not supposed to look.
RACHEL:	Your milk dried up because you were undernourished, Admira.
ADMIRA:	Rachel, you are so rational.
RACHEL:	Somebody has to be rational around here.
ADMIRA:	Rational is not enough.
SYBIL:	There are certain things men should not see. It frightens them.
JAMIE:	I disagree. Men need to see.
RACHEL:	It's important to try to understand what you've been through.
ROBERT:	It's important to be in the present. Right now. In the safety of this moment. Surrounded by love.
ADMIRA:	My city was like a light in the dark night. My city was like Troy. We all intermarried in my city. We all carried one another's blood.
ROBERT:	I went to your city with Dora several times. It was very beautiful.
JAMIE:	Just today, I came across the section in your diary. It impressed me so.
	(He opens the diary and reads.)
	'Each night at dusk we sit and drink on the terrace of the Hotel Europa and watch the white doves fly in the air.'
ADMIRA:	We would meet there to talk about all kinds of things. Like we do today.
JAMIE:	May I read this to them, Robert?
ADMIRA:	Now it is spoiled, that hotel. Gone. Yes, read it to me, please.

JAMIE:	*(Reads)* 'Situated around the square in front of the hotel in this most cosmopolitan of cities are a mosque, a synagogue, an orthodox and a catholic church; there are sounds of the men and of the bells calling us all to prayer. Last night, as we sat sipping wine, the entire city seemed to be praying as cities do in the dusk when the golden light is thrown down on their stones by the sky gods, those golden ghosts of our ancestors who have given us the open city, the city whose life is like a gaping wound, who suffers with us and releases that which is best inside us. Impulsively, I reached out to take Dora's hand. She moved it quickly out from under mine, resisting even this touch as she has resisted them all for many months. But just then the mosque came alive with the chanting of many men and in the fullness of the voices the doves took flight so that the soul of the city seemed to be visibly rising upward in the invisible hand of god. Dora reached for my hand and brought it to her lips, kissing it in an almost obsequious manner that sent a shiver up and down my spine. She smiled. "Robert," she said, "you have loved me better than I have had any right to be loved, but you have not made me whole. Often I hate you so much for all that you've given me that I cannot bear to have you touch me. All I can feel is revulsion for the ineffectual goodness of your love." I feel I have lost her. I fear she will not live. But then we made love in the Hotel Europa. For one night the curse seemed to lift.' *(Silence.* RACHEL *and* JAMIE *look hard at one another.* ROBERT *is visibly upset.)*
ROBERT:	It's strange to hear such things aloud.
RACHEL:	It's very moving, father. I'm glad I heard it.
JAMIE:	I wonder if the men of my generation will dare to risk such selfless love?
ADMIRA:	These days I think my self can begin to feel. But not if my city falls.
RACHEL:	The city won't fall, Admira.
ADMIRA:	When I walked alone in my city, then I felt I knew who I was.
JAMIE:	As women rediscover their ancient powers, men have become terrified again. That is why men fight with such fury as now.
RACHEL:	The city will survive, Admira.
ADMIRA:	Yes, yes, my friend.
RACHEL:	We should bomb the bastards with their guns. We should bomb them.
JAMIE:	Who should bomb them?
RACHEL:	The West. Europe. Us.

JAMIE:	Some poor kid in an airplane.
RACHEL:	*(To* ROBERT*)* You're a poet. People read what you write. You should issue a statement.
ROBERT:	No doubt, but what should it say?
RACHEL:	Bomb them. Lift the arms embargo.
ROBERT:	There has to be a better way.
RACHEL:	Do you know what they do up in the hills? They shoot to kill the women and the children.
ADMIRA:	I don't want to live in the world.
JAMIE:	That's why we live here.
RACHEL:	But they aim at the men below the waist.
ADMIRA:	My friends have no legs.
RACHEL:	To maim them.
ROBERT:	That's enough, Rachel, enough.
	(Silence)
RACHEL:	Pass the grapes.
	*(*JAMIE *hands her a bunch. She eats and hands grapes to* ADMIRA. *Suddenly everyone begins to eat grapes with an increasing, almost rhythmic, intensity, passing one another the ripe lush fruit. For quite a while there is no sound except the sounds of the grapes being sucked on and swallowed.)*
JAMIE:	Dionysus comes from the East, to possess, to release…
ROBERT:	'These blessings he gave:/ laughter to the flute/ and the loosing of cares/ when the shining wine is spilled/ at the feast of the gods.'
JAMIE:	Women need to invite men into their mysteries.
SYBIL:	Then they wouldn't be mysteries.
ROBERT:	Woman is the mystery.
JAMIE:	She needs to invite the man in.
RACHEL:	Nonsense.
	*(*JAMIE *jumps to his feet, a bunch of grapes held over his crotch.)*
JAMIE:	Just try to imagine, for a moment, how terrifying it is for the new god to stand completely open and vulnerable before the herd of strong and vital women, to stand full like a ripe fruit. An incredible, edible, disposable display.
RACHEL:	You are ridiculous.
JAMIE:	A sacrificial beast to be torn apart. Eaten raw.
RACHEL:	I'm not interested in men's problems.
JAMIE:	But you are. You are obsessed by male violence. You love to recite each gruesome detail. It turns you on.
RACHEL:	How dare you.

JAMIE:	But you refuse to let yourself enter into the real complexities of human relationships. You've barricaded yourself behind your own considerable brain because your mother was Dora Deming and you're afraid of feeling.
RACHEL:	To you everything is just a game without consequence. That's why you're a literary critic.
JAMIE:	It's impossible to discuss anything with you.
RACHEL:	You're the impossible one.
ROBERT:	Children, please.
RACHEL:	Pass the grapes.
	(JAMIE *moves toward her, holding the bunch of grapes in front of his crotch, like a full ripe sex.*)
ROBERT:	'Handle with holy care/ the violent wand of god!'
JAMIE:	Eat. They are all for you.
	(*He bends* RACHEL's *head into the grapes; she eats.*)
RACHEL:	They're so sweet.
	(JAMIE *laughs, kneeling in front of her, he takes her hands.*)
JAMIE:	But of course, they are sweet. That's what I've been telling you all along. Is it so hard for you to taste a little sweetness, Rachel? On your tongue?
	(*The intimacy between* RACHEL *and* JAMIE *startles* ADMIRA *into a sudden flashback. She screams.*)
ADMIRA:	No. No. I don't want to see.
SYBIL:	Look at me, child, look at me.
ROBERT:	I'm taking the baby to the house.
ADMIRA:	Don't touch me. Don't. Please, don't.
SYBIL:	Sybil is with you. It's all right.
ADMIRA:	I am broken. Broken. Inside.
RACHEL:	Damn it. I've been stung. I've been stung by a bee.
ADMIRA:	In her own blood, they push her down.
SYBIL:	Sybil will keep you safe.
	(ADMIRA *buries herself in* SYBIL's *body.*)
ADMIRA:	So cold. Wet. The stink.
SYBIL:	Sybil's going to wrap you in a feather quilt. Feed you some nice warm soup.
ADMIRA:	They have a knife, a knife to her throat.
	(SYBIL *breaks from* ADMIRA; *she chases the imaginary demons with her cane.*)
SYBIL:	Get! Get out of here! Get!
ADMIRA:	Leave them alone. Let them go. Don't make her do that.
SYBIL:	Leave my child alone!

ADMIRA:	Over and over again.
	(ADMIRA weeps in SYBIL's arms.)
SYBIL:	There. They're gone, now. Sybil chased them away. They won't come back.
ADMIRA:	I can't. I can't.
SYBIL:	You don't have to, anymore. You don't have to do anything you don't want to do. Sybil will rock you to sleep.
	(SYBIL takes ADMIRA off, singing to her; RACHEL tries to follow but with her cane, SYBIL signals to RACHEL to stay away.)
JAMIE:	Your mouth is puffing up.
	(RACHEL is mortified, also in pain from the bee sting.)
	I'll get some ice.
	(He dips his hand into the cooler, applies ice to her mouth.)
RACHEL:	Leave me alone. It's just a bee sting.
JAMIE:	Quiet. You can barely talk. Your lip is a mess.
	(They are staring at one another. Silence)
	You've been stung. Rachel, the invulnerable. It had to happen, you know. On the mouth.
RACHEL:	Look what you've done to Admira.
JAMIE:	What I've done? But she needs to remember. You keep saying she does.
RACHEL:	Not that way.
JAMIE:	There is no gentle way. It's bound to be a shock to the system.
RACHEL:	You did it on purpose, all of it.
JAMIE:	You ate.
RACHEL:	Oh, god.
JAMIE:	You were insatiable.
RACHEL:	You planned the whole thing.
JAMIE:	Not the bee sting. No, the bee sting is divine intervention.
RACHEL:	I'm frightened.
JAMIE:	But I'm frightened of you, too.
RACHEL:	Then please leave me alone.
JAMIE:	I didn't expect you to gobble up those grapes like that.
RACHEL:	Go away.
JAMIE:	Let me put some more ice on that lip.
RACHEL:	I'll do it myself.
JAMIE:	You can't live as a witness. Life has to touch you. The bee stings, you know.
RACHEL:	To say the most obvious thing, my father fancies himself in love with you.
JAMIE:	You've broken out in a sweat.

RACHEL:	You purposely tried to upset us. You planned it.
JAMIE:	It was fated from our first night.
RACHEL:	I am not possessed by you.
JAMIE:	Do you think your refusal makes a difference to me?
RACHEL:	I'm afraid nothing makes a difference to you.
JAMIE:	You want me to adore you from afar. You want me to burn silently. I will. But listen to me, Rachel, you'll make me more unfaithful to Robert doing that than if I could admit my desire openly and live it out. Love is not lethal, Rachel. I'll protect you and Robert, both. Safe sex for the heart.
RACHEL:	My head is throbbing. My lip hurts.
JAMIE:	Well, then, come, I'll walk you back to the house. No one will be the wiser.
RACHEL:	I will be leaving soon, in any case.
JAMIE:	In a way, I'm glad to be spared the drama of it all.
RACHEL:	I think I shall be exceedingly glad never to have to see you again.
JAMIE:	I feel positively light-headed
RACHEL:	Lucky you. My head feels like it's being operated on with a sledgehammer.
JAMIE:	See how you suffer. Just observe. I'm not asking anything more.
RACHEL:	I'm going back to the house. Admira needs my help.
JAMIE:	I think I'll take a long slow swim in the sea. I don't think it's fair to burst in on Robert now. You see, there are rules of decorum which I do find it necessary to keep.
RACHEL:	Why did I ever have to set eyes on you, Jamie Knox.
	(They exit different directions.)

Scene III

The Forest

(The pine forest, dark and mysterious, sweet smelling, dappled by light. People appear and disappear from behind trees into several small clearings.)

	*(*JAMIE *and* ROBERT *are walking;* ROBERT *carries the baby.)*
JAMIE:	Why, I wonder, did she decide to have it? That child, I mean.
ROBERT:	It's strange.
JAMIE:	It seemed all right for a while, possible, but now…
ROBERT:	She's become a prisoner of her past, as if some strong hand reached up and yanked her back.
JAMIE:	She's all but abandoned it.
ROBERT:	Rachel is working with her.

JAMIE:	She won't even touch it.
ROBERT:	It's a slow process.
JAMIE:	She flips whenever she hears it.
ROBERT:	I have enormous faith in Rachel's powers.
JAMIE:	Meanwhile, you've become a dedicated nursemaid.
ROBERT:	It's odd. I've fallen in love with this child. I never paid much attention to Rachel when she was this age. Once she began to talk, though, I rather liked her. She was so quick and snotty.
JAMIE:	Why the hell didn't she abort that child? So that you could experience all the joys of fatherhood, in your dotage?
ROBERT:	That's rather extreme. I'm hardly feeble-minded yet.
JAMIE:	Why didn't she get rid of it?
ROBERT:	*(To the baby)* Don't listen to him. *(To* JAMIE*)* She thought he might be a love child. She thought she might have been pregnant before they raped her with the child of a man she loved who most likely has been killed in the war. Now, it torments her that she can't pick him up. She says she'll give him to me.
JAMIE:	For all practical purposes, she already has. You hardly ever put him down.
ROBERT:	I can't take my eyes off him. It's the most astonishing feeling. When I look into this baby's eyes I can see him seeing himself being seen. I feel as though I am giving birth to him as a person, as a human being. I am giving birth to him by my act of looking. Inside my look, he finds the power to make himself and, at the same time, I'm allowed to watch while this happens. My look is the womb in which he is able to grow his own idea of what it is to be him. I shudder when I think what the looks must have been like in the eyes of the young men who forced his life onto Admira. Somehow, by looking, I feel I am also redeeming them, or, at least, perhaps I am softening that memory transmitted to him through the traumatized flesh of his mother. This boy who has only a mob of crazed warrior kids for a father. This child of the twentieth century.
JAMIE:	Very eloquent.
ROBERT:	You're jealous, Jamie.
JAMIE:	I'm against jealousy on principle.
ROBERT:	So are we all, on principle. Still, there is a father/son aspect to our relationship. One could say it has been primarily that and…
JAMIE:	I've fathered you, too.
ROBERT:	… now, I seem to have a new child.
JAMIE:	I believe in every human being's inalienable right to maintain as many loves as he or she can satisfy at any one time.

ROBERT:	I see. Then surely you'll let me have a baby.
	(Silence)
	Let me put him down. He's sleeping.
JAMIE:	Go ahead.
	(He lays the child gently on the ground at the edge of the grove.)
ROBERT:	There, now.
	(Silence)
	You've always initiated our love making.
JAMIE:	Perhaps you should try.
	(ROBERT sits next to JAMIE, seducing him with his words.)
ROBERT:	Do you remember before Admira and Rachel came we spent the entire day here in this grove. We were insatiable. Like centaurs, I said, animal bodies with men's heads. We whinnied and pawed at the ground. You were my Orpheus, I said. And I 'a tree rising. What pure growing!/Orpheus is singing! A tree inside the ear.'
JAMIE:	Very nice.
ROBERT:	'To praise is the whole thing! A man who can praise/ comes toward us like ore out of the silences/ of rock. His heart, that dies, pressed out/ for others a wine that is fresh forever. / When the god's energy takes hold of him,/ his voice never collapses in the dust./Everything turns to vineyards, everything turns to grapes,/ made ready for harvest by his powerful south.'
JAMIE:	I've always found your translations of Rilke even more strikingly effete than the originals.
ROBERT:	Effete? That's ridiculous. Those are muscular lines. Sometimes I think you're not much of a critic.
JAMIE:	Effete from effetus. 'Worn out by childbearing.'
ROBERT:	Jamie, let me touch you.
JAMIE:	Take me.
ROBERT:	Take you?
JAMIE:	Take me anyway you want.
ROBERT:	Anyway I want?
JAMIE:	Ravage me. Here on this ground.
	(JAMIE is like stone.)
	Go ahead.
	(ROBERT kisses JAMIE. JAMIE doesn't move.)
JAMIE:	Do it to me for a change.
ROBERT:	What an odd thing to say.
JAMIE:	Is it?
ROBERT:	Do you want to be brutalized?
JAMIE:	Go ahead. Try.

ROBERT:	Are you playing some sort of a game?
JAMIE:	Not exactly.
ROBERT:	Let's talk.
JAMIE:	Talk. Talk. I'm sick of talk.
ROBERT:	Well, then, let me hold you. You must tell me what's wrong. Surely, it's not just the baby.
JAMIE:	Our life is so changed.
ROBERT:	Believe me, I know. Sybil used to be able to tend her bees and keep house for us. Now I'm taking care of a baby; you're doing the cooking. They've domesticated us.
JAMIE:	All for Admira's sake.
ROBERT:	I suppose so, yes.
JAMIE:	Admira is controlling all of us.
ROBERT:	She was so brutally controlled, now her needs must take precedent.
JAMIE:	It's hard. That's all. It makes everyone irritable all the time.
ROBERT:	It is eerie, isn't it? With Admira one always feels a bomb is waiting to go off.
JAMIE:	I think that bomb has already exploded.
ROBERT:	How so?
JAMIE:	Don't be coy with me, Robert, I really can't stand it.
ROBERT:	Coy?
JAMIE:	I know what you're writing.
ROBERT:	Do you? I can hardly tell. The images have a life of their own.
JAMIE:	You're just not man enough to act on your feelings. You know what? You disgust me, Robert.
ROBERT:	Don't say that.
JAMIE:	Why not. It's true. You're weak. You have no courage.
ROBERT:	Don't say such things.
JAMIE:	Why don't you take her if you want her so much.
ROBERT:	Who? What are you talking about?
JAMIE:	Admira. That's who.
ROBERT:	Take her? You're crazy.
	(JAMIE *slaps him.*)
ROBERT:	What's come over you?
JAMIE:	Don't call *me* crazy.
ROBERT:	Don't ever hit me again.
JAMIE:	Don't lie to me, then. First of all, don't lie to yourself.
ROBERT:	I don't know what you're talking about. Admira is an invalid. If I'm gentle with her…
JAMIE:	Wounded women, you can't resist them. The Dora Deming syndrome. I've been studying it. I can tolerate anything from you except dishonesty.

42

ROBERT:	You've flipped out. The tension of this house has gone to your head.
	(JAMIE *grabs* ROBERT.)
JAMIE:	You're in love with her and you don't know it. I am crazy. You're driving me crazy.
	(He throws ROBERT *to the ground.*)
	Don't you see how it's hurting me? How it's making me act? Don't you see it.
ROBERT:	Jamie. Jamie.
JAMIE:	Say it. Tell me the truth. 'I want her' say that. 'I want her so much I can't help myself.' Say it, goddamn it, say it. Tell me you dream about her. Tell me you want to fuck her.
ROBERT:	Who are you? What has happened to you?
JAMIE:	I can't respect you. You don't respect yourself. You don't know your own feelings. You're a coward, Robert. Why don't you take her? Take her if you want her so much. Tell the truth for a change. Get up.
	(ROBERT *grabs* JAMIE; *they fight.* ROBERT *pins* JAMIE.)
	Get off of me.
	(He does.)
ROBERT:	You're not yourself. Your whole body feels changed. You can't mean what you said. The words you used.
JAMIE:	This place is a mad house. There's too much pain.
ROBERT:	Don't you see, we're all in the grip of what was done to her. Her torturers have crawled inside our flesh.
JAMIE:	Rachel loves me.
ROBERT:	Don't say that.
JAMIE:	Why not? It's true.
ROBERT:	Perhaps. But I don't want to know.
JAMIE:	You can't hide from reality all the time.
ROBERT:	You're wrong about my feelings for Admira. I feel for her, yes, who wouldn't? And Rachel also needs comfort; she's seen the worst of men…
JAMIE:	I want her. I can't stop myself.
ROBERT:	Don't say that.
JAMIE:	I can't lie to you, Robert.
ROBERT:	She's my daughter.
JAMIE:	So what? She's an adult.
ROBERT:	Why do you want to hurt me so much?
JAMIE:	I want to give her some pleasure. She's suffered too much. I feel possessed. And I must tell you the truth.
ROBERT:	Fine. Now get a grip on yourself.
JAMIE:	Do you think I haven't tried? I've tried. The denial, the game, is driving me mad.

ROBERT:	What do you expect me to do?
JAMIE:	Stay out of our way. There, I've said it. Forgive me. I don't mean to be brutal.
ROBERT:	No?
JAMIE:	Give us room. Rachel deserves something good.
ROBERT:	Oh, yes, without question.
JAMIE:	So, there, you see, that's how it is.
ROBERT:	You accuse me because you are guilty. You are the guilty one.
JAMIE:	I have the courage to say what I want.
ROBERT:	Get out of my sight.
	(JAMIE *goes.* ROBERT *lets out a huge, animal bellow, a wounded bull.*)
	(RACHEL *enters.*)
RACHEL:	Don't make that awful sound.
ROBERT:	Don't judge me, Rachel.
RACHEL:	What did he tell you?
ROBERT:	What do you think?
RACHEL:	It's not true. I promise you there is nothing between us.
ROBERT:	Don't lie to me.
RACHEL:	Nothing has happened, father. Nothing will.
ROBERT:	You're a hero, home from the war. Naturally, he would fall in love with you. But how could you do this to me?
RACHEL:	I've done nothing to you.
ROBERT:	Don't lie, Rachel. It doesn't suit.
RACHEL:	Father, believe me, there is nothing between us.
ROBERT:	You might as well have made love with him all last night. You might as well be making love with him now.
RACHEL:	I didn't and I won't.
ROBERT:	I don't believe you. I can't believe you.
RACHEL:	You won't believe me.
ROBERT:	He's mad for you. He's possessed. How did it happen? Who did that?
RACHEL:	It's not my fault.
ROBERT:	What do you want me to believe? That I'm too old for him? That he needs some young blood?
RACHEL:	That's disgusting. He disgusts me if he says that.
ROBERT:	At least admit that you love him. At least give me that. You've been brutalized by what you've seen. He's gentle and kind. You're both young. It's inevitable. I understand.
RACHEL:	Will you shut up. Your sexual libertarianism is really too much.
	(*Silence;* ROBERT *turns away.*)
	You're terribly hurt.

ROBERT:	You love him, don't you? I can see it in your eyes.
RACHEL:	There is nothing between Jamie and me. There won't be.
ROBERT:	Why not admit you're attracted to him? We can all see that much. It's natural. It's normal. It's human. You're attracted to him and he's taken it to heart.
RACHEL:	A new love drama, that's what you want.
ROBERT:	We simply have to be adult about all of this.
RACHEL:	Another sickeningly gooey 'love' triangle of the Dora Deming variety; only the roles are slightly changed. You've thrown your own daughter into the boiling pot.
ROBERT:	Why not? It's a new age with a new plot. Why shouldn't my daughter dare fall in love with her father's lover? Why shouldn't we deal with this new complication of the heart?
RACHEL:	Because I won't give you the satisfaction of turning every complex human encounter into adolescent passion stew. If it's really going to be a new age all you flower children ought to grow up.
ROBERT:	We could revert to the past. I could drive a knife through your throat, you moralistic little twit.
RACHEL:	Go ahead. Go ahead. I'd rather be dead than sacrificed on the altar of your uncontrollable libido.
ROBERT:	You'll live to regret those words. As if passion can be controlled. As if it should.
RACHEL:	Yes. Threaten me. Because I won't do what you want. Because I won't destroy myself by falling in love with a homosexual.
ROBERT:	He's bisexual.
RACHEL:	'Bisexual' is just another word for totally irresponsible.
ROBERT:	You are the most narrow-minded young woman I have ever met.
RACHEL:	Mother was bisexual.
ROBERT:	You'll end up doing far more harm than good.
RACHEL:	She killed herself.
ROBERT:	I know, Rachel. I'm sorry about that.
RACHEL:	I'm not. I'm furious.
ROBERT:	What gives you the idea that your self-righteous rage is more benign than my addiction to intimacy, to love? You brought your rage into my house and ruined my life.
RACHEL:	Why don't you wake up and join the twentieth century. You live on an island where you invent the rules of decorum but a few hundred miles away from here men are cutting off other men's testicles and disemboweling pregnant women. I have a right to my rage. I have a right to rub your nose in it anytime I please.

ROBERT:	And I have a right to a vision of another way of being, where every passion flourishes and people are kind to one another precisely because they've been freed from the anti-life morality of fanatics of every persuasion.
RACHEL:	Sure, but don't be so squeamish when a little reality forces its way into your romantic bliss.
ROBERT:	I can take it, Rachel. The real question is whether or not you with your addiction to righteous misery can tolerate a little happiness. It's not a sin, you know.
RACHEL:	You're forcing me on Jamie.
ROBERT:	No, I'm not.
RACHEL:	Why? Why? I don't understand you at all. Why don't you protect yourself?
ROBERT:	I don't know. I've never been very good at that. I suppose I don't believe in boundaries of any sort.
RACHEL:	You never protected me. You never set limits. I always felt like an experiment of yours and mother's.
ROBERT:	You've turned out quite well, Rachel. I'm proud of you.
RACHEL:	Well, thanks.
ROBERT:	You're welcome.
RACHEL:	So let's not speak any more about Jamie Knox.
ROBERT:	No, except that he's in love with you and I just want to know if you return the feeling.
RACHEL:	You can't stop, can you? You never could. It's disgusting.
ROBERT:	Look, we're all living at rather close quarters on this island. I don't want to play the fool.
RACHEL:	And I don't want to end up a hysterical lump on the floor so that you and Jamie Knox can glory in a new drama that makes you suffer then draws you closer and leaves me out just like I've been left out all my life.
ROBERT:	This is the revenge plot for your mother's suicide.
RACHEL:	I have no plot. Unlike you, I have other things on my mind besides sex.
ROBERT:	You've always been so quick to judge. So quick that you have no life.
RACHEL:	Quick? I've had years of practice, don't you think. I grew up in your house. Tell me how happy it was.
ROBERT:	Happy? Happy? You want to be happy? You grew up in a house alive with poetry, passion, love. I loved your mother. I treated her like a goddess. Like a goddess she had room to roam, to explore, to be. I never felt I owned her. I didn't want to own her. I wanted to

adventure through life with her. We did that. She and I. We were free. And we made art from every hurt, from every experience we made something beautiful not only for ourselves, but for the world. We pushed forward the boundaries of the possible. We made everyday life wildly exciting. And human love heroic. What did you learn from our example? How to sacrifice yourself on an altar of self-righteousness. How to cling to misery, war and violence.

RACHEL: I'm not a poet; I'm a human rights worker.

ROBERT: Then give yourself some human rights. Give yourself the right to admit your passion.

RACHEL: My passion really pales in the face of the cruelty in the world. Maybe it was all right for your generation to indulge every sexual whim but aside from the obvious physical danger of such a life style now, I must say that what compels me most is not sex but the hope that I could make some small difference in the balance of terror which currently controls the world. I simply don't think the best way to accomplish my aim is by fucking my father's boyfriend no matter how pleasurable it might feel for twenty minutes. But I am not a prude. You're wrong if you think I can't imagine pleasure. You're wrong if you think I can't love; only I don't intend to upset everyone's life because of it.

ROBERT: You have already upset everyone's life.

RACHEL: Oh, yes. You can't bear to look, can you? Not at real suffering. You like to manufacture esthetic grief. But you can't bear the real stuff. People whose lives have really been destroyed through absolutely no fault of their own.

ROBERT: Suddenly there's an enemy behind every tree.

RACHEL: At least Jamie has the grace to end your charade.

ROBERT: You do love him. I know you do. Oh, Rachel. Rachel. How could you?

RACHEL: How could I what?

ROBERT: Fall in love with Jamie. How could you do that?

RACHEL: Stop it. You're driving me mad.

ROBERT: Don't lie to me any longer. The damage is already done. He's treating me like a stranger. You might as well live your passion out. I give you my blessing. I promise you, it will be worse if you don't.

RACHEL: Where's the baby?

ROBERT: He's over there, on the ground.

RACHEL: He's been lying here the whole time.

ROBERT:	He's an infant.
RACHEL:	You're not fit to have a child. You never were. You make me sick to my stomach.

(ROBERT *slaps her.*)

ROBERT: There's my blessing. Go give yourself to Jamie Knox. You are the only person I know who is more calculating than he is.

RACHEL: I'm taking the baby back to the house.

(RACHEL *picks up the baby and leaves.*)

(*Another part of the forest.* SYBIL *is painting.* ADMIRA *is sitting on the ground a few feet away.*)

ADMIRA: What are you painting, Sybil?

SYBIL: I'm painting your inner demons.

ADMIRA: Those are your inner demons, Sybil. My demons are not so inner. They are all on the flesh.

SYBIL: You will have a full life.

ADMIRA: How can you say that?

SYBIL: What is a full life but a life lived down to the bone. You should paint.

ADMIRA: I can't paint anymore. My hands don't know how.

SYBIL: I didn't paint before.

ADMIRA: Before your life broke?

SYBIL: Yes, before that.

ADMIRA: I heard it in you. The branch snaps.

SYBIL: The beasts that enter one's dreams, you can paint those.

ADMIRA: I have no dreams.

SYBIL: You don't know what you dream.

ADMIRA: I don't want to know any more. I want to be left alone.

SYBIL: But they are everywhere. I see them everywhere I go. Cold eyes looking down. There is nothing in those eyes. I am painting them so they will leave us alone.

ADMIRA: Don't say such things.

SYBIL: You brought them here. They are all around us in the air.

ADMIRA: You have all tried so hard. But they will kill you, too.

SYBIL: I'm painting to tie them down. To give them a place to go. I have hundreds of paintings like this. I paint all the time. I never show them to anyone. But your demons are not mine.

ADMIRA: I was happy when I died. I looked down from the sky. I saw a woman chained to a bed. I heard the laughter of men. I don't want to live again.

SYBIL: I don't know what colors to use.

ADMIRA: I want to kill the child, too.

SYBIL:	Of course you do.
ADMIRA:	I want the child dead. It would be better for him. Then I could rest. I begged him not to join the fight. I pleaded with him. He had to, he said. He had to try to save something of what we had. He was also a writer. Like Robert. I hope he has died. We used to be happy. We drank wine. We talked. We held hands. Walked. *(RACHEL enters with the child. She is distraught.)*
RACHEL:	Take the baby, Admira.
ADMIRA:	No.
RACHEL:	Hold your son.
ADMIRA:	Don't. He's not mine.
RACHEL:	Yes he is; I want you to take him.
ADMIRA:	Go away. Can't you see anything? They are everywhere. All around.
RACHEL:	No one is here, Admira. But you and Sybil, me and the baby.
SYBIL:	Stop, Rachel.
RACHEL:	No. It's time. She has to touch him. She has to connect. She's done enough damage to herself.
SYBIL:	Enough? Rachel, enough! *(SYBIL approaches RACHEL and takes the child.)*
RACHEL:	I want you to speak. I want you to tell me what you remember.
ADMIRA:	You don't want to know.
RACHEL:	I can't stand the silence anymore.
ADMIRA:	I can't tell you.
RACHEL:	You must.
ADMIRA:	I can't speak before you. You are like a nun. You are too good.
RACHEL:	I'm not going to let you destroy yourself. Do you understand? I want you to tell me everything.
ADMIRA:	I'm dead. The dead don't speak.
RACHEL:	*(She shakes ADMIRA by the shoulders.)* You're alive, dammit. You're alive. You're alive and you're going to talk.
SYBIL:	Rachel! *(RACHEL pushes ADMIRA who falls to the ground, where she cowers. RACHEL backs away, stunned.)*
RACHEL:	Oh, my god, oh, my god, oh, my god. I could kill her.
SYBIL:	You see how they get inside of us.
RACHEL:	I could wring her neck. Help me. Somebody help me.
SYBIL:	I must paint them. *(RACHEL exits.)* *(SYBIL sits on her stool, rocking back and forth with the child on her lap.)*

ADMIRA:	I want to kill my child.
SYBIL:	I know, child. I know that.
ADMIRA:	No one should live. Not anymore. Beasts. Only monsters should walk the earth. He is too weak. I won't let him. I won't allow it. They took babies by their heels, hit their heads against rock. I saw what came out.
SYBIL:	I did. I did it. No one believed me. It was an accident. The wall came out of nowhere. I turned right into it. I had my foot on the gas. The air smelled like spring. I had the pedal to the ground. I could smell her sweet flesh.
ADMIRA:	They did it all in front of everyone. They took four of us. In front of everyone. On the ground. They did it. Everyone saw it. No one moved.
SYBIL:	It was a long time ago. Before even Rachel was born. Then no one could believe such things. I didn't believe it myself. Even with my black eyes, I couldn't see. Now people try to believe. They read in the newspapers. They see on the television.
ADMIRA:	I itched so. The smell. I couldn't stand the smell. They made me smell like that. I can't say these things to anyone. I want to shout. All the time I want to shout. I am so dirty inside. I must be dead. No one lives with so much dirt.
SYBIL:	She used to talk in poetry. She said to me when she was three and a half, 'mama, where do the stars go in day? Do they go down under the earth to dance with the dead bones.' When she was just two, she asked: 'Mama, why doesn't light always come colored like in rainbows?' I wrote the things she said down in my head. They were going to take her away from me. They were going to take her away. Because I watched him one night from the door, when he hurt her. I watched. My tongue turned to ash in my mouth.
ADMIRA:	I wanted to kill them all. I want to go back and I want to kill. I want to kill everyone who looked at me. Everyone who watched. Everyone who knows anything. Rachel knows too much. Some nights I want to take a knife. I want to cut out her heart. So she'll know. So she'll know what it felt like.
SYBIL:	Robert was already a poet when her words stopped. I thought that a big fist was behind us pushing us. Now, she would only whine. She would sit on my lap and cling. She would hold onto my knees all the time. She had been free. Now I saw how he had stopped her. He had put a big fist in her mouth. No one would believe. I didn't believe myself. It wasn't my life.

ADMIRA:	I knew them. I knew them because I had taught one year in their village. They were village boys. They used to do the things village boys do. It was so strange that I knew them. Ordinary boys. I knew one or two of their names. They looked in my eyes. No. I am dead. No one survives.
SYBIL:	My husband said I was crazy. He said I made everything up. For a long time I didn't know the truth. He said they were going to take her away from me because I was making her crazy. I knew something else. But I didn't know how to say it out loud. I was afraid he would kill us both. Afraid he would hit me again on the head, afraid he would use his gun.
ADMIRA:	I didn't mind for me. I was dead already. But I saw what they did to the others. To young girls and old women. And their eyes were so cold. They had no life in their eyes. A mother held her child to protect him. To protect him, she held him tight. So they couldn't take him away, she wrapped her arms around his chest. She held him tight to protect him. While she held him; they cut his head off.
SYBIL:	It was not an accident. No. I planned it all. I planned it when I saw the wall. I put my foot on the gas. I thought I would run the wall through both of us. I never saw her again. They wouldn't let me go to her funeral. They sent me away to live with Robert. My teeth were scattered across the cement. I saw her bright blue headband alone in the middle of the street.
ADMIRA:	If it was for myself, I could stand anything. But for the others, for them, I couldn't help. I was too dirty to live. I knew this man. He was a high school teacher of mine. He was dripping with blood. He held a knife in his hand. He looked at me in the eyes. 'Now you see how strong I am.' I was dead already, I had died so all I could do was hang from the top of the ceiling and look down.
SYBIL:	That's how I learned to keep bees. Dora bought me a hive. Dora was always very good to me. I found out that bees live the same way in captivity or in the wild. No one has ever been able to change the essence of bees. All we have ever been able to do is steal their honey, but the bees go on being bees just the same as always. They live as if they were free. They talk to each other with their wings. They make up dances. In times long ago, people used to understand the language of bees but now we've forgotten how to understand them.

(The sound of ROBERT's *flute. He is playing as he wanders around the forest.* ADMIRA *drops off to sleep. As this happens,* RACHEL *runs into* JAMIE *at the house.)*

RACHEL:	I don't care, anymore. I love you.
JAMIE:	I love you.
RACHEL:	There I've said it.
JAMIE:	We'll take the child and go. I'll rub your breasts until they give milk. We could take Admira. If you want to. Our love will heal her. We'll go somewhere beautiful.
RACHEL:	Quiet, don't talk.
JAMIE:	We are somewhere beautiful.
RACHEL:	I thought so.
JAMIE:	You are beautiful.
RACHEL:	I tried so hard not to want you.
JAMIE:	Today I think I'm crazy. I'm crazy with longing.
RACHEL:	I'm going mad. I'll go mad if I can't have you.
JAMIE:	May I kiss the back of your neck?
RACHEL:	If you promise me you won't stop.
JAMIE:	I'll kiss you all over. I'll kiss all the pain out of you. *(He kisses her softly on the neck.)* Rachel, brave Rachel. I'll be so careful. *(RACHEL takes JAMIE's hand, leads him out of sight. ROBERT walks into the grove where SYBIL is seated and ADMIRA sleeps.)*
SYBIL:	She's sleeping.
ROBERT:	Sweet oblivion.
SYBIL:	The earth shifted.
ROBERT:	She reminds me of Dora, somehow, when I see her like that. *(He kneels next to her, touches her lightly on the neck.)* How does one live without touch?
SYBIL:	Bees.
ROBERT:	You never wanted something else, Sybil, after it was all in the past?
SYBIL:	I wanted to see you happy, Robert. You and Rachel. But I am afraid of Jamie Knox.
ROBERT:	So am I, Sybil. I'm afraid of what he makes me feel.
SYBIL:	I am afraid of the power of that boy. Jamie Knox is not like us. He hasn't suffered enough.
ROBERT:	That's why I loved him, at first.
SYBIL:	He will destroy Rachel.
ROBERT:	Rachel will destroy Rachel, I'm afraid.
SYBIL:	It's not right that the innocent are not saved, that the innocent are sacrificed all the time.
ROBERT:	It's the hardest thing to accept. One must bow one's head.

SYBIL:	Admira was hurting no one. She was minding her own business. Rachel wants me to suck the pain out of her. *(She spits.)* Such poison is in the world. I've grown fat on it.
ROBERT:	At least she's sleeping.
SYBIL:	Rachel believes we can act against evil. Rachel believes in human beings, in the power of the rational mind. That's why she'll be destroyed. Here. *(She hands the child to* ROBERT, *gets up, takes her paints and easel and goes.)*
ROBERT:	If I can just rest here awhile, next to you, dear, in the sun. *(*ADMIRA *stirs.)* Hello. You've been sleeping.
ADMIRA:	Oh, Robert how sad you are.
ROBERT:	I think so.
ADMIRA:	I bring such suffering here. I should go. I should take away my child.
ROBERT:	This island is your home as long as you want to be here. It's your home and your child's.
ADMIRA:	Can I have my son? I woke up wanting to hold him. I think I had a dream.
ROBERT:	Here he is. *(*ROBERT *puts the baby into her arms.)*
ADMIRA:	It's not so hard to hold him.
ROBERT:	No, it's not hard.
ADMIRA:	I didn't know. Sometimes he looked like them. Sometimes like the other one. I couldn't tell. But Jamie doesn't have a father.
ROBERT:	Maybe I should try to be Rachel's father for a change.
ADMIRA:	It sounds simple as it should be. But nothing is so simple in the flesh. So you are sad.
ROBERT:	I am.
ADMIRA:	I'm sorry to have mentioned Jamie. I can see he's hurt you.
ROBERT:	You are very wise.
ADMIRA:	Wise? No, but now I can look through people. It's like an x-ray machine, my eyes, I look in. I can't help myself. I would rather not. Hush, now, my sweet child. *(*RACHEL *calling as she enters;* ROBERT *blocks her path.)*
RACHEL:	Admira.
ROBERT:	Rachel.
RACHEL:	Father.

ROBERT:	I'm sorry.
RACHEL:	Don't be.
ROBERT:	I'm sorry I slapped you.
RACHEL:	It's all right.
ROBERT:	I'm sorry I doubted you.
RACHEL:	Can we talk about something else.
ROBERT:	I think Jamie should leave.
RACHEL:	It's quite all right with me to have him here.
ROBERT:	He made me turn on you. I've never hit anyone in my life.
RACHEL:	It's all right. I was wrong to be angry with you, Admira. Please forgive me.
ADMIRA:	Look, I'm holding my child.
RACHEL:	Admira, oh, look, I didn't even see.
ADMIRA:	Rachel. Oh, my friend. You have suffered so much because of me. I am worried for you. I need to go change him.
RACHEL:	I'll take him.
ADMIRA:	No, please, let me. Sybil will help me.
	(ADMIRA *exits.*)
ROBERT:	Jamie made me doubt your integrity.
RACHEL:	Father, please.
ROBERT:	He can be gone in a day or two.
RACHEL:	You needn't do it for me. I'll be leaving soon myself.
ROBERT:	Jamie should go at once. We should be together as father and daughter for a change. Isn't that what you want?
RACHEL:	I don't know. It seems late to start.
ROBERT:	How can you want him to stay after what he's done to us?
RACHEL:	It's just… I don't know… Do what you want to do. You always do in any case.
	(RACHEL *leaves.* JAMIE *enters.*)
JAMIE:	It's quite all right. I'll go pack my bags. I can catch the last ferry.
ROBERT:	I don't want you to go.
JAMIE:	Well, that's simple, then. I'll stay.
ROBERT:	Rachel promised me there is nothing between you.
JAMIE:	Did she?
ROBERT:	Is there?
JAMIE:	I will go if you want me to. The house belongs to you.
ROBERT:	I want things the way they were.
JAMIE:	For a wise man, you are terribly naive. I think that's what I love about you.
ROBERT:	Do you?
JAMIE:	Rachel is going soon. Back into the war.

ROBERT:	I want you both to stay.
JAMIE:	In that case, you can have what you want.
ROBERT:	But I need to know there is nothing between you. She's my daughter, after all.
JAMIE:	Don't interrogate me, Robert, please. What good does it do? Rachel will be your daughter forever. Someday, you'll find I'm completely expendable; that I've been your fantasy all along.
ROBERT:	I'd like to walk for a while alone.
JAMIE:	I'll wait for you at the house.
ROBERT:	You are some kind of a monster.
JAMIE:	I haven't done this by myself. I think we're all a bit possessed.

Scene IV

The Sea

(ADMIRA *is dressed in black. She is sitting on a stone bench at the edge of the cliff going down to the sea.* RACHEL *is with her. The sound of the ocean intensifies, a storm is coming up.*)

RACHEL:	All right, Admira, here's some nice warm soup. I want you to take the spoon. (ADMIRA *takes the spoon and throws it.*) Then, I'll have to feed you. Come on, Admira, it's pistou. Jamie made it and you like it. Remember the first time we had it for dinner, you said you would like to learn how to cook this. It's full of fresh basil and ripe tomatoes from the garden. It's delicious.
ADMIRA:	Let me see it. (RACHEL *shows her the soup.*) Give it to me. I want to smell it. (RACHEL *hands* ADMIRA *the bowl; she smells it, blows on it, and then dumps it down the front of her dress.*)
ADMIRA:	I don't want your food.
RACHEL:	It's not my food, Admira.
ADMIRA:	Covered in filth.
RACHEL:	Look what you've done to yourself.
ADMIRA:	Look.
RACHEL:	Admira, I'm a person, like you are. We don't always act in ways that please one another. But you're not punishing me by not eating. You're hurting yourself and your baby.
ADMIRA:	I'm dirty. You can't see.
RACHEL:	You were so much better, Admira. What happened to you?

ADMIRA:	To you. What happened to you.
RACHEL:	I thought I could have something I needed for myself. I thought you were strong enough. Maybe I didn't think very much. I'm sorry.
ADMIRA:	Sorry.
RACHEL:	Sorry if I've upset you. Sorry, yes.
ADMIRA:	I don't care what you do. It doesn't matter to me what happens to you.
RACHEL:	Well it matters to me what happens to you. I don't want you to ruin your health.
ADMIRA:	You use me to make yourself feel good. People like you need to feel good about themselves. You pick us up out of the garbage. You pick up our bones. You hold us together for a while with your hands. All the time, you are thinking how good you are. How much better than we are you are.
RACHEL:	That's not true.
ADMIRA:	How privileged you have been. How chosen. Still, you have trouble feeling like a person. So you find someone who has been shamed. Someone who smells bad. And you say to yourself, 'look how kind I am. Look how good.' But it is still a lie. You still don't feel whole. You still feel rotten on the inside.
RACHEL:	I feel rotten because you won't eat. That's why I feel bad.
ADMIRA:	Don't worry about me. I'm done needing people to worry about me. It's no way to live.
RACHEL:	I won't worry anymore, if you will take some food.
ADMIRA:	I'm not in my body anymore. I pretend.
RACHEL:	You're sitting right in front of me. Your words are coming out of your mouth. You hear what I'm saying through your ears.
ADMIRA:	That's because you don't know anything.
	(RACHEL takes her hand.)
RACHEL:	This is your body, Admira. You can feel my hand.
ADMIRA:	You can do anything you want to me. I don't feel anything. Not your dirty hand.
RACHEL:	I just want to give you some food.
ADMIRA:	I can't eat because my mouth is gone.
RACHEL:	You're talking through your mouth right now. You can eat through your mouth, too.
ADMIRA:	My mouth is not mine.
RACHEL:	It's been a week since you've had solid food. Three days, Admira, since you've had any water. I know because I've been watching you around the clock. I'm very tired now. You must be very weak.

ADMIRA:	I am strong like a bull.
RACHEL:	You were getting strong. Remember? You were strong enough to swim in the sea. Would you like to swim, again, Admira?
ADMIRA:	Like an eel in the mud; like a fish with poison in its tale.
RACHEL:	I know you're very angry at me. You have a right to be angry if that's the way you feel. But you're only punishing yourself by refusing to eat.
ADMIRA:	I want to hurt.
RACHEL:	But none of us deserves to be punished. You don't deserve to punish yourself.
ADMIRA:	I want revenge.
RACHEL:	Starving yourself is not the way to accomplish that. You need to get strong, then you can come testify at the war crimes tribunal. You could help all the women.
ADMIRA:	I want revenge but you won't let me have what I want so I left myself.
RACHEL:	Look, if you won't eat, we're going to have to force feed you. Do you know what that means?
ADMIRA:	Go away.
RACHEL:	Sybil will call the doctor and he will pry your mouth open and run a tube down your throat. Do you want her to do that?
ADMIRA:	You understand none of this.
RACHEL:	He'll have to tie your hands to the bed so you don't pull the tube out. Do you want us to torture you like they did, Admira? Why do you want us to do that?
ADMIRA:	I am gone.
	(JAMIE *enters.*)
JAMIE:	Hey, I worked hard making that soup. There's more in the kitchen when you're ready. It smells really good, doesn't it?
	(ADMIRA *is silent.*)
RACHEL:	Shall I get another bowl from the kitchen, Admira? Would you take some?
	(ADMIRA *is silent.*)
JAMIE:	You've got to eat, you know. Everyone has to.
RACHEL:	I'm at my wits end.
JAMIE:	Poor Rachel.
RACHEL:	You were with my father last night.
JAMIE:	He wanted to talk.
RACHEL:	What did you say?
JAMIE:	Look, nobody said it wouldn't be difficult.
RACHEL:	I promised myself I'd never play their game.

JAMIE:	'Their game'? You are the eternal cynic.
RACHEL:	What do you want me to call it?
JAMIE:	How about a rare and beautiful, complicated love?
RACHEL:	How about insane.
JAMIE:	We can stop anytime.
RACHEL:	We can stop. Admira can eat. Why don't we do it? Why don't you eat your soup for god's sake?
JAMIE:	Here he comes. Let's go for a swim. Come on, before you totally lose it.

(ROBERT *enters; eating chocolate. He hands some to* ADMIRA.)

ROBERT:	Here's a chocolate bar, Admira. Bittersweet. Eat.
JAMIE:	We're going swimming.
ROBERT:	The wind is up.
RACHEL:	We'll be fine.
ROBERT:	You have each other.
RACHEL:	Father...
ROBERT:	I've been thinking that perhaps we could work out a schedule so we won't be getting in one another's way. That must be the civilized thing to do in such a case as ours. It's a pity the house is so small. Did you know that chocolate produces the same hormonal changes in the body as being in love? Eat your chocolate, Admira, it's good for you.

(*In the middle of his speech,* JAMIE *and* RACHEL *go down to the shore, hand in hand.* ROBERT *sits down on the bench.*)

I used to believe in the nobility of the human project. I believed that the human being's ability to create beauty had secured us a necessary place on the earth. I believed that poetry is rooted in love, and love in desire, and desire in hope of continued existence. I believed poetry alone could transmute pain. Everything ugly and base, everything cruel beyond comprehension could be washed clean by the creative act. So you see, they've taken my work from me. They can't help it. Rachel is starved. She has starved herself. It's dangerous, Admira, to deny the self.

ADMIRA:	I am hungry for one thing, Robert, only.
ROBERT:	I would like to take revenge against both of them. I would like to break their happiness as mine was broken.
ADMIRA:	I want to raise my son to take revenge for me. I want to raise him to know he must fight to the death. That there can be no peace.
ROBERT:	A storm is coming up.
ADMIRA:	I want to raise my son to be a killer.
ROBERT:	They've gone swimming in this weather.

ADMIRA:	My son will avenge my honor, the honor of my people. He will wash the stain from his mother.
ROBERT:	I should give them my blessing. I've cursed them. Yes, I've cursed them a thousand times. I should write a play in which they both die because of my curse and I am suddenly seized by remorse; I learn by suffering but only when it is too late. I learn what I've lost over the mutilated bodies of the two I cursed. Or maybe only she dies and he returns to me, full of remorse for what he's done, but by then it doesn't matter anymore. Happiness is beyond us. Grief for our loss is all we can share. I send him away. He goes as an exile to atone. I imagine their naked bodies intertwined. I am tortured by my own ability to see their love. It's as if I am sleeping with her myself. Of course, they know that. They've whispered about it to themselves, maybe they've even laughed out loud. There is nothing more exciting than the laughter of guilty lovers. It's despicable to grow old. My flesh smells rotten. I shouldn't be telling you this. It's bad for you, I'm sure.
ADMIRA:	So I must die. If I don't die I will make my son into a murderer. There is no other way.
ROBERT:	But if your pain is the only real pain then what is this thing I'm feeling?
ADMIRA:	When I go away from my body I stop wanting my son to kill for me. You must listen to what I am saying.
ROBERT:	If I could make them suffer. If I can kill what is happy in them.
ADMIRA:	If I die, my son can live. He won't have to grow up to be a killer. If I die, he won't have to remember.
ROBERT:	Admira, what are you talking about?
ADMIRA:	If I die, he can live. He won't have to carry my rage.
ROBERT:	My god, Admira, listen to what you are saying.
ADMIRA:	What am I saying, Robert. What? I want to die to protect him from me. I want to die. Let him live. Pretend he is clean. You can pretend that for him.
ROBERT:	You have to tell him that yourself. He will have to hear that from you. You will tell him you were innocent, that he is innocent, too.
ADMIRA:	All I could see, Robert. All I could see. Suddenly all I could see were swollen bellies. In the room all around were women crying. I was one of their voices. All alone, shivering. But all I could see were bellies heaving. Like the bellies of the sea. Swollen sea bellies. And the sea was singing to us; she opened her mouth, swollen bellies heaved out. I tasted sea salt in my mouth. I cannot explain what I saw. We were each one of us waves, all the women alone

59

in that room were like the waves on the sea; I saw it all in that moment. I remember I said to myself, 'I am going to live.' That is my story, too, isn't it, Robert?

ROBERT: A storm is coming up.

(He takes her hand.)

They shouldn't be swimming. Come with me. I can't face them alone.

(They exit. SYBIL *enters, a piece of paper in her hand.)*

SYBIL: I've been praying for a miracle. Now it's come. God bless the fax machine. The sea is up. There's going to be a storm.

JAMIE: *(Dripping wet from the ocean)*

Where is she, Sybil? Where's Rachel?

SYBIL: I thought she was panting after you.

JAMIE: She swam away from me. I had no idea she could swim so fast.

SYBIL: Like a fish.

*(*SYBIL *exits.* ROBERT *and* ADMIRA *enter.)*

ROBERT: Where is she, you bastard?

JAMIE: I've lost her.

ROBERT: I'll kill you with my bare hands. I swear it. If something's happened to Rachel, I'll pull you apart limb from limb.

JAMIE: I thought she must have come back here.

ROBERT: She was in no condition to go swimming. No one's been sleeping.

There's a storm coming.

JAMIE: She was swimming too fast for me. She simply vanished. I yelled for her. I had to turn back. The waves were too high.

ROBERT: I know the sea when the season turns. It's treacherous.

JAMIE: Why didn't you warn us?

ROBERT: It seemed fitting.

JAMIE: She'll be all right.

ROBERT: Dora drowned herself in the fall. Dora complicated her life beyond endurance. Then she told me she was going swimming.

JAMIE: My god.

ROBERT: You know all of this. You're writing her goddamned biography. You dragged Rachel with you.

JAMIE: I didn't know the sea was so rough.

ROBERT: You want life to imitate your miserable art.

JAMIE: It's not true.

ROBERT: Demigods. Puffed up. I know the type. We're all alike.

JAMIE: I never thought she'd swim straight out. I tried to follow, then, suddenly, I couldn't see her anymore.

60

ROBERT:	If you've drowned my child I'll wring your miserable neck. You charlatan. You gigolo.
JAMIE:	If anything has happened to Rachel, I'll never forgive myself.
ROBERT:	I'll kill you with my own hands.
JAMIE:	Go ahead. Do it. It's my fault.
	(ADMIRA, *who has been staring out to sea, begins ravenously to eat her chocolate bar.*)
	(SYBIL *enters, breaking into* ROBERT *and* JAMIE's *fight.*)
SYBIL:	Rachel's gone.
ROBERT:	What do you mean, gone?
SYBIL:	Left.
ROBERT:	Tell me the truth.
SYBIL:	Fled.
JAMIE:	Gone? That's not possible.
SYBIL:	Packed her bag in a hurry.
JAMIE:	Where is she?
SYBIL:	Already on the ferry. A fax came to the house. She read it and left.
ROBERT:	Thank god, she's safe.
JAMIE:	She went back to the war.
ADMIRA:	I must go.
ROBERT:	No, dear, you mustn't.
SYBIL:	Rachel is needed to gather facts.
ROBERT:	Your home is here, Admira, as long as you want it. Look, you've got chocolate all over your face.
JAMIE:	Robert, forgive me.
ROBERT:	It tastes good, doesn't it?
JAMIE:	Robert…
ROBERT:	Let's go eat something hot.
JAMIE:	Forgive me for loving you both.
	(ROBERT *is holding* ADMIRA's *hand. He looks at* JAMIE *and almost smiles.*)

Epilogue

The House

(ROBERT *and* JAMIE *are on either side of a table, writing.* SYBIL *is painting at a large easel in the center of the room. A playpen full of toys reminds us that the child is sleeping in the next room. From outside there is a tremendous, rhythmic clatter. The sound of metal hitting stone. Adding to it, the sound of the ferry horn. Everyone is lost in work.*)

JAMIE:	It's amazing the child can sleep.

ROBERT:	Actually, I think he finds the noise comforting.
JAMIE:	It's insane to try to work like this. I keep saying I'll build myself a hut.
ROBERT:	I find the noise comforting myself.
JAMIE:	I'm going to do it.
ROBERT:	In the woods. I'll come to you.
JAMIE:	I'm thinking of going to Paris for the winter.
	(The men look at one another. The sound outside stops. ADMIRA *enters. Dressed in white, a white bandanna tied around her forehead, holding her sculptor's tools. She has been carving marble.)*
ADMIRA:	I'm starved. But I've found an amazing vein in the marble to expose. I'll have to twist the mother's belly but I think can do it. I am calling it 'The Survivors.' After supper you will look.
ROBERT:	I'll look now.
ADMIRA:	After we eat. Someday, maybe I can bring it home. Put it outside in a square so the children can climb on it and the doves…
ROBERT:	Someday soon.
JAMIE:	Someday at sunset, we'll have the unveiling. Drink champagne.
ADMIRA:	I'm so hungry.
SYBIL:	Rachel will be here in time for dinner.
ADMIRA:	We didn't tell you.
SYBIL:	Rachel's coming.
ADMIRA:	She asked us to keep secret.
JAMIE:	Coming here?
ROBERT:	Rachel?
	*(*RACHEL *steps in through the open window. She is very pregnant; she stands with her hands on her belly. Everyone is silent, looking at her.)*
SYBIL:	Rachel, Rachel, Rachel. Look at you.
	*(*ADMIRA *has a sudden feeling of fear.)*
ADMIRA:	Rachel. No! Not you. This I will not stand.
	*(*RACHEL *goes to her; the women embrace;* RACHEL *calms her.)*
RACHEL:	It's all right, Admira. I want to be pregnant. No one hurt me. I wrote you. You remember.
ADMIRA:	Rachel, my friend, of course, for a minute… I am so… always so…
SYBIL:	Come, come, you're stronger all the time.
	*(*ROBERT *moves to embrace her.)*
ROBERT:	Daughter.
RACHEL:	Father.
ROBERT:	We worried about you, Rachel.
RACHEL:	I've been working on the war crimes tribunal. Gathering testimonies from refugees. It's important.

ROBERT: We missed you.

JAMIE: It's our child, isn't it? It's ours. It must be. Oh, Robert, oh, Rachel. I'm sorry. I'm thrilled.

RACHEL: Father...

ROBERT: It doesn't matter. I love you.

RACHEL: I've married a journalist from Sarajevo. To get him out of the slaughter. He's waiting outside on the path.

JAMIE: But, Rachel...

RACHEL: I don't know who the father is.

             (RACHEL *smiles at* ADMIRA. ROBERT *and* ADMIRA *move to embrace* RACHEL.)

END

Several lines and fragments of Jamie's and Robert's in The Beehives scene are from *The Bacchae*, translated by William Arrowsmith (University of Chicago, 1959). Grateful acknowledgment is made to David Young for permission to quote lines from his translation of *The Sonnets to Orpheus* by Rainer Maria Rilke (Wesleyan Poetry Series, 1987). Robert's line: '... poetry is rooted in love, and love in desire, and desire in hope of continued existence,' is a direct quote from Robert Graves, *The White Goddess* (Farrar, Straus and Giroux, 1966: 408).

On *The Beekeeper's Daughter*

Christen Clifford

On The Zookeeper's Daughter

Chapter Eleven

W hen I sat down to write an afterword to *The Beekeeper's Daughter*, a play I acted in three times over twenty years ago, my thoughts fragmented. I couldn't separate my knowledge of the play from my knowledge of the playwright, from my own corporeal experience, from my feminisms. But one thing was clear: we have a popular feminism now, as we did not then, with which to hear this play.

The Beekeeper's Daughter takes on rape culture, care-giving, cultural privilege and do-gooderism, gender norms and transsexuality, toxic masculinity and war: and all of this twenty-plus years ago, before our culture had named them as such. If a two-hour poetic play about rape and war was a hard sell in the 1990s when even the theater was touched by grunge and minimalism (downtown – think Richard Maxwell and Mac Wellman; uptown – think David Ives and Jez Butterworth), then in 2016 the play seems perfectly of its time. Culturally, we can see these issues without cringing so much. We can even laugh.

I first met Karen at New York University, where I took every class she taught. First a 'Theater History 101' course, then 'Modern Drama' (Chekhov, Ibsen, Shaw, Strindberg through a feminist lens), then 'Women in Theater'. I have performed in several of her plays: *Going to Iraq: Blue Heaven, The Beekeeper's Daughter* and *Another Life*. She taught me about Aphra Behn, Ana Mendieta and introduced me to Judith Malina and Hanon Reznikov of The Living Theatre. She has led by example how to live a good life filled with art, love and conviction. Social justice defines her life and work and she is a constant inspiration to me. I love her. Like any New Yorker, and anyone who works creatively, and anyone that loves truly, to quote Taylor Swift, we drive each other crazy sometimes.

As an actor I got to go back to *The Beekeeper's Daughter* three times. Each time, I learned more about Admira and more about myself. These are experiences actors love, and since we don't have rep companies anymore, these are increasingly rare. Admira is in me, a part of me. This play influenced me to want to make positive change in the world. To tell untold stories. To tell women's stories. To activate the personal and political.

I have seen Karen's influence on other classmates from NYU, most notably Anohni, an ecofeminist musician formerly known as Antony Hegarty of Antony and the Johnsons. I see Karen's influence in such songs as '4 Degrees,' 'Dust and Water' and 'Another World': 'I need another place will there be peace? I need another world, this one's nearly gone.'

Of course, I was terrified of this play, of this character. Of course, that's what made it so satisfying.

We performed *The Beekeeper's Daughter* the first time in Veroli, Italy, at the Dionysia Festival of Contemporary Drama, in 1994. The Bosnian war was still going on. We rehearsed in New York and in Italy. Veroli is a medieval hill town. When I wore the costumes by Sally Ann Parsons, I was transformed into Admira. A secular Muslim. I entered in a dirty denim dress with a fake belly underneath. It was heavy. I wore brown low heels. I'm a bit of a shoe actor. When I appeared as Admira, pregnant in the pale blue jumper, men yelled at me, 'Madonna!'

When Rachel realizes Jamie has a penis, she says: 'I don't want to be around men.' Jamie: 'I have nothing in common with my brothers in the grip of testosterone poisoning who are butchering one another for land and nation.'

People didn't talk about rape that much in the 1990s.

I felt like it was my fault that I had been raped.

Karen had a psychiatrist from Yale as a consultant. I said to him, 'I feel like what happened to me doesn't matter because what happened to these women, to this character Admira, is so much worse.' He answered: 'By that logic the women who were raped by 6 men would feel that their pain was worth nothing compared to the women who were raped by 7 men. Is that true?'

Radical feminism has helped me understand that it was not my fault that I was raped. Feminism has given me a lens with which to see war, and the war on women in particular, as part of the systemic sexism that has been in place since the beginning.

Karen listened to me. I was able to talk about rape and abuse. In whispers and with sideways looks, but still. Still. That was what we had then. Now we have bell hooks memes and I get to teach a class called 'What Is Rape Culture?'. Women now speak up. There is still so much work to do. There was a trending hashtag #SurvivorPrivilege on Twitter by activist Wagatwe Wanjuki after conservative pundits said that being a rape victim was a 'coveted status' (McDonough 2014).

I remember being on stage, naked in the bathtub, with Lee Nagrin pouring water on me and singing to me. Lee was a large and larger-than-life woman. A performance art legend and Obie Award winner (for Bird/Bear; she was in Meredith Monk's ensemble and collaborated with Basil Twist on her last piece, which is now a film Behind the Lid). In the 1990s she wore loose white-and-gray layers and had long white hair. She laughed as she told me that people occasionally stopped her on the street and pressed a quarter or dollar in her hand. It's just that she carried things in plastic bags!

While we have to struggle with Toxic Masculinity in 2016, Malpede had the title of the book Jamie is writing: Robert Blaze: The Feminized Male and the Future of Life on Earth.

In the hives, the lovely picnic scene, Jamie asks Robert if he experiences 'breast envy.' They speak of breast feeding and love. Admira has a flashback. I was always terrified to play this scene, and only became comfortable once I had it translated into Serbo Croat.

I was raped twice. Once at 15, and I fought, scratched him and yelled and got away repeating in shock 'He put his dick in my cunt.' Cunt was not a word I used then, at 15, having grown up a Catholic girl in Buffalo. No matter how rebellious you were in 1986, you didn't say 'the C word.' The second time was an assault by a boyfriend, and that time I was not active, I was frozen, on the wall, looking down at myself, naked, legs splayed. My shock language repetition was 'He-me.' This started the next day, I bundled myself in a friend's bed and couldn't even say, 'Help me.' I stayed there for two days, until my boyfriend called a friend who sent a doctor with drugs.

Jamie and Robert argue about Rilke, but they are really fighting over being new parents. Robert: 'Effete? That's ridiculous. Those are muscular lines. Sometimes I think you're not much of a critic.' Jamie: 'Effete from effetus. "Worn out by childbearing."' It's always about the childcare.

Sybil tells her story, the real story that is *The Beekeeper's Daughter*. The story of hidden violence in the family. She and Admira weave their pain together.

Malpede's plots get heightened and more convoluted, till the comparisons to the Greeks and soap operas become one and the same.

I knew the boy who raped me at 15. He was the friend of my best friend's boyfriend. She married her boyfriend; they have two kids now. I could look up the guy who raped me. I could find him on Facebook. I haven't. I don't know if I want to. Admira says, 'I knew them. I knew them because I had taught one year in their village. They were village boys.'

It was a wild experience seeing something from the outside I had been inside of for four years, twenty years prior. The play worked. I can't believe that I ever laughed at ecofeminism. (Me as 22-year-old-sex-positive-fishnet-wearing-1990s-feminist finding something to not like about 1970s feminists.) I thank generations of women for their work.

I had the script in December 1993. I took a photojournalism class instead of acting during my last semester. I borrowed $3000 from my family, and from January to March of 1994, I went to Europe by myself. I decided I would go to a refugee camp, by myself, and volunteer. I met a journalist from a Midwestern paper on the train. I told her I was a photojournalism student just graduated from NYU. I'm not sure why I lied. She took me into her ticketed car and shared her wine. She recognized my … youthful idealism? Stupidity? Recklessness? And convinced me not to get off in the countryside at night in a snowstorm and took me to Zagreb with her. She let me sleep on her couch and the next day introduced me to a writer who had an extra room. She arranged for me to get on a medical transport through the Red Cross. The front lines were an hour away. I would take photos and show the world what I found. But when they put the flak jacket on me, I started to cry. The garage was so cold and the cement was cracked and there were black oil stains. I was scared. I took the bulletproof vest off. 'I'm an actor,' I thought. 'What am I doing here?'

But that's what Karen inspired me to do: to take risks. I'm not saying she told me to go; she certainly didn't.

Lee used her own paintings on stage, round-moon-faced shadows in purples and blues and grays. I loved them. I think I was too shy to ask for one.

The poignancy of Sybil's bees also seems prescient. Karen wrote this before the rapid bee die-offs. Colony Collapse. Neonicotinoid pesticides have been blamed. Climate change has been blamed. Beekeeping has become a fad; at the same time new fears surface about the quality of the honey in the United States. I got a bee sting on my head this summer. I had a swollen spot for a week. Sybil uses the bees to heal.

Admira wants to kill her unborn child. A child of a rape camp. Admira doesn't know which faceless man is the father. Women were kept captive and seen as vessels for impregnation so that men knew they were spending their resources on a child that was 'theirs'; in this way they were trying to destroy a people, Bosnian Muslims. At the play's end, Rachel says, 'I don't know who the father is,' about her own child. She is reclaiming matriarchal rights.

In Italy I fell in love with a Slovenian actor. I left the festival with this Balkan man and he took me to Trieste, Ljubljana, Maribor. Their war had only lasted seven days. I loved the way he looked at me, the way he fell for my sad-girl-ness. I would stare off into the distance smoking at dinner and he would ask me what I was thinking. He was a fantastic actor and lover.

When I am on stage with George Bartenieff I am a better actor, he challenges me with his craft and intuition. I look at his eyes on stage and I am safe. Safe enough to be anything the writing requires. Safe enough to be a vulnerable performer. He is a legend: producing Sam Shepard's *Buried Child*, and much Irene Fornes, founding Theater for the New City and the Greenwich Village Halloween Parade, working with everyone from Harold Clurman and Uta Hagen to Vaclav Havel and Joanne Akalitis. He is also a journeyman and a laborer. A genius.

We did the second version of *The Beekeeper's Daughter* in New York, in Lee's Silver Whale Gallery. Lee was so powerful in her silence, and her vocal range surprised me on stage every night. She had studied with opera coaches as a young performer. I felt so loved by her as she washed and dried my 22-year-old-self. She sang to me. RIP Lee. Thank you for your love.

Admira's character is written with compassion and grace. She has been raped. She has been out of her body. She says, 'I was happy when I died. I saw a woman chained to bed. I heard the laughter of men. I don't want to live again.'

Admira had been raped. I had been raped.

I thought I had to use my rape as a way to portray the character. I didn't.

I needed to use my skills as an actor to portray the character, and I could use my experience of being raped to help me understand the character.

The third time we did the play was off-Broadway, on 42nd St.

In the play's 2016 production I felt I saw the play for the first time – from the outside. Di Zhu was in the role of Admira. The play is so funny. Jamie is jealous of Robert's attention to the baby. Robert calls Jamie jealous. Jamie: 'I'm against jealousy on principle.' Robert: 'So are we all, on principle.' The audience roared with laughter. I felt the world had caught up with the play. Politics in art is cool again. We have turned a corner with feminism in the United States. Rape is now regularly discussed without victim blaming – as a part of war, as a part of domestic life. There is a part of me that feels like no one wanted to see a play about rape and war and transsexuality in 1994.[1] Now, twenty years later, audiences do. Or they can. Or we can. We can now see how these issues are intertwined. *The Beekeeper's Daughter* was ahead of its time.

Note

1 [Playwright's insertion] *The Beekeeper's Daughter* was produced three times between 1994 and '96: At the Dionysia Festival in Italy in the summer of '94 and at the Whale Gallery for four weeks that same fall, *The Beekeeper's Daughter* was highly praised. But when the play opened off-Broadway in 1996, with a new director and three new cast members, it was less successful. In its 2016 revival, the play drew audiences and critical praise.

Reference

McDonough, K. (2014), 'George Will: Being a victim of sexual assault is a "coveted status that confers privileges"', Salon, 9 June, http://www.salon.com/2014/06/09/george_will_being_a_victim_of_sexual_assault_is_a_coveted_status_that_confers_privileges/.

Part II

Part I

Prophecy

In memory of my mother, Doris Isgrig, lover of theater, hater of war.

Prophecy had its world premiere at the New End Theatre, London, 8 September 2008. The direction was by Ninon Jerome. The American premiere was at the Fourth Street Theater, New York City, 1 June 2010, produced by Theater Three Collaborative in association with New York Theater Workshop. Kathleen Chalfant played Sarah Golden, George Bartenieff played Alan Golden, Brendan Donaldson played Jeremy Thrasher and Lukas Brightman, Najla Said played Miranda Cruz, Hala and Mariam Jabar, Peter Francis James played Charles Muffler. The direction was by Karen Malpede. Maxine Willi Klein designed the set, Tony Giovannetti, the lighting, Sally Ann Parsons, costumes, Arthur Rosen, sound and music.

Characters

Sarah Golden, late fifties, smart, lively, actress and acting teacher

Jeremy Thrasher, twenty-one, an acting student

Miranda Cruz, twenties, acting student

Alan Golden, late sixties, Sarah's husband, executive director of the Refugee Relief Committee

Hala Jabar, twenties, and, then, in her forties, Alan's associate; a Palestinian-Lebanese human rights worker

Charles Muffler, sixties, dean of the acting school where Sarah teaches

Mariam Jabar, twenties, Alan and Hala's daughter

Lukas Brightman, nineteen, young lover from Sarah's youth

Setting

Prophecy takes place in the early fall of 2006, in New York City, and in the memories of Sarah and Alan Golden in 1969–72 and 1981–82.

The setting need be simple, beautiful and spare. Scene follows scene seamlessly.

A back wall has two entrance ways, one to either side that serve as the *parados* of the classical theater, allowing quick and easy entrances and exits. In the middle of this wall is a bedroom alcove, inside of which is the marriage bed on a slight rake. These three openings are framed behind. Wall and floor are painted to look like light stone. Furniture, painted white, and realistic props are minimal. On stage right is a desk, with telephone and snow globe, and a desk chair. Center stage: a wooden bench. Stage left: a small wrought iron table with two chairs. Lighting defines location as does the actors' relationship to the space.

Act I

Scene I

(SARAH GOLDEN *has a quick and ironic, sometimes self-deprecating, wit; she carries a burden whose origin even she has forgotten. In a rush,* SARAH *enters from the isle of the theater, her book bag slung over her arm.* JEREMY THRASHER *runs behind her, stopping her on the lip of the stage.*)

JEREMY:	Ms. Golden! (SARAH *startles and stops, turns to him.*) Can we talk?
SARAH:	Afterwards.
JEREMY:	About a word.
SARAH:	After class.
JEREMY:	I'm in the first semester class.
SARAH:	I know. I do remember.
JEREMY:	It's just, I never read out loud, or even say anything. I'm performing today.
SARAH:	That's good.
JEREMY:	It's Jeremy.
SARAH:	Jeremy.
JEREMY:	Thrasher.
	(*He sticks out his hand to shake. She takes it.*)
SARAH:	Jeremy Thrasher.
JEREMY:	Augury.
SARAH:	Jeremy Thrasher Augury.
JEREMY:	That's it. You said to look it up. You told us any word we didn't know we had to look it up. You talked about that for a long time in class. How we've got to understand what we are saying before we can act. How we've 'absolutely got to know the precise meaning.' I looked it up. Look.
	(*He fishes a precisely folded piece of paper from his jean pocket, unfolds it, and reads.*)
	'Augury: the art of the augur.'
SARAH:	Very good.
JEREMY:	'An augural observance or rite.'
SARAH:	Right.
JEREMY:	What?

SARAH:	You looked it up.
JEREMY:	Yeah.
SARAH:	That augurs well.
JEREMY:	Sure.
SARAH:	So, now, you see.
JEREMY:	I don't. 'An omen, a portent, a token.'
SARAH:	Are augurs.
JEREMY:	Portent!
SARAH:	It's going to happen.
JEREMY:	What is?
SARAH:	Whatever has been portended, or, let's say, augured. My class, for instance. (SARAH *tries get around him to enter the room.* JEREMY *stands in front of her.*)
JEREMY:	'Foreboding, anticipation, promise, indication.'
SARAH:	Augurs, each.
JEREMY:	So which one is it?
SARAH:	You can choose.
JEREMY:	I can't choose because I don't know.
SARAH:	Listen. Foreboding. Fore. As in be-fore. But, *bode*, that has the feeling.
JEREMY:	Bad?
SARAH:	Good.
JEREMY:	Anticipation?
SARAH:	Snappy. Short. You hardly can wait – for class to start. (*She tries to move around him. Again, he stops her.*)
JEREMY:	Look, I can't say it if I don't know what it means.
SARAH:	Use it in a context. Say the word out loud, surrounded by other words.
JEREMY:	Go ahead.
SARAH:	Fine. (*Attempting to enter the room, again.*)
JEREMY:	In a sentence. Augury. Do it.
SARAH:	Right. From my place of augury I'd say Jeremy Thrasher is likely to be a good student who should speak up more during class.
JEREMY:	Look, there were no books in our house. No one in my family ever read the Greeks. The Greeks ran the diner at the end of the street. They went to the wrong church. You tell me I can't say it if I don't know what it means. You tell me to look it up. I look it up. Foreboding. Anticipation. Promise. Indication. I'm confused. I'm the one who has got to act it.
SARAH:	Just say the sentence in your script with the word 'augury' in it when the time comes for you to say it. I promise you, you'll feel it. At least for right then. You can always change your mind.

JEREMY:	Great, oh, great. You had books in your house.
SARAH:	We had books, but not what you'd call literature, art. We didn't have any of that.
JEREMY:	But the Greeks?
SARAH:	Not the Greeks, no, definitely not the Greeks. I joined the pagan church later in life.
JEREMY:	So how did you learn to feel what augury is?
SARAH:	You know what, Jeremy; it's love. That's all it is. Forget about not having books. Give yourself over. The language is your lover and you are in bed murmuring to her, or him, for that matter. Once you love, the language opens itself up. You fall in. You start to vibrate with sense. Now, we're both late for class.
	(*Quickly,* SARAH *moves by him and enters the rehearsal room. A young woman student,* MIRANDA, *sneaks up behind* JEREMY *and slaps him playfully on the butt.*)
MIRANDA:	Ready for Ms. Thing and the Greeks?
JEREMY:	I guess.
MIRANDA:	Yeah, well, I'm going to rock.
JEREMY:	Ain't nobody rocks my balls like you, baby.
	(JEREMY *and* MIRANDA *kiss, passionately; he lifts her up, her legs around his waist; they kiss again. He lets her down.*)
MIRANDA:	Just wait till you see what I do.

Scene II

(*The rehearsal room: there is a rehearsal mirror somewhere, depending upon the theater space.*)

SARAH:	Good morning, everyone. So, who is ready to present?
MIRANDA:	I'll go.
SARAH:	Good.
MIRANDA:	My name is Miranda Cruz. I will be doing a choral speech from *Antigone.*
	(MIRANDA *takes off jewelry and jacket, picks up her scarf.*)
SARAH:	Wonderful. Great. The chorus speaks in the voice of the people, for the polis, city-state, for all of us.
	(MIRANDA *begins to move across the stage in some sort of a rather bad idea of a choral dance.*)
MIRANDA:	Many
	(*She stops close to* SARAH, *gyrating her hips.*)
	the wonders but

(*She juts her bottom almost into* JEREMY'*s face.*)
nothing walks stranger than man.
(*She dances suggestively across the stage.*)
This thing crosses the sea
Making his path through the waves,
(MIRANDA *falls to the floor close to* JEREMY, *writhing sexually.*)
And she, the great god of the earth –
Ugh... old, no, ageless

SARAH:	Stop.
MIRANDA:	Ageless she is.
SARAH:	Stop. Please. The feeling tells you where to go. If you keep flitting about, you'll never know what you feel. Stand still. Stop looking at yourself in the mirror. Begin.
MIRANDA:	(*In an expressionless voice*) Many the wonders but nothing walks stranger than man. This thing
SARAH:	Listen! Wonders, strange, thing. A play of opposites, people with ideas that don't go together, but they still have to live in one city. 'Many the wonders/ but nothing walks stranger than man.' Can you feel that? Can you take that in? Again.
MIRANDA:	This thing crosses the sea (*She resumes her dance.*) Making his path through the rolling waves.
SARAH:	What kind of waves? *Roaring,* not rolling, *roaring,* so stop flitting about.
MIRANDA:	Making his path through the *roaring* waves. And she, the greatest of gods, the earth – Ageless she is, and unwearied – he wears her away
SARAH:	Wait. I can't stand it. I shouldn't be able to stand it. Not you, I mean. It's not you I can't stand. I can stand you. You're fine. You're doing well. As well as you can do without seeing or feeling one single thing you are saying. You're alive inside. Show me: the enormity. The madness driving us. Man, wonderful, strange, he wears her away. The earth on which he lives. The greatest of gods. She, ageless, unwearied, we wear her away. Why do we do such things? Greed? Rage? Is it sorrow? The death wish inside? It is very strange. Please tell. What we want from the chorus is to be made to ask the unanswerable things. Go. I'm on the edge of my seat.
MIRANDA:	Look, I worked hard on this. I had a stomachache all night, I couldn't sleep. I'm sick.
SARAH:	Right. We are both feeling ill. Rolling waves, a rough sea. But, let me tell you, for the next class, this is where you've got to end up:

Antigone appears, right then, in chains. 'My mind is split at this awful sight.' Ripped, torn in half. There's the tragic dilemma: Two sets of laws. Always two choices, but what if the gods want one thing from us and the nation-state wants something else? Next class, when your tummy ache is over, when your blood starts to flow, will you let us know if we should murder this girl? (*Pause*) Who's next?

(JEREMY's *hand shoots up.*)

JEREMY: I'll go.

(MIRANDA *gives him a furious look as she starts for the exit.*)

SARAH: Wait a minute. Where are you going?

(MIRANDA *storms out.*)

Dear me. (*To the class*) Never mind.

(JEREMY *grabs a folding chair.*)

JEREMY: (*Nervous*) I'll be doing Tiresias's speech, also from *Antigone*.

(*He sits. His voice trembles.* SARAH *leans forward, attentive, silent, watching. The presence of this young man has moved her more than she knows.*)

As I sat on the ancient seat of augury,
In the sanctuary where every bird I know
Will hover at my hands – suddenly I heard it,

(SARAH *starts writing on a half of her yellow pad, but she is speaking what is inside her mind. Something has come over her she cannot control: she has been snapped back into memory.*)

SARAH: Jeremy Thrasher grabbed me, like a hand from under the earth. I saw Lukas the minute Jeremy Thrasher started to speak.

JEREMY: A strange voice in the wing beats, unintelligible,
Barbaric, a mad scream! Talons flashing, ripping,
They were killing each other – that much I knew –

SARAH: The night we lay on the rug after love, and started talking about the war.

(JEREMY *and* SARAH *speak in unison; their words become a contrapuntal duet.*)

JEREMY: I was afraid.
I turned quickly, tested the burnt-sacrifice,
Ignited the altar at all points –

SARAH: We were more frightened than either of us knew.
We saw every night on television, flames coming.
Out of the backs of children running from the napalm.

JEREMY: But no fire,
The god in the fire never blazed.
Not from those offerings... over the embers

SARAH:	Whole villages burning up. Babies, charred,
	In the arms of their mothers, because of our bombs,
	Blood coming out of their mouths.
JEREMY:	Slid a heavy ooze from the long thighbones,
	Smoking, sputtering out, and the bladder
	Puffed and burst – spraying gall into the air –
	And the fat wrapping the bones slithered off.
SARAH:	Body counts. Body bags.
	When he moved from under me,
	When he pulled himself out,
	Lukas was coated with my blood.
JEREMY:	And left them glistening white. No Fire!
	The public altars and sacred hearths are fouled,
	One and all, by the birds and dogs with carrion.
	Torn from the corpse.
SARAH:	Blood of life, we said, not death.
	We felt we had done something sacred
	To counteract the shame in the world.
	(JEREMY *gathers force, stands, trembling, as he turns to face the mirror.*)
JEREMY:	And so the gods are deaf to our prayers, they spurn
	The offerings in our hands, the flame of holy flesh.
	No birds cry out an omen clear and true –
	They're gorged with the murdered victim's blood and fat.
	(JEREMY *grabs the chair and flings it at the mirror, which shatters.* JEREMY *runs from the room.*)
	(SARAH *pulls the curtain across the broken mirror, in the process she cuts her hand.*)

Scene III

(*The hallway:* JEREMY *is eerily calm; he is split off from what he's just done.* MIRANDA *has been waiting for him.*)

MIRANDA:	What have you got to say for yourself?
JEREMY:	Nothing much.
MIRANDA:	You sit there waving your hand. You just want to perform.
JEREMY:	I guess.
MIRANDA:	The bitch insults me in front of the whole class. You beg to go next.
	You shuffle up like a house slave, like a brownnose, kissing ass.

JEREMY:	I guess I'm paying good money to be able to act.
MIRANDA:	The chorus doesn't stand there, duh! and talk. They dance. I'm a dancer. A movement artist. She forgets about that. She stops me after each word. Then she treats me like a cunt.
JEREMY:	You do have your period.
MIRANDA:	It's no business of hers.
JEREMY:	I guess another woman can tell.
MIRANDA:	I was not up all night having cramps.
JEREMY:	No way.
MIRANDA:	You better bottle the smell. I am not some dumb chick you fuck. I worked hard on that dance.
	(MIRANDA *storms off.* JEREMY *sinks to the ground.*)
	(SARAH *approaches. She has bloody paper towels wrapped around her hand.*)
SARAH:	Jeremy, what happened in there?
JEREMY:	What'd you do to your hand?
SARAH:	I was picking up the glass.
JEREMY:	Glass?
SARAH:	What do you think?
JEREMY:	I guess I don't know.
SARAH:	You threw a chair.
	(JEREMY *jumps up.*)
JEREMY:	At you? Not at you. I wouldn't do that...
SARAH:	Not at me. Not at anyone, thank God. At the mirror. (*She understands.*) At your own face in the mirror.
JEREMY:	Man, oh, man.
SARAH:	Jeremy, you do remember what you did?
JEREMY:	I was doing Tiresias's speech. I was inside it, way inside, you know.
SARAH:	I do know, but, Jeremy, right now, you're in big trouble.
JEREMY:	Augury was easy. I started trembling.
SARAH:	Yes, that's right. It was a strong start.
JEREMY:	Really? Because I didn't think you were paying attention.
SARAH:	I was riveted.
JEREMY:	You weren't looking.
SARAH:	I was on the edge of my seat.
JEREMY:	Like you were somewhere else.
SARAH:	I was right there, taking notes. You've got talent, you know.
JEREMY:	I felt it, just like you said.
SARAH:	Yes, but, Jeremy, you threw a chair. The building supervisor notified the dean.
JEREMY:	I've got talent you said?

SARAH:	The dean wants to speak to each of us, separately. Tell me you remember what you did?
JEREMY:	It was good?
SARAH:	Look, I can't go into Muffler's office with you. You've got to sit there and nod your head. Don't disagree. Just say 'I'm sorry' over and over.
JEREMY:	About the mirror, you mean?
SARAH:	That's right. Because you put people in danger.
JEREMY:	I was frightened. Everyone was.
SARAH:	You bet.
JEREMY:	You insulted Miranda in front of the whole class.
SARAH:	I, what?
JEREMY:	You told everyone about her blood, you know. You pretended like she can't act. It's true, but it's nobody's business but ours.
SARAH:	It was a figure of speech.
JEREMY:	I was upset. She ran out of class. The more I said my speech, the worse it got.
SARAH:	That's what you're going to tell the dean?
	(JEREMY *runs out.*)
	Jeremy!

Scene IV

(SARAH *and* ALAN's *bedroom. That night.* ALAN *seems to be asleep.* SARAH *enters and begins to get ready for bed.*)

SARAH:	Alan. Are you up?
ALAN:	No, Sarah, I'm not up.
SARAH:	Alan.
ALAN:	I'm not up, Sarah.
SARAH:	Please.
ALAN:	I'm asleep.
SARAH:	Alan.
ALAN:	Sarah, honey. Stop. Let it go. Rest.
SARAH:	Right. (*Silence*) You need your sleep.
ALAN:	We went over this ten times tonight.
SARAH:	I should have stopped him, that's what.
ALAN:	I have a donors meeting tomorrow, yes.
SARAH:	A donors meeting, of course.
ALAN:	Good. So, tomorrow we'll talk some more, if you like. At dinner. I'll take you out.

SARAH:	Right. A big day coming up. You're a success.
ALAN:	Please.
SARAH:	My husband, the savior. Donors arrive at his door. The executive director of the Refugee Relief Committee doesn't have time to talk to his wife.

(She clicks on the light and sits up in bed. He reaches over her and clicks the light off. Silence. She turns on her light and his light.)

ALAN:	We talked all evening, Sarah, all through dinner. You talked to me, that is, at me, in one of your endless monologues. It's been years since I've heard that hysterical tone in your voice. Nothing I said made any difference. It never did. I know all about this, Sarah. You are obsessed by that boy. You have always been obsessed.
SARAH:	This marriage is over.
ALAN:	He's crude, but pretty. A pet.
SARAH:	You miserable lout.

(SARAH clicks off both lights.)

ALAN:	Fine. I have to be up by six.
SARAH:	I am humiliated, Alan. Not obsessed. The fine points, as always, elude you.
ALAN:	Please. I've got refugees all over the world depending on this thing tomorrow.
SARAH:	Good, because our marriage is done.
ALAN:	We'll talk about all of this, Sarah, after work.
SARAH:	Right. Such important work as yours cannot wait. If you cut through the red tape, children will be able to eat. What do I do? It's so insanely unimportant, isn't it? A kid freaks out in my class. So what. He's not from the third world. He doesn't live in a Palestinian refugee camp. He doesn't live in Iraq. He's a white kid. He doesn't count. And my job. My job? You thought you married an actress. You thought you married a star. A woman who would look good on your arm.
ALAN:	Nonsense. You weren't working when I married you.
SARAH:	And thirty years into it…
ALAN:	You were falling apart…
SARAH:	… you find out I'm a wrinkled, sag-bellied failure with thinning pubic hair who speaks in monologues without end. And you need to change things, don't you, Alan? You need to make a huge difference in the world. What do I need? I need to drudge along with the wreck of my life, the wreck of my dreams. As if you never messed up our lives.

(ALAN snaps on both lights.)

ALAN:	All right, Sarah, let's talk.
	(SARAH *turns both lights off.*)
SARAH:	Too late. This time it is really too late. I'm going to sleep.
ALAN:	Sarah? (*No answer.*) I do love you, Sarah.
SARAH:	We'll talk tomorrow. After you've massaged your donors… after that.
	(*Long silence.* ALAN *snores. The doorbell rings.*)

Scene V

(*Silence. The doorbell rings, insistently this time.* SARAH *gets up, wraps herself in her robe. She goes to the hallway door of the apartment.*)

SARAH:	Who's there?
	(*Silence*)
	You've got the wrong door. Go away.
JEREMY:	It's Jeremy. Thrasher. (*An angry knock.*) Augury.
SARAH:	Jeremy. It's three in the morning. What do you want?
JEREMY:	Open up.
	(*They enter the living room.*)
SARAH:	You didn't sit there, did you, saying 'I'm sorry.'
JEREMY:	Look, I'm sorry about that.
SARAH:	Sorry. Great.
JEREMY:	I couldn't sleep.
SARAH:	Neither could I.
	He's taken my class away.
JEREMY:	No way.
SARAH:	I get paid by the class. I don't have a full-time salary.
JEREMY:	Look, I've got to talk. (*Looking around.*) This is a pretty nice place.
SARAH:	The dean spoke with your girlfriend, what the hell is her name? Anyway, she acted up quite a storm. Wept right on cue.
JEREMY:	Look, I didn't mean…
SARAH:	To say it was my fault that you threw your chair through the mirror because I said your girlfriend had her period and that got you so upset.
JEREMY:	Right. You live here alone?
SARAH:	Because that is what you said.
JEREMY:	I guess.
SARAH:	There is someone in the next room.
JEREMY:	You're not alone.

SARAH:	From your place of augury, you don't guess, you speak. Do you normally fuck up people's lives?
JEREMY:	Look, there's no one else in the entire world I can talk to but you.
SARAH:	There, you can sit.
	(*She motions to the bench and sits beside him.*)
	Why did you lie, Jeremy?
	(JEREMY *reaches out to her.*)
	My husband is in the next room.
JEREMY:	You already said.
SARAH:	Not for long.
JEREMY:	Let me talk.
SARAH:	My husband, I mean.
JEREMY:	Oh, newlyweds.
SARAH:	Not quite. What's up?
JEREMY:	Look, I freaked out.
SARAH:	You threw a chair.
JEREMY:	I did.
SARAH:	At your own face.
	(*Impulsively, she takes a lock of his hair and puts it behind his ear.*)
	It was not because I said, whatever it was that I said, to that ditsy girl, Miranda! that's it. You wouldn't risk your career to defend that girl's honor. She's a lousy actress. She's not even that interested in you.
JEREMY:	Look, that's between me and her.
SARAH:	You get my class taken away, the least I can do is tell you. Watch out. Where is she right now, for example?
JEREMY:	How do I know? At home, asleep.
SARAH:	Right.
JEREMY:	I don't care where she is. I'm not here to talk about her.
	(JEREMY *reaches for her hand, holds it, and then brings it to his lips.* SARAH *snatches her hand from his and moves away.*)
JEREMY:	You touched me.
SARAH:	Your hair.
JEREMY:	My hair, face, so what, you touched.
SARAH:	I'm sorry.
JEREMY:	Sorry! I guess.
SARAH:	Sorry, yes.
JEREMY:	That's not what I thought.
SARAH:	I was thinking of someone else.
JEREMY:	Great. The husband in the next room.
SARAH:	Not him.

JEREMY:	Good for you.
SARAH:	It was a long time ago.
JEREMY:	Some young guy you came on to?
SARAH:	I don't 'come on to' young men, Jeremy. Let us be very clear. You arrived here.
JEREMY:	I don't know. I've been come on to before.
SARAH:	I'm certain you have.
JEREMY:	Well, it's true. By an older woman, too.
SARAH:	Perhaps, but not me.
JEREMY:	Sure, you were coming on to someone else. It was just my hair you touched.
SARAH:	(*Laughs*) That's it, you know. You are finally telling the truth. Good.
JEREMY:	Look, you've got to talk to the dean. He thinks, I don't know. He wants to send me to counseling. I've got to go, he says, if I want to stay in school.
SARAH:	Sure. I have lots of influence, you see. I have lots of influence because you lied…
JEREMY:	But, she has it. How did you know?
SARAH:	Go to counseling, Jeremy. It might do you good. Of course, the counselors at the school are fools.
JEREMY:	Listen to me.
SARAH:	Otherwise, they'd be in private practice, wouldn't they? Otherwise, I'd be on stage.
JEREMY:	Sarah, can I call you Sarah? You said we could the first day of class. I've got to stay in school. Everything I've done I've done to get here. It's so fucking stupid. It doesn't make any sense. I'm an actor. I know it. You know what my father does? He's a butcher. Mainly he grunts and waves a knife. Now, I'm acting the Greeks. I'm acting the Greeks because you taught me how.
SARAH:	Yes, Jeremy, I taught you. But, you know what, you already knew. You really can't teach anyone anything they don't already have inside. You can open them up. That's all. Your father, the butcher, was he in Vietnam?
JEREMY:	Yeah, you sure opened me. Big time. So, you have to talk to the dean. You've got to tell him I'm not fucked up. I just got opened up. I don't need to talk about that. You can explain.
SARAH:	It's late. We both have to get up very soon.
JEREMY:	You'll talk to the dean?
SARAH:	Tell me what happened in class.
JEREMY:	Yeah, okay, I will tell you. I was doing the speech of the prophet, see. Tiresias's speech, the blind guy, and he's giving this prophecy

when all of a sudden, he's saying that the fat isn't burning, that the altars are glutted with the fat thigh bones smoking, that the gods aren't hearing, that they won't take the offering in. And that's when it hits me, shit, fuck, like a truck, it hits. We've been cut off. We're floating free in space and even the gods aren't listening; they don't care anymore. We've gone too far. They won't take our offerings. I'm a Catholic. I was brought up to believe in forgiveness. In redemption, see. You say you're sorry. You say you've sinned. It's okay. God forgives you. You say twenty Hail Marys and you're back in. He's a forgiving god. But all of a sudden I think it might not work that way, you see what I mean? It might work another way. You might go too far. You might step off the end of the earth. There might be no way back. The altars might be glutted with flesh. And that's when I saw, like I didn't see out of my eyes. I was blind. I saw it inside my head. How it is when the gods can't bear to listen. They can't bear to hear anymore. They've already heard it all. You can't ask for forgiveness. The gods aren't hearing. They're fed up with us, sick. We're cut off. I got scared.

SARAH:	And you threw the chair?
JEREMY:	That's it.
SARAH:	Makes perfect sense.
JEREMY:	That's what I think. I'm not crazy. You see. I'm not crazy at all.
SARAH:	It had nothing to do with that girl.
JEREMY:	Of course not. Why do you keep talking about her?
SARAH:	Jeremy, what are you frightened of?
JEREMY:	Nothing. The idea, of course.
SARAH:	I see.
JEREMY:	You do? Because you weren't paying attention. You were thinking about someone else.
SARAH:	Please.
JEREMY:	Look, you've got to talk to the dean. You weren't listening to me. I threw the chair. You woke up.
SARAH:	Leave. You've got to go.
JEREMY:	Talk to him. Damn it!
SARAH:	Quiet! My husband is in the next room.
JEREMY:	Please. I've got to stay in school.
	(*She nods her head 'yes.'*)
	You will?
SARAH:	I will.
JEREMY:	Promise?

SARAH:	Scout's honor, Jeremy Thrasher. In the morning. Go home.
JEREMY:	Thank you. Really, I thank you from the bottom of my heart. (*Impulsively, he grabs* SARAH *and kisses her awkwardly, chastely, on the cheek. She's charmed, in spite of herself.*)
SARAH:	(*Laughing and pushing him out the door*) Out, Thrasher, out. (JEREMY *exits.* SARAH *is confused, moved. This young man has undone her, somehow. She cares for him more than is wise. A light comes on in the hall.* ALAN's *voice.*)
ALAN:	Sarah? Are you all right?
SARAH:	But, of course.
ALAN:	I heard something slam. Voices, too.
SARAH:	There's nothing. Go back to bed. (ALAN *comes in; he has pulled on pants and a shirt, half unbuttoned. He looks around.*)
ALAN:	Entertaining the doorman because your husband's a lout.
SARAH:	It was him, my student. Upset. We talked. Cleared things up.
ALAN:	Well, good. (*Pause*) I'm sorry, Sarah, I am. (*He takes her hand and leads her over to the bench. They sit. After a moment she snuggles into him, buries her head in his chest.*) The things you say, sometimes, Sarah; I never know what's coming next. (SARAH *kisses* ALAN *on the cheek.*) You've hardly ruined your life. You do wonderful work with those kids. You teach them how to feel, to think.
SARAH:	She was dancing like a chorus girl. That's what the word 'chorus' means to her.
ALAN:	That boy; he's the real thing, you said.
SARAH:	A kid breaks a mirror in my class because I'm somewhere else… what do you call that, Alan?
ALAN:	A trigger. You got snapped back to your paradise lost.
SARAH:	We each have our own never was.
ALAN:	Our marriage is all the more precious for that.
SARAH:	More improbable, in any case.
ALAN:	Our chimera of love. The odd beast we've made over time. Not of burden. That's not what I mean.
SARAH:	You don't need me, do you, Alan? Not like that.
ALAN:	Like what? Of course, I need you.
SARAH:	You're so rational, poised, in control. You pick up the pieces; put things back together, save people…
ALAN:	Go talk to Chuck Muffler. Tell him to give your class back.
SARAH:	Chuck Muffler. That I have to bow and scrape before him.

ALAN:	You can act a little superior.
SARAH:	He calls himself Charles now. Sober as a dean.
ALAN:	You are superior in every way.
SARAH:	I ought to have stopped him before he freaked out.
ALAN:	Hey, no one got hurt.
	(*She takes his hand, as if to lead him back to bed.*)
	I'll stay up. Do some work.
SARAH:	Alan, I do hate this rug…

Scene VI

(SARAH *breaks away from* ALAN, *turns, goes downstage center. By directing her comment to the audience she sets up the first of the memory scenes, which are indicated, also, by change of light.*)

SARAH:	I hate this rug because of what happened here in 1981.
	(ALAN, *nervous, moves a chair. Romantic music. From the memory entrance [center stage right] in walks a much younger woman,* HALA JABAR. *She is dressed professionally, in a slim skirt and jacket, high heels. She holds an armful of documents.*)
HALA:	Where's Sarah?
ALAN:	Sarah phoned. Technical rehearsal. Late night. Don't wait up.
HALA:	You phoned.
ALAN:	I thought, let's work here, then. You also live uptown. I'll order something in.
HALA:	Fine.
	(*She sits down on the chair, clutching the documents in front of her, like a shield.*)
ALAN:	Can I fix you a drink?
HALA:	All right.
ALAN:	My God, you're beautiful.
HALA:	Please…
	(*She stands.*)
ALAN:	Breathtaking. You.
HALA:	Alan, we must not…
ALAN:	Hala, you take my breath away.
	(HALA *backs away, yet she does want him and his speech will win her.*)
ALAN:	Hala, stop. Don't go. I'm sorry. Sometimes one has to say what's on one's mind. To clear the air. It's over now. Nothing will happen. Nothing can happen. Sarah is my wife. She was my lover before

that. She was my friend. She was a girl who needed saving. She was, always, there is, will always be, Sarah. But, Hala, you are something else. Beautiful, brilliant and so calm. Sarah is, well, Sarah is not calm. That's one thing Sarah is not, calm, that is. Brilliant, yes, in an artistic sort of way. But Sarah is not someone you can count on, really, at least not me. I was never able to count on her. I feel I can count on you. There is something steadfast in your nature. That is odd because I can see the hurt in your eyes. You have dark eyes with sorrows inside. I would like to share your sorrows, Hala. The whole of you, I would like to know. I'm making a hash of this, a mess. But Sarah is not coming home tonight until late, that is, very late. I would like to hold you, Hala, in my arms. I would like to give you what comfort I can. I can't promise anything. I can't. But I can tell you this: I will never abandon you. I will stand by you if... I would be there for you and a child.

(HALA *smiles lovingly at* ALAN, *then walks out the apartment door.* ALAN *remains standing, looking at the door. After a moment,* HALA *returns, without the documents in her arms. She walks forward to the rug.*)

HALA: Alan, I'm pregnant.

(ALAN *stands for a moment, without speaking. Then he goes to* HALA. *He kisses her face, her belly, gently, very gently, in awe. He gets down on his knees in front of her.*)

ALAN: A blessing. Thank you. My goddess. My darling. My precious. We make life.

(*His arms are around her feet. Carefully, she steps out of his embrace and exits. Alan falls asleep on the floor.* SARAH *enters the living room.*)

SARAH: Alan? Oh, sweetie, you waited up. How adorable, my adorable, sweet husband. Come on, let's go to bed. The tech was horrendous. HORRENDOUS. The producer smokes Cuban cigars. Chuck Muffler. Sips from a flask. Made a fortune in something. Now, he wants meaning in his life. What a profession. I do nothing for an entire year, now, all of a sudden... I'm not complaining. It's going to be good. Alan, I really think this one time, I will get what I deserve. I am going to be seen.

ALAN: Great, Sarah. That's great. I hope so. I really do.

SARAH: I know you do, baby. How sweet of you to try to wait up.

(*She sees something on the floor, a pair of black silk women's underwear.*)

	What are these? Whose are these? Oh, shit, Alan, oh shit. Someone was here. Answer me. Were you fucking some bitch on my rug?
ALAN:	I was not 'fucking some bitch.'
SARAH:	Are you a cross dresser?
	(*She dangles the underwear.*)
ALAN:	Sarah, it's very late. I want you to get some sleep. I'll stay on the couch.
SARAH:	What are you saying, Alan, what? The couch? So, it's true. You are not a cross dresser. I would have understood that, you know. I'm a tolerant person.
ALAN:	We should speak in the morning.
SARAH:	You are jealous of my success.
ALAN:	Of course not. This is not about that.
SARAH:	Then, why now? Why tonight? You've been faithful through everything else. Tonight, you bring some slut into my house. A ninny. Don't lie to me. Some NYU student you picked up in a bar. Who is she? Why?
ALAN:	Calm down, Sarah, please. Think about your career. It is so very important to you.
SARAH:	You're the one who wanted to be married to a star. Is this the day you've been waiting for all along? Obviously, you hoped to get caught.
	(*She flings the underpants at* ALAN. *He catches them and stuffs them in his pocket.*)
ALAN:	You won't believe me if I tell you I love you. I hardly believe it myself.
SARAH:	(*Suddenly, perfectly calm*) All right, Alan. Tell me the truth.
	(*She sits.*)
	Then I'll go straight to sleep. I'll get up in the morning. I'll use all this for my work. I'll put it right into Nora. Believe me, I can do that.
ALAN:	Promise?
SARAH:	Yes.
ALAN:	All right, then. It's Hala.
	(*She rushes at him.*)
SARAH:	You slimy bastard.
ALAN:	You want to know, I'm telling you.
SARAH:	You fucking imperialist.
ALAN:	Hala is my colleague.
SARAH:	She works for you, in your office, you prick.
ALAN:	There is nothing wrong with me.
SARAH:	No?

ALAN:	My sperm count, in fact, is rather high, above average.
SARAH:	You're an above average sort of guy.
ALAN:	I want a child.
SARAH:	Right. We'd adopt someday, we agreed, if we ever wanted that's what we'd do.
ALAN:	My doctor suggested…
SARAH:	Your doctor?
ALAN:	Just to make sure. I agreed, without thinking, really. I had no idea, Sarah, believe me, I had no idea at all, none. The desire came over me so suddenly…
SARAH:	All those sperm fighting to get out.
ALAN:	When my father died.
SARAH:	Oh my god, Alan, very good. Play the Holocaust card.
ALAN:	It is hardly, Sarah, as you insist, in your own inimitable way, 'the Holocaust card.'
SARAH:	I can't trump the gas chambers. You get to have whatever you want…
ALAN:	Shut up.
SARAH:	All those great-aunts and uncles you never knew.
ALAN:	My father, Sarah, a remarkable person. He saved many people, worked, slaved, to bring people here, to this country, as you know very well. I do not want his story to end with me.
SARAH:	Not his story, his DNA.
ALAN:	I had no idea, no idea at all I would need my own child. It's some sort of biological thing. I am not in control.
SARAH:	Forgive me, Alan.
ALAN:	Oh, Sarah, yes, long ago.
SARAH:	But, I am not able to forgive.
ALAN:	You might try, Sarah. Please.
SARAH:	You could have bought eggs from Hala, Alan, had them implanted in me, or in someone else, if my play runs, if it was blood you wanted to mix.
ALAN:	Why does this sound so crude in your mouth?
SARAH:	I can't imagine, really, I can't.
ALAN:	We are not molecules but souls. I had to be there.
SARAH:	Are you going to divorce me, Alan, if Hala is pregnant that is? Are you finally going to leave me then?
ALAN:	It is possible to love two women at the same time.
SARAH:	A harem.
	(SARAH *gets up and she begins a belly dance, slowly at first, but maniacally.*)

ALAN:	I don't know what to do.
SARAH:	(*Dancing faster*) Go away, Alan. Get.
ALAN:	Sarah, stop.
SARAH:	First wife is tossed into the garbage…
ALAN:	Enough!
SARAH:	Shame. For being infertile.
ALAN:	I still love you, Sarah.
	(SARAH *stops dancing*.)
	I don't know how to explain.
SARAH:	And Hala, too?
ALAN:	Yes, and Hala, too. We are enlightened people, let us think.
SARAH:	Who thinks at a time like this?
ALAN:	Then, let's get some sleep.
SARAH:	Sleep!
ALAN:	Come to bed.
SARAH:	Go. I will stay here on this rug. 'Stewed in corruption' in the seamy stink of your love.

(*She sinks onto 'the rug.'* ALAN *exits to bedroom.*)

I bought this rug. I picked it out so we could start fresh. White … The other rug, the red one where Lukas and I slept, I rolled up and stored in the basement because I cannot bear to throw it out. The night we protested the 'secret' invasion of Cambodia. The night we thought the war would never end. I pulled Lukas off the street. I was forever pulling Lukas away from the police. He was always aching for a fight. I brought him up here. It was a collective apartment, then. Below, on the street there was tear gas. Lukas told me he had flunked all of his classes, except one. In English composition I gave him an 'A.' He would go to Canada, he said, to avoid the draft. Or join the Weathermen, and become a real revolutionary. 'Go to Canada,' I told him, 'Please. I'll come to you, there.' I leaned down to taste him again. When finally we finished, when he lay beside me on the red rug and I cradled him in my arms, he smiled and said he had figured out what he should do. He would leave school and get himself drafted. He would join the GI resistance and organize from the inside. He sat up. He saw his destiny plain: 'When the army refuses to fight the war will end.' 'Don't be an asshole,' I said. 'Kiss me,' he said. I want your child, Lukas, but I couldn't say that to him. 'Don't be a hero,' I said. 'You know how long those guys live in the jungle.' 'I'm working class,' he said. 'Those are my men.' 'Stay here. You can make up your failing grades. I'll talk to the dean.' We lived in our grief, legs looped, sex linked. 'It's okay,' Lukas said, 'Whatever happens to me it will be fine. There's no time for personal happiness, now.' He learned to talk that way at Columbia. 'Little kids are being napalmed. This shit has to stop.' 'I'll give up Alan for you. I'll call him in Cambridge right now.' I reached for the phone. But Lukas was only nineteen. He was more frightened of me than of Vietnam.

(She exits.)

Scene VII

(The dean's office. Later that morning. Dean CHARLES MUFFLER *enters humming a happy tune. He is a commanding presence but beneath his bellicose good humor, he is hiding something. He sits behind his desk. On it there is a snow globe with a rural scene which he strokes with his free hand as he pushes the button on his speaker phone.)*

CHARLES:	Lizzie, put that call right through when it comes.
	*(*CHARLES *sees* SARAH *at his office door and waves her in.)*
	Come on in, Sarah, come. What's on your mind? At ten, I've got the Ford Foundation.
SARAH:	Jeremy Thrasher.
CHARLES:	Quite a name. Like a character in a play.
SARAH:	He does tend to make waves.
CHARLES:	Sarah, I'm going to give your class back.
SARAH:	Good. *(Pause, during which* CHARLES *drums his fingers on his desk.)* Thanks.
CHARLES:	We all make mistakes. I've put the Thrasher boy somewhere else.
SARAH:	I wish you wouldn't call him that.
CHARLES:	You were quite distraught, yesterday. You seemed in over your head. Maybe things at home…
SARAH:	Alan and I are just fine, Chuck.
CHARLES:	Charles, if you don't mind. Chuck was my Broadway name. Dean Charles Muffler. Glad to hear married life is good. Sometimes one bad egg, one rotten apple…
SARAH:	Are you speaking of Jeremy Thrasher?
CHARLES:	I'm being harsh, over-harsh; I'm overstating my case. Still, sometimes, a student needs another approach. In any case, the class is yours. No need to ask.
SARAH:	I want Jeremy Thrasher back. He's the best actor I have.

CHARLES:	It will cost us eight or nine hundred dollars to replace that mirror. Mercifully, no one got hurt. Let me handle the Thrasher boy. You get the rest of the class.
SARAH:	Jeremy, too. Trust me.
CHARLES:	Thrasher's here on scholarship.
SARAH:	So?
CHARLES:	Working class, a bit out of his element.
SARAH:	If only you could hear yourself speak.
CHARLES:	Let's not wrangle, my dear.
SARAH:	Right. I'll work with him privately. Independent study. Greek tragedy. I tell you, he's the real thing.
CHARLES:	Bad idea. I'll work with him. Let him do something light. Situate the narrative in another part of the self.
SARAH:	You wanted to send him for counseling.
	(CHARLES *drums his fingers on his desk.*)
	Charles?
CHARLES:	No. No counseling, no. Counseling is not a requirement anymore. I've gone over the boy's record. I'll stick him in my monologue class. We're doing Moliere and Goldoni. Both are smart, both are snappy. Counseling is not advised at the moment. Give my best to Alan. What's he up to, by the way?
SARAH:	Refugee policy, the usual stuff. Why no counseling, Charles?
CHARLES:	It's over and done. Best to move on. We were lucky the glass didn't fly. I shudder to think.
SARAH:	It won't happen again. What is over and done?
CHARLES:	He's a good man, Alan, officer material. A pity he never served.
SARAH:	You know Alan was a draft resister. You know that, Charles.
CHARLES:	I thought it was just an array of student deferments he got.
SARAH:	Everyone got student deferments in those days.
CHARLES:	Not everyone.
SARAH:	No, Charles. Not you. You got medals, defense contracts, too.
CHARLES:	And you got *A Doll's House* on Broadway. I apologize for nothing I've done.
SARAH:	You asked my forgiveness on opening night.
CHARLES:	I've been sober, now, a long time.
SARAH:	You asked my forgiveness for getting drunk?
CHARLES:	I don't want you fraternizing with our students, my dear.
SARAH:	What did you need forgiveness for? Mine, that is. Not the forgiveness of your three wives.
CHARLES:	Young men get hurt, Sarah, when they are pushed. The Greeks are too much.

SARAH:	I disagree. The Greeks hold us when we can't hold ourselves. Tragedy keeps us honest, in fact.
CHARLES:	Young men are vulnerable, you, of all people, ought to know.
SARAH:	Chuck it, Charles.
CHARLES:	Touché. Nevertheless, this Thrasher boy has had something stirred up, not, I think by the Greeks. When that happens, we are no longer effective teachers; pedagogy flies out the window… mirrors become shattered. Next time, a student could be harmed. Then, I could not give your class back to you, Sarah, or any class, for that matter.
	(*He walks around his desk to dismiss her, but in a warm, expansive way.*)
	Always good to have you stop by. Give my regards to Alan. We ought to get together sometime. Reminisce. Are you still such a good cook?

Scene VIII

(*Hallway, immediately afterwards.* JEREMY *has been waiting for* SARAH *and steps in front of her.*)

JEREMY:	Yeah, well, thanks a lot.
SARAH:	You're welcome, Jeremy, you can skip therapy.
JEREMY:	Big deal. You took me out of your class.
SARAH:	I took you?
JEREMY:	You told him you couldn't handle me. I'm 'unruly' he said you said. I didn't need to look it up.
SARAH:	Charles Muffler said I said that? This does not augur well because I never said such a thing.
JEREMY:	I don't care what you said. I need you. The dean said I can't have you. Why did you tell him I came over last night?
SARAH:	I did not.
JEREMY:	He said you said, he asked, I thought, anyway…
SARAH:	I have just come out of his office, as you can see since you've obviously been lying in wait.
JEREMY:	So what?
SARAH:	So I couldn't have said anything to him, could I, before he apparently spoke with you this morning?
JEREMY:	How do I know? There are cell phones, email.
SARAH:	Well, Jeremy Thrasher, contrary to your idea of yourself as the center of my life, I had other things on my mind this morning

	besides calling Muffler. I spoke to him because you asked me to. He's agreed not to send you to counseling. Although, frankly, I think you could use it. I argued to keep you in class.
JEREMY:	Great.
SARAH:	I lost. So that's the end of it. It's been a pleasure, Jeremy, I wish you well.
JEREMY:	What about last night?
SARAH:	I should never have opened the door.
JEREMY:	Now, I'm inside.
SARAH:	That was my mistake.
JEREMY:	Of Tiresias, I mean. It's going to come out one way or another. You've got to be there.
SARAH:	Look, you'll be doing Moliere.
JEREMY:	What the fuck does that mean?
SARAH:	You've been moved into Muffler's monologue class. It's an honor. You should be pleased. Don't swear at me.
JEREMY:	Oh, fuck, I'm sorry. I'm so sorry, look. Please. Let me just do the speech for you, one time. I won't bother you ever again. I can pay you. I will pay you.
SARAH:	Stop. Enough.
JEREMY:	I'll come to your house, anytime. Anytime you are free.
SARAH:	Absolutely not.
JEREMY:	Something is inside of me. They put it there. The Greeks, I mean. No one can help me but you. Tonight?
SARAH:	It's not possible. It's not right.
JEREMY:	Right. He shouldn't pull us apart. Two of us who love the Greeks. And I do, let me tell you. I love them like you.
SARAH:	Dean Muffler will tell you he, also, loves the Greeks.
JEREMY:	Look, I do believe in redemption, only now there's something new. I've been thinking about it all night, ever since, last night, you know. It's something we've got to go through.
SARAH:	That's right. That's it exactly.
JEREMY:	So, I've got to finish that speech. I can't just leave it like that. I threw a fucking chair through a mirror. I need help. I know. With the words.
SARAH:	All right, Jeremy. You win. Eight o'clock. My husband will be home.
JEREMY:	Fine, okay, anything you say. It's a date.
SARAH:	It's a rehearsal, that's what.
JEREMY:	I'm not dangerous. I would never hurt you.
	(JEREMY *exits*.)

Scene IX

(SARAH *walks downstage to announce the second memory scene.*)

SARAH:	I am a good cook. I made the pasta from scratch. Alan was leaving the next day, business trip. It was 1982. (*She exits as* ALAN *enters from memory entrance center stage left. He hangs his jacket on the back of his chair and takes two airline tickets from the pocket. He puts the tickets on the table and sits.*)
ALAN:	(*Calling to her in the kitchen*) Sarah. I want a child.
SARAH:	(*She calls back*) Fine. Good. I agree. How about Colombian?
ALAN:	No coffee, thanks.
SARAH:	I meant from Colombia, country of. I'll steam the milk.
ALAN:	No, thanks. My stomach is upset.
SARAH:	Poor dear.
ALAN:	My child, Sarah.
SARAH:	Ours. A girl math prodigy from China. So adorable. Or a little boy with an Afro. Sweet.
ALAN:	Hala is pregnant, Sarah. (*Silence. Then,* SARAH *enters. She is calm if nonplussed.*)
SARAH:	Hala miscarried. I forgave you. Over and done.
ALAN:	Hala is pregnant again.
SARAH:	How Abrahamic, Alan, really, truly, how profound. I'm impressed. Ishmael, is that what you'll call it? You can start the whole cycle over again.
ALAN:	It might have worked with us, Sarah, if you had tried.
SARAH:	My womb rotted, Alan. Fell out between my legs.
ALAN:	Don't be repulsive.
SARAH:	Me, repulsive? You're the one who impregnated your office assistant.
ALAN:	Colleague.
SARAH:	Twice. Two times!
ALAN:	Hala and I are… we are together all the time.
SARAH:	You're having a midlife crisis, my dear. And she can have an abortion.
ALAN:	Like you, and your Lukas, the only one whose child you wanted to have, the one you kept on getting pregnant with, how many times, was it, Sarah? And so when I finally got you, when I finally won you, after Lukas was dead, it was too late for us.
SARAH:	I never lied to you about the abortion. One, Alan, one.
ALAN:	And I'm not lying to you.

SARAH:	How the fuck could you do this again?
ALAN:	Because I want a separation.
SARAH:	You don't mean that. You can't. We are like, always us… before Lukas, even.
ALAN:	Stop. I promised Hala if she became pregnant again, I would be more than the father of her child. We would make a life.
SARAH:	You discussed this?
ALAN:	Of course.
SARAH:	It wasn't a mad fit of passion, a late night when you couldn't think straight, after Sabra and Shatila, or some other horrible event? Overwhelmed, distraught. It wasn't on our rug. You had sheets. You spoke about when and where in the yellow light of late afternoon. You planned.
ALAN:	Close enough, I'm afraid.
SARAH:	You're leaving me?
ALAN:	Yes. I am.
SARAH:	But I love you.
ALAN:	Sarah, don't.
SARAH:	And you love me, that's what you say, Alan, right now, please…
ALAN:	It won't be… oh, Sarah… I'll try…. I don't intend never to see you again. I don't intend to put you out of my life, that is, if you can stand it. Oh, darling, I didn't want it to come to this. But I've gone and done it. It seems that I can't have both. My dearest friend Sarah, and a child and a wife.
SARAH:	I feel like Medea. I feel like poisoning her.
ALAN:	If you were Medea, this never would have happened.
SARAH:	Right. Two sons. I am a vessel and you're trading me in.
ALAN:	Stop, darling, stop. I can't take any more.
SARAH:	Then, send her away.
ALAN:	Away?
SARAH:	Give her money; we can support it. When it's older it can come around.
ALAN:	'It'?
SARAH:	I'll forgive you. I promise I will. I want to kill you, too, now, of course, wring your neck, but we both know that won't last.
ALAN:	'It' is my child.
SARAH:	Bastard.
ALAN:	Hala will be the mother of my child. I can forget you, Sarah. I can't, of course. I won't.
SARAH:	All right, Alan. Have it your way.
ALAN:	You understand?

SARAH:	Shredding your life. It should be done every decade, I think. We were long overdue. Why, I ought to have walked out on you.
ALAN:	You should never have married me, Sarah. You never loved me.
SARAH:	I never loved you! I adored you, worshipped you. You taught me everything I know.
ALAN:	I got you by default. After Lukas died, you came back. I thought I could live with that, I wanted you so, and maybe I could.
SARAH:	What happened to Lukas in Vietnam?
ALAN:	How would I know? I was 4-F, remember.
SARAH:	Not a conscientious objector?
ALAN:	Philosophically, yes. I had a psychiatrist's note.
SARAH:	Who killed Lukas, Alan?
ALAN:	Sarah, please, our marriage is falling apart.
SARAH:	Lukas was murdered. He wanted me to know.
ALAN:	Lukas was brain dead, Sarah. Lukas could not speak.
SARAH:	Help me, Alan, with this. I won't bother you ever again.
ALAN:	Help you with what? Please. I feel like I've got to throw up.
SARAH:	I didn't poison you, I'm sorry to say.
ALAN:	I've got to lie down.
	(ALAN *exits to their bedroom.*)
SARAH:	It's just your sperm count, acting up.
	(*She sees the pair of airline tickets and she rips one up. She takes* ALAN's *jacket and exits.*)

Scene X

(*Continuation of memory scene, 1982. It's raining.* HALA JABAR *enters from the memory entrance [stage right]. She walks across the stage and mimes pushing open a restaurant door. She goes inside, looks around for* ALAN, *then she sits at the table just as* SARAH *approaches.* SARAH *enters the restaurant and sits at* HALA's *table.*)

HALA:	Sarah, how amazing, really.
SARAH:	It is, isn't it?
HALA:	Do you often come here?
SARAH:	This is our favorite restaurant, Alan's and mine. He proposed to me here. At the same table at which you were sitting.
HALA:	Really?
SARAH:	Really.
HALA:	I see.
SARAH:	He's not coming.

HALA:	I don't understand.
SARAH:	My husband, Alan, sent me instead.
HALA:	Instead? Of what?
SARAH:	Let's not play games.
HALA:	All right, let's not. I'm late.
SARAH:	Yes, but Alan is not coming.
HALA:	Then, I must go.
SARAH:	Go. Where will you go?
HALA:	Home, of course. It's late. I've a plane early tomorrow.
SARAH:	Such dignity, Hala, I'm impressed.
HALA:	I should not be dignified? Do you think so?
SARAH:	I? No. Of course not. I admire you more than you know. It's just me, I suppose. My way is, well, Alan has told you all that. My husband, Alan, you know; I've known Alan for a very long time. We were students together in the sixties.
HALA:	A long time ago.
SARAH:	I occupied buildings; Alan got the judge to drop charges. I've watched Alan operate, so to speak. Then, in a fit of grief, I married. I rather suppose I owe Alan my life. I suppose Alan has told you all this.
HALA:	Alan has told me many things; we spend many hours together, after all, at work and after. But, I really must be going. I've a lot on my mind. There is a war. I am Lebanese.
SARAH:	Not Egyptian.
HALA:	Palestinian and Lebanese. My people are being killed.
SARAH:	Not a slave from Egypt given to Abraham, given to Sarah, in fact, by Pharaoh, given to barren Sarah, to bear the patriarch an heir.
HALA:	I don't need to listen to any more. I have relatives in those camps. (HALA *stands abruptly and exits the restaurant.* SARAH *immediately follows, stopping her on the street. Thunder.*)
SARAH:	Alan wants a child, from his loins, such a strange expression that, like a cut of beef; yes, he wants a son, but Sarah is barren since Lukas's child was dug out of her, like a wad of fat cut from a lamb chop. I was half mad. I said 'yes,' that is, to Alan. I had the abortion. If I had not been grieving privately, so that Alan would not see, and what is more private, after all, than the blood from a woman's insides, tears, great globs of them, then, well, who knows, we went on. Our sex life became astonishingly good.
HALA:	Let me give you a word of advice.
SARAH:	No, Hala, that's not how it works. The other woman puts out; she does not get to talk.

HALA:	It might be correct, Sarah, if I were to tell you, now, about our plans, Alan's and mine, because, I think, perhaps, he has not.
SARAH:	Alan did not come here to meet you tonight because Alan is not leaving me. In some inextricable way, Alan and I are too tightly bound. We are barren, yet we do love. Alan gave me this ticket to give to you.
	(SARAH *hands* HALA *the ticket.* HALA *takes the ticket from* SARAH, *and looks at it.*)
	I'm sorry, Hala.
HALA:	I don't think so.
SARAH:	I admire you, Hala. Alan does, too. We will often speak of you.
	(HALA *begins to walk away.*)
SARAH:	Oh, and just one more thing. Don't wait too long to get rid of it.
	(HALA *stops and looks at her.*)
HALA:	Alan did tell me about your abortion. He was quite clear. You had just been hired to play Antigone, in a big important production. You could hardly play Antigone, could you, if you were pregnant? (*Pause*) And will you please tell Alan for me that I choose this child of ours. I will have a girl. I will call her Mariam. Good night. Alan need not worry about us.
	(HALA *exits stage right, memory exit. After a moment,* SARAH *follows.*)

Scene XI

(*The present. Outside bells. Eight o'clock. The phone rings and rings.* SARAH *opens the apartment door, in a rush, dressed as she was when she went to meet* CHARLES MUFFLER *that morning.* SARAH *grabs the phone just in time.*)

SARAH:	I just walked in. (*Pause*) You were going to take me out tonight. Right. Are you lying to me? Someone you 'absolutely must see'? Has Hala come back, Alan, after all these years? I was thinking about her, that's all. I was, what can I say? Some things you don't forget. They pop up, like pop-up books in your head. (*Pause*) I think I can tell when you're lying, Alan. Fibbing, right. All right, I'll trust you. Later, then. Bye.
	(SARAH *puts down the phone.* JEREMY *enters.*)
JEREMY:	Hey, you should be careful. Who knows who could get in? Where's the husband?
SARAH:	He stepped out for a minute, to pick up Chinese food.

JEREMY:	Okay. Fine.
SARAH:	You want to start from the beginning, of the speech, I mean.
JEREMY:	Just jump into it?
SARAH:	Why not.
JEREMY:	What if he comes back?
SARAH:	He won't…
JEREMY:	With the Chinese food.
SARAH:	… come back.
JEREMY:	Where's he gone, Taiwan?
SARAH:	Sorry, sorry.
JEREMY:	Right. You were thinking of someone else.
SARAH:	Something else, okay. There's a chair.
	(*He takes the chair, places it in the center of the room. He looks around.*)
JEREMY:	Just want to make sure there are no mirrors. (*He laughs.*) Okay. All right. Here we go.
	(*He clears his throat. He begins but it sounds very flat and he has trouble remembering his lines.*)
	As I sat on the ancient seat of augury,
	In the sanctuary where every bird I know
	Will hover at my hands –
	(*He stops, stands.*)
	Shit! I'm not into it. It's terrible, isn't it?
SARAH:	Pretty bad.
JEREMY:	Look, let's forget it.
SARAH:	Fine. You can go.
JEREMY:	Why? What's happened to me? Why can't I do it? I feel like I've lost it. It's gone. I had it. I knew it. Now, I don't have it anymore. What's wrong?
SARAH:	You're scared.
JEREMY:	No shit.
SARAH:	You lost control, now you're trying to control too much. You've got to just let go.
JEREMY:	I'm worried your husband will open that door, and I'll freak out.
SARAH:	Don't be. He's out until late.
JEREMY:	You lied?
SARAH:	I didn't know.
JEREMY:	No Chinese food.
SARAH:	Maybe, but not with me.
JEREMY:	Does he do that a lot? It's not right.
SARAH:	Look, you do the speech and then I'll order us something to eat.
JEREMY:	Sure. Okay. Fine.

(She goes to him and begins to rub his shoulders.)

SARAH: First, relax. Breathe.

(They stand there, breathing together. And then JEREMY *begins to speak, looking at* SARAH. *He gets better and better. He's got it, this time, and the speech is so real to him that it takes him back to the moment he's been hiding.)*

JEREMY: I was afraid,
I turned quickly, tested the burnt-sacrifice,
Ignited the altar at all points – but no fire,
The god in the fire never blazed.
Not from those offerings… over the embers
Slid a heavy ooze from the long thighbones,
Smoking, sputtering out, and the bladder
Puffed and burst – spraying gall into the air –
And the fat wrapping the bones slithered off
And left them glistening white. And no fire.
I had my gun, I took my gun. I jabbed
My gun into that Haji's head, talk or I'll
blow your fucking brains out. I kicked that
bastard until he bled. Where's the Fucking IED?

SARAH: Jeremy.

JEREMY: Where's the bomb, rag head? Tell me, I'll let you
Go. I'll let your sorry ass live. The motherfucker
Grabs at my leg. I take my rifle, hit him hard.
His jaw breaks. Blood spurts out and bone.

SARAH: Jeremy. Stop.

JEREMY: Stop. His wife starts to scream. She starts pulling
At my jacket. Begging. She grabs for my gun.
My gun starts to go off. She's screaming, stop.

SARAH: Jeremy, please. That's enough.

JEREMY: Shut the fuck up. It doesn't stop.
I can't take my hand off. I don't know
She's pregnant. I see pieces of baby fall
Out. He's down on his knees, begging.
And we're crying. We are, all of us,
Crying. My gun is on the floor, next
to her. Her hair comes loose from that scarf.
Her black hair spreads out on the floor.
He's kneeling, stroking her hair.

(Silence. JEREMY *is on his knees, staring at the spot.* SARAH *pulls herself together and speaks calmly.)*

SARAH:	Jeremy. Jeremy?
	(*She touches him gently and he jumps, crouching behind the table, screaming.*)
JEREMY:	If you tell anyone anything you heard here tonight, I'll kill you I swear I will. I'll blow your brains out.
	(*She is behind a chair, but, again, she speaks softly, reassuringly.*)
SARAH:	Hush. I won't tell. Trust. I'm here for you, Jeremy.
	(JEREMY *falls to the floor, moaning and sobbing.* SARAH *gets down next to him and she gently lays a hand on his back. Slowly, he quiets. She sits next to him, lightly stroking his back. For a time, there is only the sound of their breathing. Then,* ALAN's *voice is heard from the hall, speaking to someone.*)
ALAN:	Go on in.
	(*Louder*)
	Sarah! I have someone I want you to meet!
	(*A young woman,* MARIAM, *dressed in jeans, sneakers, a long-sleeved form-fitting top, with a hijab on her head, steps into the room in front of* ALAN. SARAH *shakes her head, and waves her other hand in a gesture that says 'go away.'*)
SARAH:	(*In a whisper*) Get out of here, Alan, please. With her.
ALAN:	(*Expansive with pride*) Sarah, this is my Mariam. My daughter.
SARAH:	Jesus Christ.
	(JEREMY *jumps up, terrified as he sees the woman in the hijab.*)
SARAH:	Jeremy, it's all right. This is my husband, Alan, and this lovely young person is his daughter, Mariam. Amazing, but true. This is Jeremy Thrasher, my most gifted acting student. We've been here tonight working on quite a difficult speech from *Antigone.* Jeremy found a whole new truth... (*To* JEREMY) It takes great courage to speak like that. Your work was very honest, very brave.
ALAN:	Hello, Jeremy. Sarah has spoken very highly...
MARIAM:	*Antigone* is my favorite play.
	(JEREMY *is staring all the while at* MARIAM.)
JEREMY:	I've got to get out of here.
SARAH:	Stay. We'll have supper. I said, we'd eat.
JEREMY:	Can't. My girlfriend. Got to go.
SARAH:	Jeremy, come to class tomorrow.
JEREMY:	Yeah, okay, sure.
	(SARAH *moves very close to him.*)
SARAH:	Look at me, Jeremy.
	Go straight home. Tomorrow, come to me, first thing.

JEREMY: Sure, whatever you say.
            (JEREMY *exits. Silence*)

ALAN: So, Sarah, I always imagined Lukas to look like that.
            (SARAH *is too upset to respond to him. She speaks to* MARIAM.)

SARAH: You look like your mother. That's lucky, you know, you might have had Alan's looks. You remember what Bernard Shaw said to who was it, Mrs. Somebody or Other, about looks and brains. She wanted his child. My god, I've lost my mind. I can't think who it was. Anyway, in your case, the analogy doesn't hold up. Hala was brilliant and beautiful. Is, I should say. I do hope she's all right. You can see, I suppose, why I was jealous. Here you are, a grown woman in our living room, standing on our rug, and it all seems amazing. Because, it doesn't seem to matter what happened then. None of that matters anymore, not after, well, it doesn't matter, now, after all. Here you are. I'm extremely grateful that you are here. In one piece. Look, how lovely, Alan, she is. With such beautiful hair. Spread out. On the ground.
            (SARAH *is completely undone.*)

Act II

Scene XII

(CHARLES MUFFLER *sits behind his large desk, talking on the phone. Outside his open office door,* MIRANDA *paces, agitated; she reacts with scorn to what she overhears.*)

CHARLES: Yours is truly exceptional foresight, Mrs. Gifford, extraordinary. Jennifer is our most gifted student. I had no idea she was your niece, none, when she auditioned for us. Juliet. Who could forget? The balcony speech. I wept. A bronze plaque. Right in the center between the two doors, as you enter. 'In loving memory …' yes, and something, a few words, a couplet, perhaps, about your late husband's love of the bard. This has made my day, Mrs. Gifford, my year. I can't thank you enough. By pure coincidence, it happens, our senior project is to be *Romeo and Juliet,* beating out Moliere and Goldoni. With our Jennifer, of course. Mark Gant adores her work. The Mark Gant, yes. He will direct. (*He laughs at something she says.*) You are very kind. And I will call

her in and let her know. I'm certain she'll phone you directly after. Ciao for now.
(*He clicks the speaker button on his phone.*)
Lizzie, send the young lady back in.
(MIRANDA *has a black eye. She's full of manic energy; she shifts her weight from foot to foot.*)

MIRANDA: The 'young lady' has a name. Miranda Cruz.

CHARLES: Take a seat, please, Ms. Cruz.
(*She plops onto a chair. Silence. He ignores her, jots some notes.*)

MIRANDA: I did Juliet for my audition, too. I won't be cast as her, though. My aunt works at Wal-Mart. I'm going to have a scar. And, I'm going to sue. I will need plastic surgery. And, if I want to work, I'll need a theater with my aunt's name on a plaque, 'Sonia-Lynnette Cruz,' in the center, between the two doors… Where the fuck is she?
(CHARLES *sees* SARAH *outside the door and waves her in.*)

SARAH: Charles, thanks for seeing me right away.

MIRANDA: Damn straight.
(SARAH *wheels around and looks at her.*)

SARAH: What happened to her?

MIRANDA: Miranda. Miranda Cruz. She doesn't even fucking know my name. No one in this place knows who I am. You will.

CHARLES: Sit down, Miranda. I'm on your side, believe me. I only ask you to control your tongue. You'll get further in life. So, Sarah, what have you to say for yourself?

SARAH: What happened to you, Miranda? Not Jeremy?

MIRANDA: What do you think?

CHARLES: I'm afraid so. The worst.

SARAH: Jeremy beat you up?

MIRANDA: She acts surprised. (*Under her breath*) The bitch.

CHARLES: Let's watch our language, please, Ms. Cruz, I don't want to tell you again. The Thrasher boy has a concussion, from a frying pan, I believe, wielded by our Ms. Cruz.

SARAH: Shit.

CHARLES: You, also, Sarah, please, your tongue.
(MIRANDA *jumps up.*)

MIRANDA: My face is ruined. Destroyed because of this cunt.

SARAH: I beg your pardon?

CHARLES: Sit, Miranda. Not another word. (*To* SARAH) You were with Jeremy Thrasher last night. We know that.

SARAH: Jeremy came to my house.

CHARLES: After I'd strictly forbidden you to see him?

SARAH:	Come on, Charles. You took Jeremy out of my class. I told you that was a bad decision. He needed to finish work on that speech. Believe me, he has his reasons.
CHARLES:	And what are those reasons, if I might be so bold as to inquire?
MIRANDA:	I know damn well what his reasons were. Ms. Thing here is trying to break us up.
SARAH:	Wrong.
MIRANDA:	You slept with my boyfriend.
SARAH:	Don't be ridiculous.
MIRANDA:	Me? You could be his mother, his grandmother. You're his teacher. Mine, too. *Were.*
SARAH:	I would never.
MIRANDA:	I saw how you looked at him from the first class. You knew we were together, that's why you hated my work.
SARAH:	I'm afraid that's not why…
CHARLES:	'I did not have sex with that woman,' excuse me for quoting our former president.
SARAH:	Stop this nonsense.
CHARLES:	I spoke with the boy by phone from the emergency room.
MIRANDA:	He came home at four a.m., drunk, smelling of sex. We had a fight. What do you think? He told me he was with you.
SARAH:	At my house…
MIRANDA:	The bitch admits.
CHARLES:	Silence, Ms. Cruz. Sit.
	(MIRANDA *sits.*)
SARAH:	He worked on his speech.
MIRANDA:	I'm suing your ass. I want you out of this school.
CHARLES:	Miranda, you have crossed the decency line too many times.
SARAH:	Jeremy left by nine, nine-thirty at the latest. I begged him to go straight home. He told me he would go to his girlfriend's, you, Miranda. He did. My husband came in with his daughter. Amazing, but true. I have witnesses. Alan's daughter. Charles, I must speak with you alone.
MIRANDA:	Blame the victim. It's illegal what she's done.
CHARLES:	Well, ill-advised. And prohibited at this school.
SARAH:	You can't believe this… Miranda, I did not do what Jeremy has said, if he even said it, that is. Jeremy is disturbed. He's lying to protect himself. I can't believe you hit him on the head.
MIRANDA:	The prick had a gun.
SARAH:	Fuck.
CHARLES:	Ladies, enough.

MIRANDA:	I love him. He tried to kill me.
SARAH:	You saw the gun?
MIRANDA:	That's why I grabbed the pan. I love him.
CHARLES:	No gun was found.
MIRANDA:	He threw the gun out the window; I told the police.
SARAH:	Charles, we must talk, alone.
MIRANDA:	He was kissing me. Then, he grabbed my hair. He was acting so wild. Saying dumb things about the war.
SARAH:	I see. Miranda, why not wait outside, for a minute, please.
MIRANDA:	I've been sitting outside the whole morning. I'm not rich, but I've got an uncle on the force.
CHARLES:	I have great respect for the NYPD.
MIRANDA:	New Jersey.
CHARLES:	Miranda, take a seat outside.
MIRANDA:	They talk…
	(MIRANDA *glares at them through her tears and goes out. Silence*)
SARAH:	Charles, Jeremy Thrasher was in Iraq.
CHARLES:	We know that.
SARAH:	I did not know that until last night.
	(CHARLES *does not respond.*)
	Charles! You might have told me. After the mirror incident. That's what they call them, don't they, 'incidents,' 'regrettable incidents,' in fact. We regret the loss of each civilian life. But, they are all civilians, aren't they, until they sign up. Jeremy did it for the tuition money, so he could get out of his godforsaken life and come to this school. The Tiresias speech became the minefield he had to walk through.
CHARLES:	More matter, less art.
SARAH:	Right. Jeremy Thrasher killed someone in Iraq.
CHARLES:	Naturally, my dear, it's a war.
SARAH:	He murdered a woman.
CHARLES:	Innocent people get killed. Regrettable, always, of course.
SARAH:	I see.
CHARLES:	We go on.
SARAH:	Is that what 'we' do?
CHARLES:	Did you have sex with the Thrasher boy or not?
SARAH:	Stop this. Jeremy flashed back during the speech.
CHARLES:	Jeremy Thrasher should not have been at your house.
SARAH:	Did he threaten that girl with a gun?
CHARLES:	A little provocateuse, that one.
SARAH:	Did Jeremy have a gun?

CHARLES:	Absolutely not.
SARAH:	Are you certain of that?
CHARLES:	The gun story is hers.
SARAH:	She made it up?
CHARLES:	Trust me. (*Pause*) Thrasher got the thrashing he deserved. Nevertheless, Jeremy Thrasher is out of this school.
SARAH:	Don't be ridiculous, Charles; you can't throw him out.
CHARLES:	No? We're a conservatory, not a mental hospital. I might as well expel that foul-mouthed little tart, also.
SARAH:	This is the wrong approach. The worst idea…
CHARLES:	I believe your class starts at ten.
SARAH:	You must not expel Jeremy Thrasher.

(CHARLES *picks up the snow globe and appears totally lost in it.* SARAH *pulls up a chair and sits facing him, waiting.*)
Charles?

CHARLES:	I cannot tell you what comfort it is to get lost in a snowstorm for a bit. It takes me back to my boyhood on the farm. Mother would send me out first thing in the morning to gather the eggs. The whole world was new, sparkling with frost. Icicles tinkling in the wind. The chickens would be hunkered down, feathers plumped up, a brown egg hidden under each one. They'd flap their wings and screech, trying to scare me away. It was a loss, of sorts. My fingers were stiff from the cold but the eggs were warm. I'd have my pockets full. There'd be snowflakes on my nose.
SARAH:	I see.

(CHARLES '*comes back.*')
Charles, did you know Lukas Brightman in Vietnam?

CHARLES:	I had many young men in my command.
SARAH:	You asked me to forgive you on opening night.
CHARLES:	Enough. This Thrasher fellow was honorably discharged. There's not a stain on his record. It's a pity. What can I do? We're an acting school. In the long run, we may be doing him a favor by asking him to go. Adversity builds character, it's so.
SARAH:	I don't believe you, Charles.

(*He stands to usher her out.*)

CHARLES:	No more, now. No more of this. I know a good man at the VA; I'll send the boy to him. Thanks, Sarah, for dropping by. Your class awaits. A great source of satisfaction, our students. Go, give them your best. Lose your cares, Sarah, in art.

(SARAH *looks hard at him and then leaves.*)

Scene XIII

(*The hospital:* SARAH *enters an empty room.*)

SARAH: I visited Lukas at Walter Reed in 1972. The place was full of young, beautiful bodies with unlined faces, only they were missing one or two of everything: arms, legs, private parts, and a few, like Lukas, were missing themselves. They lay about like detritus on a beach ... 'Urns with ashes that once were men.'

(SARAH *walks closer to the chair where she imagines* LUKAS *to be sitting.*)

He was alone, in his own room. So as not to upset the others, I suppose. He was tied to a chair. 'Lukas?' His glorious hair was all gone; his scalp wrapped. His head hung like it was barely attached to his neck. But, his eyes were open, with a faraway look. Lukas was breathing through a plastic tube in his nose. I started to cry. Then, I thought, what if he can still see? I closed my eyes; I saw Lukas, the beauty he was. I sat down on the stool next to him. 'Hi, Lukas. I'm here.'

(*She sits on the bench next to the empty chair.*)

I took his hand. His flesh was soft, moist. He smelled sweet. He gripped my fingers like a baby does. He held tight. We sat for a long time like that.

'Lukas, can you hear me? Let me tell you... Please, can you hear? Yesterday, there was a great protest, Lukas, the best. The vets took their medals and they threw them over a chain-link fence back at Congress, right into the faces of those smirking, self-righteous bastards. One by one, the vets ripped their medals off of their chests and heaved them over the fence. It was on television, Lukas, on Walter Cronkite. The whole world watched it. Your friend, John, he had your Purple Heart. He said into the microphone, 'This one is from Lukas, who hated this mother-fucking war, and who is in fucking Walter Reed because he was going to talk about what he saw,' and he threw your Purple Heart back. I asked John what he meant. 'What the fuck difference would it make?' But it does matter, Lukas, doesn't it.

'Lukas, what did you see in Vietnam? What were you going to say? Who did this to you, Lukas? Please, tell me.'

Lukas tightened his grip. He jerked himself straight. I felt him tremble. I heard him roaring inside like the ocean. A wave rushed through him.

And, then, there was nothing. Lukas slumped in his chair. His fingers fell from mine. Lukas was gone.

I couldn't tell him I carried his child. If I had… never mind. Two weeks later, Lukas was dead. Lukas used himself up trying to speak. Lukas wanted me to know.

(JEREMY *comes in the door. A white bandage wound around his head.* SARAH *startles.*)

JEREMY: Jeeze, Ms. Golden, you're here.

SARAH: Jeremy, what happened to…

(JEREMY *paces as he unwinds the gauze from around his head. There is another smaller bandage underneath.*)

JEREMY: Wounded. See. Took a hit. Discharged. Ready to go. Said I'd talk to a shrink; they took the cuffs off. (*Pause*) You know what the shrink said? (*He paces, laughs nervously, and says in a mocking voice*) 'Well, young man, you are not a risk to yourself or to anyone else.' So, that's that. Fixed me right up. Stitches. X-ray. Had counseling, too. 'Not a risk.' Fine. Inside and out. Good as new.

SARAH: Jeremy, stand still.

JEREMY: Look, I don't have a gun if that's what they said.

SARAH: How do you know they told me that?

JEREMY: She starts screaming. I yell back.

SARAH: Be honest with me.

JEREMY: I stopped to have a few drinks. She throws a frying pan. If I'd had a gun, I'd a blown her head off. I smacked her, instead.

SARAH: Very smart.

JEREMY: Ms. Golden, Sarah, look, I can control this stuff, if I can act. I know I can. Trust me. Please.

SARAH: Jeremy, Muffler has thrown you out of school.

JEREMY: Right. Sure.

            Fucking dickhead. Jerk.

            (JEREMY *slumps into the empty chair.*)

            It's over. See. I fucked up.

            (SARAH *sits on the bench next to him.*)

SARAH: It was war, Jeremy.

JEREMY: Sure. That's what it was.

SARAH: You can tell me. Anything. Anything at all.

JEREMY: Help me. I've got no one else.

SARAH: I promise.

JEREMY: Stop looking at me.

SARAH: Trust me, Jeremy. I will help. I know how hard…

(She reaches out to him. He flies into a rage.)

JEREMY: I told you not to talk about that. Never, I said. Shit. Fuck. You know what: just get out of my life. Stop following me around. Asking me stuff. Pretending you know. That's right. Give up and leave us alone. Miranda and me.

(JEREMY storms out the door. SARAH, stunned, waits a moment and then leaves.)

Scene XIV

(The desk phone is ringing in ALAN's office, later the same day. He enters, nervous and excited, he speaks into his phone.)

ALAN: Yes, I'm free. Send her right up!

(SARAH enters, carrying several large shopping bags from an expensive boutique.)

(Surprised, not altogether pleasantly) Sarah!

(She kisses him.)

SARAH: Surprise, sweetie. Give me a minute. I'll slip into something smashing, cashmere, décolletage. You'll take me some fabulous place. We'll drink, fuck.

ALAN: Sarah, it's two o'clock.

SARAH: I'll forget.

ALAN: My afternoon's booked.

SARAH: Everything was on sale.

ALAN: I'm certain it's lovely.

SARAH: I can't take anything back.

ALAN: Sarah, truth is… I've a meeting.

SARAH: Whenever I get near a hospital, my life falls apart…

ALAN: Darling, later, I promise, my head will be clear.

SARAH: I see. What exquisite timing. Isn't it amazing how life works? All our ghosts.

ALAN: Don't say that.

SARAH: Alan, help me. I'm afraid.

(He goes to her and holds her.)

ALAN: Don't be, darling, I'm here, with you.

(MARIAM opens the door. She clutches a large leather lady's handbag to her chest and stands awkwardly.)

MARIAM: I'm sorry, I'll…

(ALAN moves quickly away from SARAH.)

ALAN: Mariam, please, come in. I'm so happy you're here.

(*He moves to hug her, but she steps away. Everyone stands in awkward silence.*)

SARAH: Is your mother in town?

MARIAM: My mother?

(*Silence*)

My mother is in Beirut.

ALAN: Sit down, everyone, please. Coffee? Tea? I've cleared the whole afternoon just for us.

(*He points out the two chairs around the table, and he holds one out for* MARIAM. *The women sit.* ALAN *sits on the bench. He is effusive.* SARAH *is distracted.* MARIAM *tense.*)

Here, everyone. Good. Now, how long will you stay in New York?

MARIAM: Long enough.

ALAN: Great. I'll show you the city. We will, won't we, Sarah? What would you like to see? Do you like opera, museums, food, we have the best restaurants, shopping, do you like to shop? Read? Hip-hop? There are mosques. We have quite a few Arab neighborhoods. There are so many people I'd like you to meet. You'll stay for a while, I hope. You could think of studying here, at Columbia.

MARIAM: I won't stay that long.

ALAN: No?

MARIAM: I don't think you know why I've come?

ALAN: I had hoped to see me.

MARIAM: That's true. I want to know about you.

ALAN: You do? Sure. That's so nice. Well, what's to know? I'm still executive director here.

SARAH: Your mother's office was right next door.

(SARAH's *cell phone rings; she fishes for it.*)

ALAN: Yes. Well, I'm rather overwhelmed at the moment. We're trying to figure out how to get some aid into Tyre, then, of course, there's Gaza. There's always Gaza, as we say around here. Not to mention Iraq.

MARIAM: It's an overwhelming moment, yes.

(*Silence.* SARAH *is listening, intently, to the voice on her phone.* ALAN *and* MARIAM *lock eyes.*)

SARAH: Yes, Jeremy, of course, I know just where it is. Right away.

(SARAH *gathers her things, getting ready to leave.*)

ALAN: It's fine, Sarah, stay.

SARAH: Can't.

ALAN: Tonight, then. Be careful, will you.

(ALAN *kisses her.*)

SARAH:	(*To* MARIAM) I leave Alan to you.
	(SARAH *exits.*)
ALAN:	Well, then, good. Sarah stopped by out of the blue… I had planned for us to be, well, here we are, now, just we two. (*Pause*) I will work hard, Mariam, to become a real father to you.
MARIAM:	There's no need. I'm grown.
ALAN:	Even for a grown-up, a father is… I miss my own father quite a bit. It went so fast, your growing up. I thought about you every birthday, what you'd be wearing, where I would take you. I always wanted you to ride the merry-go-round in Central Park. I never knew the actual date.
MARIAM:	June 27.
ALAN:	Close! I always thought the first of July. Somehow, I think, I was not surprised to see you as you are now, in the hijab, too. A father knows his daughter, somehow, even if…
MARIAM:	I never felt I knew you.
ALAN:	You look so much like Hala.
MARIAM:	I have your nose.
ALAN:	Sorry, that was a mistake.
MARIAM:	Don't be sorry about that.
ALAN:	Does Hala ever speak about those years? (*Silence*) All right, Mariam, look, I will tell you. I never intended to leave your mother while she was pregnant. It was Sarah. By the time I had sorted things and Sarah was, well, resigned, your mother didn't want me anymore. How is she? How is Hala?
MARIAM:	Hala was traveling the road north from Tyre with a convoy of women and children when the road was hit. The first ambulance, clearly marked, it could be seen from the sky, was destroyed. Deliberately targeted, Hala says.
ALAN:	We heard. (*Pause*) Hala would be in the thick of it all.
MARIAM:	Everyone, now, is in the thick of it, I think.
ALAN:	True. Does she know you're here? That you've come?
MARIAM:	It was a beautiful summer in Lebanon, Alan. Our house on the Corniche overlooks the sea. In the morning there were birds, at night music. So many friends had come home. We were laughing all the time. Hala made me leave, to go to London, she thought. I never left Heathrow. I got on a plane for New York.
ALAN:	I'm very glad.
MARIAM:	I am glad, too.
ALAN:	I'm happy about that.
MARIAM:	Happy?

ALAN:	Thrilled, I'd say, yes.
MARIAM:	I don't think you know why I've come.
ALAN:	I had hoped to see me.
MARIAM:	Yes, to see you at work. I wanted to be here in this building with you and all these good people, all these innocent civilians, at this particular time, when so many innocent civilians in my part of the world... You do good work, all of you. You send aid to people like me. You send protein bars and bottles of cooking oil, not olive oil, of course, vegetable oil, but still, we can cook up the dried chick peas, and rice, if we have clean water, that is. If the water purification plants have not been bombed, if crude oil has not been dumped in the sea, killing the fish. Never mind. You send ready meals, if you have to, dump them on us from the sky. And you send little pieces of paper telling us to leave our houses before they are bombed. That is very kind. The good people in the United States continue to think they are good because of the work you do here helping refugees. The more refugees your country makes, the more people like you try to help.
ALAN:	That is one way of looking at it, I suppose.
MARIAM:	Do you look at it another way?
ALAN:	I try. There is always evil in the world, and there is always good.
MARIAM:	True.
ALAN:	I do what I can to tip the balance our way.
MARIAM:	That is admirable, Alan.
ALAN:	Thank you. Your mother, too, Hala feels the same way. Felt. I'm certain, still does.
MARIAM:	Oh, yes. My mother thinks exactly like you. But let me ask you, Alan, one thing. I have come here just to ask you. Why when you tip the balance, as you say, why is it always Muslims who must die? Why does the balance never tip the other way? There is a bomb ticking right now inside my bag. Please answer soon.
ALAN:	Don't talk like that. Not even inside my office. It's fine to be outraged, of course. I am, also, outraged. But someone might overhear you, even here. That would put you at risk.
MARIAM:	I understand.
ALAN:	Fine, then, okay. We all know what's going on. What do you think I do day in and day out? But I want to tell you something else: My father, your grandfather, he lived in times worse than these, and he never gave up. He wasted not one instant on revenge. He got people out. Snatched from the Nazis. He saved lives. Often, of course, it does feel useless. I feel hopeless... but I learned from

	him, from what he did, individuals can make a difference to other individuals. That may be all we can do. But we must do that much.
MARIAM:	That is true.
ALAN:	My father left a legacy to me. I intend to pass his legacy to you. I have letters to you, Mariam, a drawer full, returned by your mother, unopened. I wanted to know you. I tried to imagine what you needed to hear at every time, every age. You can read them. Tell me if I got anything right.
MARIAM:	That would be nice.
ALAN:	I sent money, too.
MARIAM:	Naturally. Of course.
ALAN:	I wanted you to have the best. Be the best. Your mother and I spoke about a new race. It was foolish, romantic talk, of course. But we believed it in those days, and we still do, Hala, too, I am certain of that, in peace, somehow, in justice, in living together, side by side, that someday clearer heads will prevail. We believed in you, too, Mariam. We believed that in making you from our flesh we were going to give something beautiful not just to ourselves but to the world. I am so sorry I wasn't there to see you grow up.
MARIAM:	In Lebanon for the Civil War? In East Jerusalem? Where?
ALAN:	I am sorry, Mariam. I have a great deal to be sorry for. But, please know, how thrilled, how blessed I feel, truly, I don't use that word lightly, that you came to find me. Amazing at this time in my life to have one more chance.
MARIAM:	One more chance?
ALAN:	I might live to know my grandchildren, a wonderful thought. I am a fortunate man, Mariam, because you've come.
MARIAM:	I see. I thought it would be nice if you knew me, if you understood everything in your last minutes, if your whole life flashed before you, and you got to know at the very last moment that this child who was supposed to bring in the new world, only you never got to watch her grow up, unfortunate, that, but there was always a war on, after all, and how could you leave your important job to go there, anyway. It was always so unsafe. But, I wanted you to know, now, at last, about the new world you made with your big dreams, your empty words, and the murderous actions they cover up, the peace plans, the road maps running every which way, they have to bulldoze so many houses to get there, and put up such a big wall, build a fence around Gaza, such a nice prison they built, to keep the fishermen from being able to fish, and there is nowhere to run, you get blown up if you go to the beach, if you

leave, you can't get back in, and, then, why not send Lebanon back to the stone age, the people, after all, are so primitive. But none of that matters, now, at all, because most of all I wanted to see your face at the moment you understand it is your own flesh who is going to blow you up.

(*At this,* ALAN *makes a lunge for her and grabs for her bag.*)

I wouldn't open the clasp.

(*He lets go of the bag and takes a step back.* MARIAM *laughs.*)

We are all terrorists, after all.

ALAN: Forget about me. I'm an old man. Don't ruin your life.

MARIAM: Get ready, Alan. I'm going to give you a treat. Parents are always already dead. They don't get to hear this:

(MARIAM *begins to recite the Kaddish, the Jewish prayer for the dead.*)

Yeetgadal v'yeetkadash sh'mey rabbah

B'almach dee v'rah kheer'utey

V'yanleekh malkhutei, b'chahyeykhohn, uv' yohmeykhohn

Uv'chahyei d'chohl beyt yisrael

(ALAN *is frozen in terror; he doesn't want to believe her, yet he does.* MARIAM *opens the bag and dumps its contents onto the floor: lipsticks, pens, her passport, a diary, a wallet, keys, the usual stuff, a book.* ALAN *feels like a fool, but he relaxes.* MARIAM *picks up the book.*)

See Under Love by David Grossman. A great Israeli novelist. A great Holocaust book. And do you know that David Grossman had a son, Uri. He was a tank commander in the ground invasion. His father had just signed a petition with other Jewish intellectuals calling for an end to the fighting. This war could have ended before Uri Grossman got killed by a Hezbollah rocket. He was twenty years old. And you think we are the only ones who love to make martyrs? Do you think we are the only ones who love death?

(*She trembles.*)

Like an ocean, like two seas crashing together between the rocks and that is my bloodstream, that churning is always my heart. You cannot imagine the power with which my heart beats. How does my heart not jump from my chest? How does my blood not rush out? You wanted something else. I believe you wished for a son. In your mind I would be a great man. I would have had a bar mitzvah. I would have done good. I would have figured out how. Like your father, like you.

ALAN:	No, Mariam. It was you I wanted. All the time, I wanted you.
	(ALAN *goes to her and he holds her and comforts her.*)
MARIAM:	It's too hard.
ALAN:	I know that, believe me, my dear one, my daughter, my child, I do understand.
	(ALAN *helps her up and they walk out together.*)

Scene XV

(*That night.* SARAH *is in bed.* ALAN *enters the bedroom.*)

SARAH:	I'm awake.
	(*He kisses her head.*)
	I can't sleep.
	(*She sits up and turns on the light.*)
	Poor kid…
	(ALAN *sits on the bed.*)
ALAN:	She pulled quite a stunt.
SARAH:	He was crying when he called. I met him in the park at Strawberry Fields. He got down on his knees and apologized.
ALAN:	Well, good for him. Mariam threatened to blow me up. She said she had plastic explosives in her bag.
SARAH:	You didn't believe her?
ALAN:	She was quite convincing.
SARAH:	You believed her.
ALAN:	For an instant.
SARAH:	It's your guilt.
ALAN:	Afterwards, I felt like a fool. Worse than a fool. Some kind of criminal. At least, I didn't show her how angry I was.
SARAH:	He promised me he doesn't have a gun.
ALAN:	A gun? Sarah, stay away from that kid.
SARAH:	He would never hurt me.
ALAN:	Don't be so sure.
SARAH:	He never threatened to blow me up.
ALAN:	He's not your flesh and blood.
SARAH:	Right.
ALAN:	I looked for them, Sarah, more than once. Hala was good at covering her tracks but it wasn't Hala by then I cared about.
SARAH:	We went to a stupid movie to clear our heads, stuffed ourselves. We laughed, Alan, like kids. I won't let that boy go off on his own. I promised I'd get him back into school.

ALAN:	Somehow the pain dulled over the years. Days would go by when I wouldn't even feel the ache.
SARAH:	Alan, what have we done?
ALAN:	Abraham rode twice to Egypt to see Ishmael, Sarah, did you know that? He could not get off his white horse. Sarah forbade his feet touching the ground; still, she let him go.
SARAH:	I let you.
ALAN:	He left signs for his son to interpret so the boy knew he was loved.
SARAH:	Mariam found you.
ALAN:	Daughters are impossible, it turns out.
SARAH:	You deserved a fright – look at it from her point of view.
ALAN:	She recited the Kaddish.
SARAH:	Really?
ALAN:	Perfectly, yes.
SARAH:	You couldn't do that. I suppose she can do it, someday, for you.
ALAN:	It was ghastly, really, I thought. I know, it's ridiculous. That beautiful, brilliant girl… to think such a thing.
SARAH:	Like Hala, really.
ALAN:	Quite.
SARAH:	I always liked Hala, actually. I thought of having an affair with her myself.
ALAN:	No.
SARAH:	Yes. It's a line from a Pinter play. Robert says to his wife, 'I always liked Jerry rather more than I liked you. I should have had an affair with him myself.'
ALAN:	Something else happened to me when I thought I was about to die.
SARAH:	What?
ALAN:	Lukas.
SARAH:	Lukas, of course. I've never been unfaithful to you, Alan, not since.
ALAN:	That's something, I suppose.
SARAH:	It most definitely is. All our friends had open marriages, then.
ALAN:	Then.
SARAH:	Well, that's how it was.
ALAN:	Years after the war, a man, he said he was in Muffler's command, came to see me. He was having nightmares. His therapist suggested we talk. He knew Lukas, Sarah.
SARAH:	Was his name John?
ALAN:	John, yes, that was his name. I talked to the guy. He was pretty distraught. Paranoid I thought.

SARAH:	You didn't believe him?
ALAN:	It's not that I didn't believe him. I was no longer practicing law.
SARAH:	You believed him. John was Lukas's friend.
ALAN:	After that, I went to see Muffler.
SARAH:	To accuse the bastard.
ALAN:	Not exactly, Sarah, I needed to hear his side of the story.
SARAH:	His side!
ALAN:	Muffler was a mess. Incoherent. Drunk. Shortly after we spoke, he dropped out of sight.
SARAH:	You'd always been jealous of Lukas. Perhaps you were grateful to Muffler, in your heart of hearts.
ALAN:	Nonsense. He canceled the play you were in.
SARAH:	*Uncle Vanya*. I was the Yelena.
ALAN:	Right. You were pretty upset.
SARAH:	I loved the part.
ALAN:	I felt I had undermined your career for no reason. It would have been impossible to prove, and what would have been accomplished after all? Muffler had disappeared.
SARAH:	But, today when you thought you were going to lose your life in a terrorist attack carried out by your own flesh and blood, this scene in your office with John flashed through your head and you decided that you don't want to go your final destination, however hot that may be, Alan, without making a clean breast, so you decided to tell me tonight that I owe my career to the decorated war criminal who shot Lukas in the head.
ALAN:	We don't know that.
SARAH:	I ought to have known, Alan, all along. But, I didn't want to know, did I? I wanted to act.
	(SARAH *looks at him. She takes her robe and leaves the bedroom.*)

Scene XVI

(*Split scene:* SARAH *enters her living room. Her cell phone is in her hand. A phone rings. Day in Beirut and* HALA's *living room is drenched in Mediterranean light.* HALA *enters, her cell phone in her hands. Both women use ear-pieces and hold their phones, allowing them mobility. The scene has a strange sort of physical intimacy; though the women cannot see one another and never look in the other's direction, their movements indicate a growing synchronicity of feeling.*)

SARAH:	Hala?
HALA:	Hala, yes.

SARAH:	It's Sarah.
HALA:	Sarah?
SARAH:	Alan's… you know…
HALA:	Ah, Sarah! Hello.
	(*They laugh a bit nervously; then, they begin to speak at the same time.*)
SARAH:	How are you?
HALA:	How are you?
SARAH:	You're well?
HALA:	As usual. And you?
SARAH:	I'm fine.
HALA:	You are?
SARAH:	I am, yes.
HALA:	I'm glad.
SARAH:	I'm glad you're all right. Mariam is in New York.
HALA:	I sent her out of here to England. I had no idea.
SARAH:	She's a wonderful young woman. Amazing, really.
HALA:	I'm glad you think so.
SARAH:	I do. She's ballsy, if you know what I mean.
HALA:	(*Laughs*) I do.
	(*Pause*)
	I don't want to speak to Alan.
SARAH:	Alan's asleep.
	(*Pause*)
	Hala?
HALA:	Yes, Sarah, what?
SARAH:	Something has happened. Not to Mariam; she's fine. Really. Lovely.
HALA:	Has she taken off the headscarf in New York? Tell me, yes. She started that at boarding school in England, not in Beirut. Here she was disco-dancing. Here, before, I worried about sex, drinking, usual things. Now, who knows what to fear. The young are putting on the scarves. If my mother were alive, she'd…
SARAH:	Something's happened, Hala, to someone else. To me, too, I think. I couldn't sleep. I haven't been. Sleeping, that is.
HALA:	I know.
SARAH:	You do?
HALA:	I don't sleep.
SARAH:	Oh, my god, of course not. I'm… what can I say?
HALA:	The bombing has stopped. The truce might hold.
SARAH:	I hope so.

HALA:	We are relieved.
	(*Pause*)
SARAH:	Hala, I have something in my head. A woman. I had to tell someone. You. I thought: Hala, I could tell. You've been to Iraq.
HALA:	I was there, yes. At the start. Afterwards, there was no room for the UN.
SARAH:	How can such things happen? This war, I mean, we let it, not you, we, here, and, now, well.
	(HALA *puts her head into her hands.*)
	I teach, you remember, do you? A talented young man in my class. She was pregnant, Hala. I don't know what I'm asking. He can't forget. That's good, I think, he shouldn't. But now? I mean, I know. I see. It's an indelible image, really. (*Pause*) I don't know. What do you do?
HALA:	Do?
SARAH:	With such things? With the things you've heard, things you have seen, I mean. How do you?
HALA:	Go on?
SARAH:	I suppose. I don't know. You go on. Obviously, you do. But it's in my mind. Like a scene in a play. I didn't see it, firsthand, like you, like I suppose you have seen, and worse things, still, I can't forget. I cannot stop looking. Sometimes I feel I am her.
HALA:	I see.
SARAH:	You do? Because I'm afraid I'm completely unhinged.
HALA:	There's a concept the therapists have, secondary traumatization, it happens from the things you hear, things that the people tell you. They tell you, and you see it all in front of you. You take their story into your body. It happens to everyone, everyone who listens, that is. Is this what you wanted to hear?
SARAH:	What do you do?
HALA:	Do?
SARAH:	Yes, Hala, please.
	(HALA *gets up and as she does* SARAH *sits down and gently rocks herself back and forth.*)
HALA:	You weep with them. You hold them, if you can. If they let you. If they are not so stiff they can't be touched. You try to hold them, until, you hold them until they can start to shake. You want to know this?
SARAH:	I know it, yes…
HALA:	Sometimes they bury their heads in your lap, even if they are men, sometimes, often, if a wife has been killed. They cry. Or if

	their children… Grown men. They tremble in your arms. They were not home when the house was bombed. They come home. Everyone they love is gone. They dig. They find, maybe, a hand. I can't tell you, Sarah. I will not do it, not over the phone, not in your West Side apartment with all those white walls.
SARAH:	But I know, I mean, I read, I watch the news, we do see, but, please, it is this boy I have, he was a soldier.
HALA:	A soldier.
SARAH:	A boy, innocent, really, then all of a sudden… he shot a pregnant woman, Hala, many times. (*Silence*) Hala?
HALA:	I will tell you about the survivors, the ones who remain alive, after soldiers like yours. Let me tell you about their eyes. Their eyes have a look you do not see in anyone else. They are looking, trying to look, from very far away. They cannot believe themselves what they tell you that they've seen. They do not anymore know how to believe.

(*Silence. Both women are very still.*)

Sometimes, I think we are held here by threads, each one of us, by threads slim as the web of a spider, to the people we love, to our children. How easy it is for someone to walk through our web without seeing, to wipe it away with one move of the hand, without ever knowing what they've done. If you cut a person's threads, they go spinning, all by themselves. They are whirled out to the other side of a divide, to a place where there is no one they can touch; there is nothing to hold them. They are a long distance from us. (*Pause*) Here, in my part of the world, family is so important. Now they have no one. 'I am no more a man.' 'I am no more a woman.' They do not, anymore, know how to be. This frightens me. It should frighten us all. They look at us with dead eyes from very far.

(*Long pause in which both women walk closer.*)

Sarah, I am sorry that I took your husband. That from him I had my child, my Mariam, with her headscarf and her rage. I didn't want this life. I wanted, yes, of course, my child, I wanted her, and Alan, I wanted him. I did. We wanted, he and I… We forgot the moment, the present in which we lived. I forgot the thread connecting me to you. We had no idea, then, what would come. We wanted to weave… I wanted strings, Sarah, threads.

(HALA *turns toward* SARAH *who turns around to face her.*)

I am glad you called, Sarah, I have wanted to tell you this.

(*It is almost as if they can touch.*)

SARAH:	Thank you, Hala.

HALA:	Thank me?
SARAH:	Yes.
HALA:	I am to be thanked?
SARAH:	Not for taking Alan, not for that. For making Mariam, for making threads to keep you, to keep us, you and me, attached. For telling me what you have. Somehow, it helps. It does.
HALA:	Good morning, then, Sarah, it must be very early.
SARAH:	It is. Good afternoon, Hala. Take care.
	(*They each listen, for a moment, to the other's breathing in the phone, unable to hang up.*)
HALA:	Your country has caused a great shame with this war.
SARAH:	I believe that, too, Hala. I don't know what to do.
HALA:	Shame drives people mad. (*Pause*) Good luck, Sarah.
	(SARAH *goes toward her bedroom stage right.* HALA *exits stage left.*)

Scene XVII

(SARAH AND ALAN's *living room, the following evening.* JEREMY *is alone and is busy going over his lines.* SARAH *enters from her kitchen.*)

SARAH:	You know what, Jeremy, get up.
	(*He stands.* SARAH *takes the chair away.*)
	For the audition with Muffler tomorrow let's cut the chair.
JEREMY:	'I sat,' he says. He's sitting down.
SARAH:	No. He appears; he comes, led by a small boy, to confront Kreon. Jeremy, have you read the whole play?
	(JEREMY *hangs his head.*)
	Wonderful. How can you act, if... never mind. Read the play, Jeremy. It's good for you.
JEREMY:	He's sitting there talking to the general.
SARAH:	No, he's on his feet in front of King Kreon, yes, general, too.
JEREMY:	The commander-in-chief.
SARAH:	Close enough. This is the big moment, the turning point. The highest spiritual authority confronts the temporal... it's like the Pope coming from Rome to say 'stop the war.'
JEREMY:	The Pope would sit down.
SARAH:	Well, you're going to stand. Look, I had quite a talk with Muffler today. He just needs to see...
JEREMY:	If he thinks I'm good.
SARAH:	You are good.
JEREMY:	At least, you think so.

SARAH:	Well, that's what you've got to go on so far. My word. Plus what you feel, inside. Are you good enough Jeremy?
JEREMY:	Good enough?
SARAH:	As an actor, I mean.
JEREMY:	Are they two separate things?
SARAH:	Sometimes, yes. Sometimes, usually, in fact, I would say all the time, we are better in our art than we are in our lives. After all, we get to rehearse. So, let's begin.

(JEREMY *stands.* SARAH *sits.*)

JEREMY: Okay, here goes. (*Pause*) You'll catch me?

SARAH: I most certainly will.

(JEREMY *tosses his head so that his hair falls down around his eyes.*)

JEREMY: As I sat on the ancient seat of augury... (*He stops.*) See! 'Sat.'

SARAH: 'As,' Jeremy. As in 'when I sat.'

(*The doorbell rings.* SARAH *shrugs, goes to the door.*)

MARIAM: Sarah, hello.

(*There's an awkward moment, then* SARAH *hugs* MARIAM. MARIAM *is wearing a headscarf, jeans and a form-fitting, long-sleeved shirt.* JEREMY *stares at them.*)

SARAH: Come in. (*To* JEREMY) You've met Alan's daughter, Mariam. (*To* MARIAM) He's held up. Crisis at work. No time to talk. And we're just in the middle...

JEREMY: Salaam, Mariam.

MARIAM: Salaam.

SARAH: We're rehearsing, Mariam.

MARIAM: I'm sorry. I'll go.

JEREMY: Stay. It's good. An audience, you know...

SARAH: Fine, then, sit. You can start at the top, if you like, or anywhere.

(MARIAM *sits.* JEREMY *stands, smiling at her.*)

JEREMY: Hey, the Arabic worked.

SARAH: (*A bit annoyed*) Whenever you're ready. I'm here.

(*Split scene:* CHARLES MUFFLER *enters and sits in his desk chair, opposite. He's attentive to Jeremy's audition and disturbed by it.* SARAH *sits between* JEREMY *and* CHARLES. *There are two time periods here: the confrontation between* SARAH *and* CHARLES *earlier that day and the rehearsal at Sarah's house that night. As the scene unfolds, there will be a third,* JEREMY's *audition in front of* MUFFLER *the next morning.*)

JEREMY: They were killing each other – that much I knew.
The murderous fury whirring in those wings
Made that much clear!

I was afraid…
(*Freeze:* JEREMY *is completely committed to the speech and* MARIAM *is paying complete attention.*)
(*Action:* SARAH *turns toward* CHARLES's *desk. They are in the midst of the confrontation they had earlier that day.*)

CHARLES: You're correct in one thing, Sarah, one. Lukas Brightman was on that patrol. He volunteered. It's a village, he said, those were his words. It's a village full of women and children, old men. There are no Vietcong. Well, they shot him point blank in the head. His brains blown away by someone's little, old grandmother in black pajamas.
(*Action on the other side of the stage:* JEREMY *continues with his speech, becoming strong and angry, he speaks directly toward* CHARLES.)

JEREMY: And it is you –
Your high resolve that sets this plague on Thebes.
The public altars and sacred hearths are fouled,
And so the gods are deaf to our prayers, they spurn
The offerings in our hands, the flame of holy flesh.
(CHARLES *is becoming undone.*)

CHARLES: (*The scene in Vietnam playing out in his head*) Stop! Why should I be made to watch? I see the whole thing in my head. I give the order to open up. I use overwhelming force, yes. I use everything I have. Lukas is the only soldier I lose on that patrol.

SARAH: Lukas was going to blow the whistle on you.

CHARLES: Enough. I know about that man who rants about massacres. Poor devil, he's not in his right mind. He came after me, stalking. Proof of what? He made a grab for me right on the street, screaming obscenities, threatening. A passerby called 911. I was supervising the men putting up the signs for our *Uncle Vanya*. I blame Alan. Putting absurd ideas into a crazy vet's head. I was afraid for my life. A murderer, believe me, I'm not.

SARAH: Right, Charles, have it your way. But if you don't let Jeremy back into school, I will not be able to stay.

CHARLES: Don't push me, my dear.
(SARAH *turns back to* JEREMY *as the speech continues to build. He is still speaking as if directly toward* CHARLES *who drums his fingers during the speech, then puts his head into his hands, visibly shaken.*)

JEREMY: Take these things to heart, my son, I warn you.
All men make mistakes, it is only human.
But once the wrong is done, a man
Can turn his back on folly, misfortune, too,
If he tries to make amends, however low he's fallen,

And stops his bullnecked ways. Stubbornness
Brands you for stupidity – pride is a crime.
(MARIAM *begins to applaud energetically; she's completely taken with him.*)

SARAH: Well done, Jeremy. It gets better and better.

MARIAM: You are very, very good. You will put some truth into the world.

JEREMY: (*To* MARIAM) Ma'am, I'm not good.

SARAH: It was, Jeremy, really. Very fine.
(*He steps closer to* SARAH *and hits his heart.*)

JEREMY: What do you think I see when I talk?

SARAH: You got through it. You used it. The speech will hold you. The words become your container. You can pour your heart in.

JEREMY: I never don't see it; that's the thing. But he says you can get up, no matter how low.

SARAH: Sophocles was a general; his actors had all been soldiers. You're not alone, Jeremy. Stay, both of you. I'll order in.

MARIAM: No, it's fine.

JEREMY: Me, too, got to go, home, read the play, you know.
(JEREMY *smiles at* MARIAM.)
I can walk you to the train.

SARAH: Jeremy, call me, if you need anything. Call me, anytime, tonight, tomorrow morning before the audition. Call me the minute you hear.
(SARAH *kisses* MARIAM. JEREMY *exits with her.* SARAH *reenters the earlier confrontation scene with* CHARLES.)
I don't push, Charles. I'm telling you. I will be forced to resign, quite publicly, in fact. I know what happened to Lukas in Vietnam.
(CHARLES *is shaken; he is humbler, more fragile than we've ever seen him. This is the memory that haunts, and he has never told anyone before.*)

CHARLES: You think I never think about that night? You bet. There's Lukas and all the rest of it, too. Over and over it plays. A film in my head. Machine guns. Grenades. Blood-curdling yells. Wings beat the sky, shatter the rays of the sun. Birds squawk, trying to fly. Flesh drops to the ground. Feathers flying like snow. A boy falls out the door. Two eggs in his hands. Yolk breaks on black dirt. Eyes roll in his head. A white feather lands on his nose.
(*Pause*)
So, I am aware, yes. I see. I ask myself: Did I let Lukas volunteer to go first because I hated the little commie bastard? If true, I'm not saying it is, if subconsciously, that's what I felt, well, that was a good decision,

	wasn't it? Lukas was turning my men against my command. He was a fifth column. You don't take prisoners in a jungle. We needed bodies.
SARAH:	Come, Charles, we are members of one another. Lukas, me, you, Jeremy, too. For your own sake, as well, Jeremy Thrasher should come back to school.
CHARLES:	I have done you some good, Sarah, have I not?
SARAH:	True. Now, you can help Jeremy, too. *You will* help him – for all of our sakes. He belongs in this school. He's got the stuff. He needs to be here.

(*He's had it; he stands to usher her out.*)

| CHARLES: | Enough. We've spoken our minds. I'll take a good, hard look at the boy. |
| SARAH: | Thank you, Charles. |

(SARAH *exits the office.* JEREMY *enters, stage left, where he was standing before. He is at the very end of his audition, full of the force and fire he displayed in* SARAH's *living room. He finishes his audition speech.*)

| JEREMY: | Stubbornness
Brands you for stupidity – pride is a crime.
No, yield to the dead!
Never stab the fighter when he's down.
Where's the glory, killing the dead twice over?
I mean you well. I give you sound advice.
It's best to learn from a good advisor
When he speaks for your own good. |

(*The words hit* CHARLES *like a blow to the thoracic.*)

| CHARLES: | Well, well. (*Pause*) That's… |

(*He clears his throat; he's undone by the words and force of the speech. It's all too much for him. He struggles to pull himself together.*)

Thank you very much, young man.

JEREMY:	Sure. I mean, thank you for the opportunity, sir.
CHARLES:	That's enough, then.
JEREMY:	I could do it again. If you have… I could try… anything, you want. Do you want anything else?
CHARLES:	No need to do it again.
JEREMY:	It was okay? It felt good, I mean.
CHARLES:	Yes, yes. We'll give you a call, Jeremy.

(*He looks at his watch, in a hurry to end this.*)

I've got… something else. Young man, you can go.

| JEREMY: | Yes, sir. |

(*Awkward pause.* JEREMY, *defeated, exits.* CHARLES *stares, terrified, into space as if in the middle of his recurring flashback – he sees it all again, the little boy falling out the door, and* LUKAS, *being shot, blood bursting out of his head. He exits.*)

Scene XVIII

(*Split scene. That evening, after* JEREMY'*s audition.* SARAH *enters her living room. She looks nervously at the phone, which has not rung, and sits on the bench.* JEREMY *and* MARIAM *enter stage left into a Japanese restaurant and he pulls her chair out. They sit.* MARIAM *wears the hijab, a pretty top, jeans.* ALAN *enters the living room and begins to massage* SARAH'*s back. They become increasingly loving;* JEREMY *and* MARIAM *are flirtatious.*)

SARAH:	Alan, how kind.
ALAN:	My heart feels light for the first time in years.
	(*Silence. Both couples smile at each other. The two conversations alternate.*)
JEREMY:	I'm glad you like Japanese food.
MARIAM:	I do.
JEREMY:	You eat the raw stuff. I can't do that. I like this steak teriyaki. I'm a red meat sort of guy.
	(*He laughs, nervously.*)
MARIAM:	I suppose you are.
SARAH:	Amazing, really. The absence of hurt.
ALAN:	I've passed through something with Mariam.
JEREMY:	How did you learn to eat with chopsticks?
MARIAM:	Maybe in London, maybe Beirut, probably not East Jerusalem.
JEREMY:	Wow. You've seen plays in London?
SARAH:	There's a dreadful staying power to grief. Suddenly, we've loosened its grip.
ALAN:	I wish she'd stay here, go to school.
SARAH:	Jeremy's good. I hope Muffler saw it that way. Jeremy's raw. Muffler likes crusted over, as he says, 'in control.'
ALAN:	Muffler liked you.
SARAH:	I'll blow the bastard's cover if he doesn't let Jeremy back into school.
MARIAM:	You were quite wonderful the other night.
JEREMY:	Thanks. (*Pause*)
ALAN:	She learned Hebrew, this Lebanese-Palestinian girl with a headscarf when she found out who her father was.
JEREMY:	I think you're pretty wonderful, too.

SARAH:	Proof that she has a good mother.
MARIAM:	I began to applaud. That's what you liked.
JEREMY:	It sure sounded great. I thought just wait till that sound of two hands clapping is multiplied by a thousand, you know, like on Broadway.
ALAN:	I thought Hala would refuse. Instead, she said, 'If you wish to find him, go ahead.'
SARAH:	I think Hala might have been pleased.
JEREMY:	It's hard being an actor you know. It's harder than (*He stops.*) It's the hardest thing I've ever done. It's terrifying.
SARAH:	I told him I'd quit.
ALAN:	You should audition, again. Act.
MARIAM:	When you want something very much, it's always difficult. There is so very much to lose.
SARAH:	Right.
JEREMY:	After the speech, my audition, I mean, the dean, he didn't applaud.
MARIAM:	I don't think the dean would.
SARAH:	I stopped by his office; he'd left. He didn't return my call.
ALAN:	Relax. He's pulling rank.
SARAH:	But why hasn't Jeremy phoned?
ALAN:	Jeremy has a date, with Mariam, in fact.
SARAH:	I see.
	(*Both couples are silent.*)
MARIAM:	I only came to meet my father. To confront him, I thought…: finally, to get it all off my chest. And then I find out that I like him, despite myself. That he listens and understands, that, in many ways, we think the same.
JEREMY:	My old man… forget it, you don't want to know.
SARAH:	Hala is an extraordinary woman.
ALAN:	I thought so. I still do.
SARAH:	It must have been hard very hard.
ALAN:	I also think so about you.
SARAH:	You forgave.
JEREMY:	I wanted us to celebrate tonight, wanted to, except the dean, he hasn't called.
MARIAM:	He will.
JEREMY:	I don't know… it was like he didn't like… (*Imitating* CHARLES's *pompous voice*) 'Thank you very much, young man.' (MARIAM *laughs.*) I swear to you, that's how he talks.

ALAN:	We must, in order to live. Forgive. Ourselves, too. That's the one thing we must do.
JEREMY:	Look, I'm a Catholic. I haven't been to Confession for years. I feel like, I don't know. There are things no one forgives.
MARIAM:	God does.
JEREMY:	Maybe, but you're talking to priests. (*They sit in silence;* JEREMY *reaches for* MARIAM'*s hand and they toy tentatively with one another's fingers, smiling into each other's eyes.*)
SARAH:	Alan, come to bed. (ALAN *and* SARAH *exit to their bedroom.* MARIAM *carefully removes her hand from* JEREMY'*s. Something about the way he is looking at her…*)
JEREMY:	I thought only married women wore that scarf. I mean I like it, it's pretty, it looks nice on you and all that, but I would like to see your hair. I bet you have beautiful hair.
MARIAM:	That's why I wear the scarf. So I don't have to talk about my hair.
JEREMY:	I could talk about your hair for a long time. I could say all sorts of wonderful things. I could talk about it a lot longer if I could see it. If I could wind a curl around my finger…
MARIAM:	(*Pulling back*) I'm certain you could.
JEREMY:	Hey, don't get upset. You are a beautiful woman. I'm a guy. It's only natural, that's all. We can talk about something else. (*Pause*) We can talk about London.
MARIAM:	London, fine.
JEREMY:	Look. Can I tell you something? Can I just talk? There's something about you, not just that you're pretty, beautiful, like I said. There's something in your eyes, some deep thing, a sadness, that's what I see. You remind me of… you look so much like this woman I saw in Iraq. Someone I didn't even know, but she was beautiful, like you. Met. Ran into, I guess. Someone who, well, she had black hair. Her scarf came loose and her hair spilled out all over the floor. How beautiful, that's what I thought, how beautiful.
MARIAM:	Please, don't say any more.
JEREMY:	They tell us everyone is armed and dangerous. They tell us all the women have bombs under those robes; they just look pregnant. That they'll blow themselves up just to kill us. They tell us not to trust.
MARIAM:	I can't listen to this.
JEREMY:	Please, forgive me. Just forgive me, please.
MARIAM:	I must go. Excuse me.

JEREMY:	Please, I'm so sorry, really I am. I'm so sorry, goddamn it. I'm telling you. You're beautiful. You're smart. You're gorgeous. I think. I thought. The minute I saw you, I thought you were perfect. Then you applauded. You clapped for me, for something I'd done. It was the most amazing feeling. I think I fell in love with you then.
MARIAM:	Stop. You come on to me because I wear a headscarf. You know nothing of my life. Then, you use the word 'love.'
JEREMY:	I'm sorry. I'm telling you that. You can't go. Not like this.
	(JEREMY *roughly grabs her from behind; they struggle.*)
	You've got to. Damn it. Let me.
	(JEREMY *pulls off her hijab.*)
	You're beautiful.
	(JEREMY *runs his hands through her hair.* MARIAM *frees herself from him, stands her ground.*)
MARIAM:	I won't listen. I don't want to know. Go to your priest if you need forgiveness. Go ask your government for help.
	(MARIAM *pulls the hijab out of his hands.*)
	Why is it an Arab who must forgive?
	(MARIAM *exits.* JEREMY *becomes completely undone.*)
JEREMY:	Forgive, please. Fore, but *bode,* that has the feeling, Foul, yes, deaf. Splatter and burst. Cut off. Gorged on the flesh. With such beautiful hair. Cracked jaw bones glisten. Please. Stop. No, not listening. Glutted with blood. Not good. Not good enough.
	(JEREMY *runs out.*)

Scene XIX

(*Early morning.* SARAH *comes out of the bedroom. She is still halfway inside a dream. This is her memory of the boy she loved.*)

SARAH:	Before he shipped out we went away for a weekend. The last weekend, really, of Lukas's normal life. A history professor lent us his cabin on the beach on the North Shore of Long Island. The idea was Lukas and I would spend the weekend writing one paragraph we could duplicate many times on strips of paper telling why the war was wrong and how the enlisted men could organize on the ground to stop it. Lukas could hide them inside cigarette packages, hand them out, palm them to guys. Oh, how we argued, cut and pasted, reworked and reworded to get it all into one paragraph. Basically, we just wanted to tell them to say 'no,' just to say no and to stop. I think he was a little bit excited,

intoxicated, somewhat; Columbia had felt like a betrayal to him. His people were car mechanics, waitresses. We fell asleep on the floor in front of the fire. Early the last morning we got up and decided to walk along the shore. It was late summer, the early morning was cool and the sun was just coming up from under the sea. One of us began to sing:

(SARAH *begins to sing.*)

Morning has broken like the first morning.

Like the first morning.

But we didn't know the rest of the words. So we began to make things up:

(LUKAS's *voice is heard.*)

… praises to be.

(LUKAS *walks forward, he's a lovely, young, long-haired boy dressed in jungle fatigues in the style of the sixties, a bandana around his curls.*)

The mist is rising, like the first morning,

Like the first morning, praises to be.

(SARAH *stops singing, and* LUKAS's *voice grows stronger.*)

All hearts are open, like the first morning.

All hearts are open, praises to be.

(*They sing together, almost holding hands. But they never touch. They are gentle, tender with one another, aware this may be the last time. Their love and sadness are palpable.*)

Praise to ocean, praise to the tides.

Praise to the new sun, red in the sky.

SARAH: Our feet were wet and caked with sand. I had gone off the pill while Lukas was in basic training but I hadn't told him and he didn't know.

LUKAS: (*Singing, directly into her eyes*) Morning has broken, like the first morning.

Like the first morning, praises to be.

SARAH: When we got up from the little beach, I was pregnant. I felt the collision, the blasting apart of what was. I felt like Lukas felt, intoxicated, everything up in the air, my life at risk, suddenly, too. Lukas could have had no idea, but he was smiling at me like he knew.

LUKAS: (*Singing*) Black bird has spoken like the first bird.

(*Lukas vanishes.*)

SARAH: And now, after all these years, Jeremy Thrasher walks into my life, asking me if he's good enough. I would so like to hand a new morning to him.

ALAN: Sarah, my love.
(SARAH *turns.* ALAN *looks at her, unable to speak, and she begins to intuit something is terribly wrong.*)

SARAH: No. Don't, Alan.

ALAN: I am so sorry, my darling. That was the police on the phone. Jeremy Thrasher shot himself this morning… A note pinned to his shirt: 'I am not good enough. Forgive.'
(ALAN *holds* SARAH *while she cries, and she writhes in his arms. Her face an agony. She is like a mother animal whose cub has been taken.*)

SARAH: No. No. No.

ALAN: My darling, my dearest, hush, now. I'm here.
(SARAH *struggles. Alan quiets her a bit and holding her up, they exit.*)
(MIRANDA *enters, from the stage left door, and walks to the center of the space. She is speaking at a classroom memorial service for* JEREMY. *She says her name and then she speaks the final chorus simply and feelingly.*)

MIRANDA: Miranda Cruz.
Numberless are the world's wonders, but none
   More wonderful than man.
We have all done this thing. Not one
   Young man with a gun
   or a bomb strapped to a chest.
These things are in the hands of men.
So, let the weeping start. Let
Mourning come, dawn will break.
   The Divine inside
   hallow this ground

END

Because much of the history of the movement against the Vietnam War has been obscured from common memory, it is a little-known fact that growing G.I. resistance inside the military leading to the army's inability to field an effective fighting force contributed mightily to the US government's decision to finally end that war. Fragging, i.e. shooting, of their officers by enlisted men was not unheard of. In the play, Muffler sends Lukas into battle and shoots him from behind out of fear that Lukas is stirring up the men and, thereby, putting Muffler's life at stake.

Grateful acknowledgment is made to the Penguin Group and the estate of Robert Fagles for permission to use the Tiresias speech from *The Three Theban Plays* by Sophocles and translated by Robert Fagles. First published in 1982 by The Viking Press, Inc. Penguin Classics © Robert Fagles, 1982, 1984.

On *Prophecy*

Najla Said

I first met Karen Malpede in 2004, when I responded to an email about an event she was organizing. I did not know Karen at all, and I don't know through what channel I received her email, but volunteering to help read the names of the dead in the beautiful vigil she put together at the close of the first year of 'Operation Iraqi Freedom' was one of the most serendipitous decisions I have ever made.

In September of 2001, having already embarked on my professional theater career, I was stopped in my tracks by the events of September 11th, which affected the only 'safe' home I thought I would ever have (New York City), and gave me a sudden, new and ill-fitting identity ('Arab-American') that I felt pressured to fully inhabit on a moment's notice, despite the fact that it meant nothing to me.

2003 brought the invasion of Iraq and my father's death, so by the time I met Karen in 2004, I knew right away that there was a reason I had impulsively come to help her out.

After the event, we stayed in touch and became friends. By early 2006 she had expressed her interest in writing a play for me and Kathleen Chalfant, my theater idol. I was completely flabbergasted and flattered by her offer. Karen, Kathy and I began to meet frequently to discuss what we might want to work on together, and for the first time in my professional career, I felt I had found 'my people.'

Our conversations veered from the Abraham, Sarah, Isaac story in the Bible back to modern-day Iraq and Palestine, circled back around the Greeks and classical theater and culminated, ultimately in *Prophecy*. With Kathy and Karen, I felt I had found the people who understood the complex connections always firing in my brain; connections that took my thoughts everywhere and back and always turned the personal into the political and vice versa, while still delighting in the lyrical constructions and rhythms that only a deeply gifted, sensitive writer can compose.

Prophecy did not really begin to come together until the summer of 2006. I was alone in Lebanon, visiting family, and the summer quickly turned from a beach holiday into a nightmare, as Israel invaded on July 12th and a month-long attack began on my mother's home country once again.

My Post Traumatic Stress Disorder (that up until that point I didn't even believe really existed) jolted me into a heightened state of awareness and fervor, and I began sending long email missives to everyone on my contacts list, one of whom was Karen.

Karen Malpede bears witness; she listens to what her collaborators are saying and feeling and to what they are not saying and feeling. By the end of the summer she had finished *Prophecy*, and it was beautiful and full and magnificent.

Somehow, she had taken everything I had said and expressed and created three different women for me to play, each of which had a substantial story line, an empathic heart and her own very clear ideas and thoughts; each of the women she wrote for me to become – Miranda the Puerto Rican American acting student, Hala the Lebanese human rights worker and Mariam, Hala's angry, half American-Jewish daughter – contained, at her core, an essential truth that Karen had found inside of me, simply by reading my words and listening to my feelings.

Ultimately, I performed *Prophecy* in countless readings, as well as in both the London and New York City premieres. We never spoke of it, but I think Karen knows quite clearly what she did for me, and did it consciously and gently (as is her way): she allowed me to process my trauma through art. Each of my characters had a kernel of me inside her, and each of them went on a full, satisfying and cathartic journey throughout the play. I was then given the opportunity to work through all of my current re-surfacing traumas and fears, on the stage, in the only way that has ever worked for me.

Moreover, the story of *Prophecy* is also the story of the healing power of theater, of art. Jeremy's journey from soldier to actor, though it doesn't end as happily as my own, is meant to remind us of the healing power of words, storytelling, bearing witness and working through pain in order to find the strings that draw us together as human beings from all over the world. Hala's beautiful speech to Sarah over the phone toward the end of the play embodies this idea, and beautifully, simply and affectively allows for the actress playing her (and Mariam and Miranda) to give voice to the greater themes and ideas at work.

It was an honor to work on *Prophecy*, both as an actress and as a human being. To have been given the opportunity to dive into three separate parts of my soul and confront the discomfort and passion inside each one (while also being given an actual paying job) allowed me to heal from the overwhelming experiences that had recently come back to haunt me, without actually having to make sense of them in my own words.

Prophecy remains for me, the greatest opportunity for professional and personal growth I have ever had, and to Karen I must always bow my head in thanks and love, for she allowed her play to actually BE what it was about. Rare is the playwright who can bring the conscious and unconscious together as she does, and I am forever grateful.

Part III

Another Life

In memory of my dear friend and great artist, Judith Malina.

Another Life was performed in workshop at the National Theatre of Kosovo, 2011; it *premiered* at the 2011 Art of Justice: 9/11 Performance Project at the Gerald W. Lynch Theater, NYC, directed by Karen Malpede. Lights: Tony Giovannetti. Costumes: Sally Ann Parsons and Carisa Kelly. Set: Robert Eggers. Music: Arthur Rosen. Video Projections: Luba Lukova. George Bartenieff played Handel; Christen Clifford played Tess; Eunice Wong played Lucia; Omar Koury played Abdul; Dorian Makhloghi, Georff; Ariel Sharif, David Abbas. It was restaged with the same director and designers in 2012 at the Irondale Theater, Brooklyn and in 2013 at Theater for the New City. The cast: George Bartenieff played Handel; Christen Clifford, Tess; Di Zhu, Lucia; Abbas Noori Abbood, Abdul; Alex Tavis, David Abbas. London, Rada Festival of New Plays, 2013, with the same cast.

Characters

Handel, late seventies, a mogul, founder of Deepwater, a private contracting firm

Tess, forties, his wife, beautiful, originally from Chechnya

Lucia, thirties, his adopted daughter, born in China

Abdul, forties, a livery cab driver, originally from Egypt

David Abbas, forties, half-Syrian, half-American, formerly with the FBI

Geoff, thirties, Lucia's fiancé; he was a union organizer, killed in the Twin Towers

Setting

The play, 2001–08, is set in Handel's expansive downtown loft; in a fancy mid-town restaurant; at a detention facility outside Bagram Air Force base in Afghanistan; a hotel in Baghdad; and a congressional hearing room. Parts of scenes occur in the mind of Lucia where she encounters Geoff. There is, of course, no need for and no time for realistic settings. Locations are established minimally. Where slides are indicated it would be nice to have them.

The set should be very simple. There are three areas moving stage right to left: Tess's studio; Handel's living room, center stage; and Lucia's space. Handel's large executive's desk chair, on wheels, dominates center stage. To stage right is Tess's work table. To stage left a larger, rectangular table, with sturdy legs which is the restaurant table in Scene III. In Scene IV, turned upright, it becomes the doorway to the interrogation room, and there is small window cut out of it to be the window into the room. In Scenes II and IX, the table is the bed, first Lucia's bedroom, and then the bed where David and Lucia have sex. In Scene VII, this same table, tipped the horizontal, long-way, becomes the hotel balcony. Behind each of the two table areas hang two large rectangular panels, and there is a square panel upstage center for the projections; and behind those, a cyclorama.

An early version of Scene I was originally published in the Kenyon Review, fall 2010, under the title *Another Life*. The play, obviously a fiction, is based on much research. While none of the characters bear a relationship to anyone living or dead, the torture stories are factual. Ibn al-Shaykh Al-Libi committed 'suicide' in prison after 'admitting' to ties between Saddam Hussein and Osama bin Laden. Abu Zubaydah, still in Guantanamo and unlikely ever to be released, was water-boarded some 90 times before 'confessing' to similar knowledge. No charges have ever been brought against him but the extent of his torture prevents his trial. The torture story of Emad Khudayir Shahuth Al-Janabi was taken verbatim from the testimony that journalist Donovan Webster provided to me. Special thanks to the lawyers Susan Burke and Martha Rayner for sharing with me their knowledge and for their legal work, suing private contractors and defending torture victims and Guantanamo detainees.

Scene I

(A slide of a burning World Trade Tower appears stage right. A large, modernist loft-living room in downtown New York. HANDEL enters, agitated, a glass of scotch in his hand. He is corpulent, elderly yet strong of voice. He looks out his window. Hurries off stage. A CRASH. Stage left a slide of the other Tower, hit and burning, appears. HANDEL stares for a moment and then, he uses a remote to draw the heavy drapes. The light in the room dims.)

HANDEL:
So, now, once more, Handel left. Handel left by himself. Not to look. Not to look at... End of thing. End of one. Was. Is not. *(Pause)* Yet already something grows, is growing from, up from, the end of... that. Memory remains, calamitous, no less. Which is what one is or has. Mine being what to me remains. Handel says. *(HANDEL sits in his large executive office chair.)* Why left if not for this? To say. Sway. To have my way. At the ready of, begin, again. If not me, who then? So many gone.

I, Handel, myself, was, came of, out of, from, born to humble parents, them, humdrum humdudgeon, not, at least, not they, hypochondriac, of course, humanoid, just. I early on was humbled by their humbleness. My own, my lack of, impossible to, without. Timidity, itself. Humility. My father, he a watchmaker, yes, tinkerer with time, minute minutia, minutes, jerking, leaping, exploding seconds, a hand limping limpidly, swirling wildly might occupy him for a day. Out of mind, time immemorial, time out, time of life, time-of-flight, time-wise, time like no other it has always been. Adjust then readjust and all the while, while a way, he listed, wilted. Shrunken fellow. Barely large enough at last to reach his nose upon his desk. He sat on books; his arse astride… never mind. My mother had been before my birth and was soon to be again, after spilling, spitting out, disgorging, disengaging, yes, a seamstress, sewer, that is, of seams that bind, a seer of strings, threads attached, undone. Her teeth, between her teeth she chomped and cut, snapped. Corkscrewing in upon herself. Her mind morose, who knew, not I, standing, attentive at her side. So it was so. Hoping, longing, even… Both small ones, each emanated from his or her own inhospitable place. Each escaping, at the final moment, by the last means of transportation, separated from luggage, small reserves of money stolen, alone, with no one, nothing, each fled from a hideousness never to be spoken of again in a language not to be passed on. Worked from dawn to dusk, side by side, at a bench; humped, humbled, content. Without complaint. I stood needle in hand to hand to her, to him a small screw-driver. Anticipating each desire.

A small silent boy, a rather frightened little fellow, standing at his father's side, watching springs and screws explode, standing by his mother's knee, her needle ripping through the cloth, eyes crossed, a whir, fingers stabbed straight through, skin grayed, red dots upon her nails, watching them toil, watching them shrivel and shrink, observing them at honest work. The yellow smog of early morn, late afternoon. No, not look, those two had been given a child, a boy, borne a son, to carry on.

Quietly to shut the door. Never knew, they why, wherefore. Me to reap the benefits, beneficence of public education, in schools finally to be beaten with a yard stick, yes, wooden, sliver of metal siding sharp, made to stand eyes to the wall, to memorize, recite, to count, multiply, divide, learn by rote, to think, son of a simple watch maker and a simple dress maker, into whom what little they had had was put, their life they would not live, through mud holes, pot holes, with shoes too small, pinched toes, pit falls to make my way.

At the window stood, not to tell don't say. He was gone out, some bread to get, a screw, a pickle for the boy, nothing more. She rose. She flew, she flung. I, Handel stunned. When he returned was gone, window shards, skirt up, she lay, around her neck, legs splayed, Handel at the window stood, alone, bright sun glittered she lay glass inlaid. Never a word said of her again.

Away. To the city university I went, on to a private school further east, further north, a private school well-endowed, scholarship granted, among the small quota to be admitted, and there to meet, there to know for the first time, indeed, in fact, always and for some, only, to become, to be, to billow, set sail on fortune's wing.

Handel worked at two extremes: fixer, fixer-upper, maker, shaper, shaker of ordeals and deals, procurer of lucidity equally liquidity. Maximizer thus of finest, best entrepreneurial and ingenuous parts of the self. My clinic for the well-endowed to motivate success. With acumen ameliorate, enhancer, yes, interrogator unmatched; intractable, untreatable, intransigent, the worst, let Handel take a look, empathize, invest. Handel fixes as he goads and gambols through the limbic regions, reassembles and dismantles; remakes, calm, concise, controllable, puts them back in better shape, lectures, writes and thinks nonstop, manager of corporate needs, maximize and reinvest, envision cures, profit driven prophet of desire.

A wealth of feeling courses through myself. That stony stare, that rheumy look, the puffed lids, sorrow of the down-turned mouth, all horrors once escaped, run, rammed through, floor a mess, with glinting shards studded she spread out below. She fell, he yelled. Sickened she was, must have been, but no. Handel saw. A simple boy born to simpletons, born to become, to be, to do, to have, to take, amass.

(There is an explosively loud crash outside.)

A shock, a bitter pill, abomination, cataclysm, treachery beyond description, despite intuiting, no prediction. Yet we grow again, up from, we step, and must, lift up, grab hold, boot straps, bold. I see them now, before me, bent. Never once, she nor he, from their endless, mindless, thankless tasks to see their son, look up, the boy, to ask what will become, whatever did become of him.

(TESS enters; she wears khaki trousers and a white sleeveless shirt; she is younger than HANDEL, attractive, wiry. She is covered head to toe in sticky white dust. She has several cameras around her neck. She opens the drapes, behind HANDEL, and begins shooting photos from the window.)

HANDEL:	And now this mess. Come back to me at last, but where else could you run? Whoever take you in? Illusion is it not? You always wished, threatened me with leaving, but now, come back. Yet, glued, what is on you, to you stuck. I cannot, will not look at you like that.
TESS:	It's how we look.
HANDEL:	She twinkling down below; you stood. You bolted out the door, thank God. Not, I, Handel here, alone, waiting for her, you, my wife.
TESS:	Your wife.
HANDEL:	Mine, yes. You dare come to me like this, bearing what, stuck stuff, remains, upon yourself. Go wash. Scrub clean.
	(She exits.)
	White against the tarry roof. Leave me trembling here, alone. Viscid you've come back. Not pearly white with drops of red. Scrub it, them, off yourself.
	(She returns wearing a long rain coat.)
	(Agitated) In vain viscidity an overcoat can't hide. Viscid Vanitas. Vanitas all human life. You are involved in shooting stars, celebrities, my pet. Why else are you in my firmament. Tess, clean up. I cannot bear to look, to touch.
TESS:	Stars, yes.
HANDEL:	Beautiful ones are who you shoot. In stiletto heels. Baseball caps. Thick hair, thin, with yachts.
	(She kneels as she photographs HANDEL *and behind him the scene outside.)*
TESS:	Poor Handel. Your world falling down inside your head.
HANDEL:	You are misguided to think thus, my dear. We are not so fragile, no, I use the 'we' advisedly, not so by half. Survive we do. Pick up. Begin again. United stand.
	They shall swarm in hordes, from the hinterlands, the heartland, the homeland, wearing T-shirts, flag pins, hard hats, helmets, they flock already to the spot in ambulances, tow trucks, SUVs, with shovels, axes, with their gloves on, vests, they come gladly, quickly. They are rolling even now down our streets in cavalcades; they will troll in from every state. They will dig and pull, enlist and go. But for you, scrub free that scum. But for us, for this, for this thing is, we, this home we've made, this fulfillment of a dream.
TESS:	Where's Lucia?
	(At this moment, the door opens, a MAN, *he is Middle Eastern, carries in his arms a young Asian woman who is loudly slurping a*

multi-grande latte with whip cream and chocolate from Starbucks. She is dressed in light blue hospital scrubs and has a stethoscope around her neck.)

LUCIA: I went to Starbucks to meet Geoff.
(The MAN *gently lowers* LUCIA *to the table. He moves to the side of the room.* HANDEL *and* TESS *ignore him.)*

TESS: Thank God. Suddenly, I thought…

HANDEL: I don't like that boy, Geoff. Not good enough.

TESS: He's not your boy.

HANDLE: Union organizer. What meaning does it have? Undermining us.

TESS: Geoff counsels and defends. Don't put Geoff down.

HANDLE: She's a specialist, heart, kidney, lung. Handel's own. Make use of her large brain.

TESS: She's going to be a general practitioner, in the South Bronx.

LUCIA: I went and stood in the line.

TESS: At Starbuck's you mean?

LUCIA: Geoff phoned.

TESS: Thank goodness. Tell him to come here. I'll clean myself up. We'll have lunch.

LUCIA: I didn't answer him. I was about to go off-duty; naturally, I didn't leave. Someone said: soon the wounded will be coming, we should get some air. We went up to the roof. I'd been up all night. The morning sky was blue, a deep, clear… A pure sky, open, expectant, somehow. It had been a quiet night. No gunshot wounds, one heart attack, mild, one acid reflex, terrified, certain he was dying on the spot. It's worse when it's nothing. They're the ones who tend to make a fuss. The ones who understand, who know, they are quiet, self-possessed. They realize no medicine can. I didn't hear Geoff's ring.
*(*LUCIA *takes several huge, slurping drinks.)*

HANDEL: Terrible noise, that.

TESS: Like suckling a child at the breast.

HANDEL: Disgusting.

TESS: The look on the face of a child at the breast, there is nothing lovelier than that.

LUCIA: We were watching, waiting. We were thinking soon the sirens will be screaming. We'll have no chance to stop. We'll be down on the street. We'll be standing in a line. We'll be getting them in. We'll be doing triage, making choices no one wants to make, but gladly, in fact, we'll be saving lives. A leg crushed, an arm, a chest, we can fix. We'll have blood bags, oxygen, morphine. It was very quiet on the roof. We could see black smoke dashing against blueness of the sky. We could see specks falling, like balloons drifting, no, like birds, flapping, trying to fly.

TESS: I have them. I caught them in the air, like fireworks bursting, astonishing colors exploding.

LUCIA: We were waiting, breathing. If only we can be of use. I had stepped out of these clogs, I'd been wearing them all night, to rest my feet on the warm roof. It was growing hotter. The tar began to bubble, melt. Blisters started on the balls of my feet, blisters puffing up between my toes. My feet were melting into the tar. We thought soon we'd be yelling, screaming for bandages, scissors, we'd be cutting off clothes. My phone was on vibrate but I couldn't feel anything. I wanted to call Geoff; I had wanted to tell him right then; I didn't want to wait. Then, the first fell, almost without effort, like a card house, a thing of ribbons rippling, gently folding into itself, delicate, as if it had all the time in the world. My feet were stuck to the roof. When I walk I'm in tremendous pain.
(She plays the message on her phone.)

GEOFF'S VOICE: 'Lucia, listen, for Christ sake, I wish you'd pick up. Look, I'll be fine. They'll send helicopters, drop ropes. Don't worry. They told us to go to the roof, stay put. I'll meet you in an hour at the Starbucks.'
(Silence)

TESS: Geoff.
(LUCIA dials her phone it rings, she speaks.)

LUCIA: Geoff, for god's sake, give it up, get out. They'll never get their union, you know that. There are bigger forces at work.

TESS: Lucia, I promise you. I watched. I saw. I have him here.

LUCIA: No one was coming, hurt or wounded. No one needed us. I went to Starbucks to meet Geoff. I could hardly walk; the skin on my feet was coming off. I crawled the last half block. I had something I had to tell Geoff.
(She plays the next message.)

GEOFF'S VOICE: 'Lucia, I love you, don't forget. Look, I'm burning up.'

TESS: I looked up, watched them jump, fly, fall. I cradled them with my sight.

GEOFF'S VOICE: 'I'm on the roof, my girl, the sky above earth below, here I go.'

LUCIA: *(She holds her stomach)* Stop. Geoff, please, please; don't jump. I've got something to tell you before. I've got something inside me. Us.

HANDEL: Let me hold you.

LUCIA: I don't want to be touched by you. Not now. Not ever, again.
(TESS turns suddenly to the man.)

TESS:	Who are you?
ABDUL:	I am Abdul Rahman Ahmed. I am a livery cab. I found her outside on the floor, as she describes. Her feet not able to walk.
TESS:	Thank you.
ABDUL:	One would do that for anyone's child. She is a kind girl. A doctor.
GEOFF'S VOICE:	'Lucia, I've got to…'
LUCIA:	Wait a minute, will you, I've got you. Inside me. I need to tell you now. Geoff, I want you to be the father of my child.
	(TESS walks toward LUCIA.)
TESS:	Caught them while they fell. People were running away. I stayed. Arrested in air. Angels held in the palm.
LUCIA:	You're covered, covered in that stuff.
TESS:	Stuff?
	(TESS holds out her arms.)
LUCIA:	Go away.
TESS:	Lucia, it's him, them, clinging like skin.
LUCIA:	But he will be the father. He is, already, our baby's father.
	(As she speaks, LUCIA begins to bleed; she is having a miscarriage, her blue pants turn red. Blood drips from between her legs. Silence)
TESS:	Oh, my dear. This happens so often, in the first trimester. Far more often than we are told. It's a common occurrence. It doesn't mean you can't carry a child. So many first pregnancies end in miscarriage. It's the shock, of course. Towels. I'll get towels.
	(TESS leaves. LUCIA bleeds. ABDUL cowers.)
	(Returning with towels) Here we are.
	(LUCIA moves away from her.)
	You will get pregnant, again. I thought my life stopped. Then Handel came. He had you, Lucia, needing someone. 'I need a mother,' he said. I got up; I went on.
	(HANDEL rises abruptly.)
HANDEL:	No pictures, damn you. All right, Mohammad…
TESS:	Abdul. Handel, for goodness sakes.
HANDEL:	… up against the wall.
	(HANDEL grabs ABDUL by the neck and roughly throws him against the wall. A smash. A small cry from ABDUL.)
	Give me a towel.
TESS:	Don't be absurd, Handel. Here, dear, let me.
	(TESS kneels and mops up some blood.)
ABDUL:	Please, I rescued your daughter.
HANDEL:	Don't give me that. I've got eyes. I can see. Blood.

TESS:	Handel, get hold of yourself.
HANDEL:	I can stop. I can stop any time I want. You want me to stop.

(HANDEL *throws* ABDUL *against the wall.* ABDUL *is silent this time.*)
Wrap a towel around his neck. I don't want to leave marks.

TESS: Do it yourself. Abdul had nothing to do…

HANDEL: Do as you're told.

(TESS, *still kneeling in* LUCIA's *blood, hands* HANDEL *the other towel.* HANDEL *wraps it around* ABDUL's *neck. He throws* ABDUL *against the wall, holding the ends of the towel.* ABDUL *cries out.*)
You like it better like that.

LUCIA: Shoot him, Tess, please.

(TESS *starts to take photos.*)

LUCIA: Good.

HANDEL: Good, yes. I do it for you, to keep you, protect, safe. All for you. No one else. Caught in the act like she caught hitting the ground. Blood everywhere. Legs splayed. You think I don't see.

(HANDEL *takes* ABDUL's *arms behind his back ties them with his belt and hooks them up behind his head, so that* ABDUL *is in stress position, his toes barely touching the floor.* LUCIA *is crying, softly.* TESS *continues to photograph.*)
And, now, he's going to talk. No more of this Mr. Nice Guy. Picked her up. We know who you are. We know what you did. You want to see your wife, again, your kids. You want your wife raped, just like that, blood on the floor. You want your daughter deflowered. You want your virgins in the sky. We'll have your eyeballs in highballs. We'll have your cock in plastic wrap. A stick up your arse. The gloves are coming off. I'll crush your balls in the palm of my hands. Eat them like olives. You'll give me what I need. Believe me. You'll tell us what we want to know.

Scene II

(*Several days later.* LUCIA *runs laps through the space, as on the panels, one by one, photographs and Xerox flyers of the dead and missing appear.* TESS *enters the street with her camera; she photographs the memorial.*)

TESS: Maybe now we open our hearts to the suffering in the world. If this could happen, then, the terrible thing would be undone. Those young men who crashed those airplanes, my first thought, it was really, I felt for their mothers. I felt for their pain of having given birth. Their care come to this. Am I wrong to think so? I watched. I saw. I felt the mothers' cries in me. Strange what thoughts come. And, I am not the only one. All around me, where I stand on the street, people are full of feelings they have never felt. Who knows why they think what they think. Quiet it is on the city streets. People are busy expanding their hearts. Feelings come they dare not say. No noise but the whoosh of each one opening up. The city so still like being held in a large hand. Each one is a new born; for the first time such sweetness. We stand. Quiet together. Mourning our dead. There is no more terror on the streets of New York.

(LUCIA enters; she runs frantically in place.)

TESS: I had watched Lucia grieve before.

LUCIA: When my mother died…

TESS: Then, also, her body was where she hid.

LUCIA: I started playing soccer; I joined the swim team. I began to compete.

TESS: Ten years old. Her body muscled up. No breasts.

LUCIA: In the water, I felt safe.

TESS: Lucia had lost two mothers by the age of ten. The one in China no one knew and Handel's first wife, the mother who raised her. I am the third mother in Lucia's life. The one lacking the most.

LUCIA: On the street, my feet pounding the cement, I can begin to breathe. The day Geoff fell, jumped, my breath stopped. I know well enough how the chest constricts, the lungs burst. Hurtling through space. The breath leaves. Like brilliant flashes of light.

TESS: I am afraid she will run until her own lungs burst in her chest. Like the brilliant flashes of light I caught. She doesn't go to work. She runs until she falls into bed.

(LUCIA collapses in her bed. GEOFF enters.)

GEOFF: Luce, are you home?

LUCIA: Geoff?

GEOFF: Hey, how's my girl?

LUCIA: Geoff?

GEOFF: Don't question, Lucia. Accept.

LUCIA: Jesus, Geoff, accept what? That you're back? That you're here? Touching me. Fine. Great. Yes. I do. I accept. Oh, my darling boy, you've come back. Hold me tight.

GEOFF: How's the little worm?

(He touches her belly.)

LUCIA: But, Geoff, it's not…

GEOFF:	Luce; it's all right. You were going to tell me. I loved looking at you with your secret inside. You said you didn't want to have the champagne.
LUCIA:	Only a sip, I said. We were so, so happy that night.
GEOFF:	The food was great. The stars. The service, Luce. They thought; we thought we could unionize.
LUCIA:	I was so proud of you, Geoff. The smiles on the faces of the waiters.
GEOFF:	The free oysters and chocolate mousse they slipped us. We were so certain we were going to win. *(They laugh together. Pause)* We are so happy, Lucia, now.
LUCIA:	I am so happy Geoff.
GEOFF:	You're dreaming, Lucia. It's a dream.
LUCIA:	Don't say that.
GEOFF:	It's okay. This is how we can meet.
LUCIA:	In my head? It's all my head. Your hand on my belly. Oh my God, you don't know what happened to the child, Geoff.
GEOFF:	I know everything you know; it's just that here, right now, we are all three together. Everything's good. This is how it was meant to be.
LUCIA:	Shit.
GEOFF:	Come on, cheer up. I know it isn't much. It isn't what we thought we deserved. But, hey, it's something. It's a slice. You feel me.
LUCIA:	If I can feel you, you must be with me, next to me. There's no other way.
GEOFF:	Inside your head there's a world. On the skin of your eyeballs. I can project myself sometimes, not all the time, usually when you are least prepared, hardly ever when you really need me to be there. It's not that I don't want to, Lucia. Obviously, I would like to be with you all the time, you and our child. Obviously, I would like to make a home, but that's not how it works. But, you won't believe this; I still do have some choice. If I really strain my astral self, well, it's not really a *self*; I am not actually anymore a single self-conscious entity. Never mind, the I I was can still enter your world through your dream.
LUCIA:	What sort of mystical shit is that? You're here, Geoff. I can see you. I can feel you. I can beat your chest. *(She hits his chest.)*
GEOFF:	Hey, that's my girl, Luce. Feisty and sweet. I've loved you and loved you for this.
LUCIA:	Don't fucking use the past tense.
GEOFF:	It's not in the past. I'm here, now, in your head.
LUCIA:	In my life.

GEOFF:	The mind is a great expanse. We can go anywhere together, you and I. We can wander. We can lean on one another like we always said we would through thick and thin. We don't have to give each other up.
LUCIA:	It's beginning to sound like bondage to me. Can't you understand, I don't want to have to make you up in my head. I want you to be.
GEOFF:	Me, too. I wanted it all. The five course meal with nuts. But, we're lucky…
LUCIA:	Lucky? You and I? What about the child? What about the rest of my life?
GOEFF:	All I know is I'm here with you.
LUCIA:	You're not real.
GEOFF:	What is real? Who? Could I talk like this even inside your dream if you were making me up? Stop being a scientist. Just experience. Just feel.
LUCIA:	Scientists experience, that's what science is all about. We observe. We taste, smell. I can diagnose by the pulse, by the color of the whites of the eyes, the breath; I can tell if someone is sick. I can tell what disease they have. And I can tell you this, Geoff: you have terminal death.
GEOFF:	It's not as fatal as all that.
LUCIA:	No? Can you come with me? Can I get inside your head? It's always got to be me who is here for you. Isn't that what this is all about?
GEOFF:	Why do you make everything so difficult? You were always like that.
LUCIA:	Oh, yes, I am the difficult one. You are the idealist, the dreamer, you are the creative soul. And now you've got me just where you want me. I'm a prisoner inside your fantasy.
GEOFF:	That's an odd way of putting it, since this is your dream Luce. You are one who wakes up.
LUCIA:	Oh, fucking great. I get to turn on the light. Whoosh, off you go, out of here. Where to Geoff? Tell me where?
GEOFF:	You know I can't tell you that. That is strictly forbidden.
LUCIA:	By whom, by what?
GEOFF:	Hey, no one knows that stuff. This is what we've got, kid. This is us.
LUCIA:	It's not enough. *(She beats on his chest; he stands immobile, unresponsive)* Geoff? It's not fucking enough. I want you in my bed every morning. I want to wake you up at 4 am when I need to talk. I want you walking the floors with our crying baby. I want

you bringing me coffee. Answer me? Say something, Geoff. *(He goes)* God-damn it. You get to go.

(Lights up on HANDEL *who sits in his chair, scotch in hand.* LUCIA *stands looking at him.)*

HANDEL: Tess! Tess! Tess? Where, oh, where? Come home. Nevermore, my pet, to roam. Lucia, daughter. Here, here, come, come.

*(*LUCIA *goes to him. She sinks down to the floor between his legs, her head on his knee.* HANDEL *strokes her head.)*

There, there.

LUCIA: I can't live without him, that's all. I don't want to.

HANDEL: So I thought when your mother died, my pet, but I had you. You must live for me, my child, for my sake. You're young. You'll find a new lease on life. You may not believe me, yet, but time will tell. The invasion has begun. We're in Tora Bora, closing in.

*(*HANDEL *takes her face in his hands and he leans down. He kisses her fully on the mouth. She extracts herself.)*

LUCIA: I'm going out.

HANDEL: Go, child. You are free. Come home to me. Tess! Tess, my wife, my heart; the time has come. Bombs away. Glorious day. Revenge is sweet.

*(*HANDEL'S *phone, the Valkeryie by Wagner is his ringtone. He answers and a greenish photo of Alan Greenspan is projected behind him.)*

Alan Greenbridge, thanks for checking in. Family first in times like these. Bonds of love. Rest assured. Handel sees inside the brain. Everyone wants houses, now; a roof over their head. Give them mortgages to pay. Bundle up. Rate them 'A.' Revenge is empty, must be fed. Their fixed rates will fast unfix. Watch them scramble, watch them fail. Bet against their loss yourself. Regulation is passé. Glass-Steagall down the toilet flush. Profits usher boom times in. Over-pricing begets bonuses stupendous. Terror begets acquisition, no restriction. Get begets gobble up. The dust? Is it toxic? But it must be, yes. Pulverized cement. Remains, what else. Still, I see them from my window, here. They dig without respite, without respirators, too. Give them loans they can't afford. When they falter, banks foreclose. Alan, good to speak with you. Free money flows from the Fed. Prime primed to explode begets sub-prime. Collateralized debt swaps all around. Between you and me, the private sector wins this war.

*(*ADBUL *and* TESS *enter her work space.* ABDUL *carries the wire sculpture and puts it on the table.* TESS *goes to work.)*

TESS:	Put it there. Thanks.
ABDUL:	It's him, her husband.
TESS:	They weren't married.
ABDUL:	She had his child.
TESS:	They would have been, I suppose. Handel was opposed.
ABDUL:	A father should wish to marry his daughter.
TESS:	*(She looks at him bemused)* That is the problem I'm afraid.
ABDUL:	A father should want the best for his child.
TESS:	In theory, yes.
ABDUL:	Let me out.
TESS:	If I could, I would; I am against all this, everything that has now begun.
ABDUL:	Open the door.
TESS:	It's locked from the inside. He keeps the keys. Since I came back. Foolish of me. Without money I don't live.
ABDUL:	You don't know where?
TESS:	On him. On his person.
ABDUL:	Asleep, take them.
TESS:	He sleeps in his chair.
ABDUL:	Still, he sleeps, sometime.
TESS:	I can't just rummage around.
ABDUL:	You're his wife.
TESS:	He keeps them under his balls.
ABDUL:	I do not understand this house.
TESS:	One window opens up. Tell me, Abdul, why don't you escape? I'll bring you bed sheets.
ABDUL:	It's my job.
TESS:	You had a job. You can go back to driving a cab.
ABDUL:	The cab was towed.
TESS:	Dear, that's hardly fair. You did a good deed.
ABDUL:	It was parked outside. Then, there was an empty spot. When he was done he took me to the window. He said I was free. I could go. He'd gotten the wrong man; I wasn't him. But two police were standing on the street below, where the cab was. They had guns. He told me I could also stay and work for him.
TESS:	Leave. You can go to the tow garage. Explain. I'll write a letter for you.
ABDUL:	I'm an illegal. They'll deport me; he knows I have no papers. The car belonged to my cousin. I cannot go back and tell him I lost it. They will find me if I run away. If they send me back to my country, I will be put into prison. What he did to me is not much.

	What they do, there, is… I don't want to think. *(Speaking of the sculpture)* It will be beautiful.
TESS:	I'm going to do it in gold leaf. Icarus. He flew too near the sun. But, his wings were made of wax.
ABDUL:	We are all like that.
TESS:	That's the point.
ABDUL:	You are happy doing your work.
TESS:	Would I be happier somewhere else? Not in my country, either; I'm afraid. It's true what he says: I was a whore, high class, a prostitute nonetheless. I still am, of course. Do I shock you?
ABDUL:	I don't think so. I think I am sad.
TESS:	I think you're very rare, Abdul.
ABDUL:	You tell me of your unhappiness. I feel sad.
TESS:	I should sculpt you. I'll sculpt you catching Icarus as he falls. He'll melt into you. I feel that way. We hold them in ourselves.
ABDUL:	The lost belong to us. They have no one else.
TESS:	Geoff was a good person. He hated Geoff and he beat you up.
ABDUL:	He is afraid. He feels better to beat someone up.
TESS:	That's a dangerous thought.
ABDUL:	It is how I understand the world. The frightened are the worst.
TESS:	Yes, but if you are the one he beats up to feel upbeat, so-to-speak, and you don't run away, what does that say about you?
ABDUL:	I tremble like anyone else.
HANDEL'S VOICE:	Boy! Fool!
	(ABDUL goes to answer the call. TESS sighs and then returns to her work.)
	Tess. My Tess.
	(TESS goes toward HANDEL's chair. ABDUL is crouching there.)
HANDEL:	Stay away from him. I say.
TESS:	Normal people don't keep prisoners, Handel.
HANDEL:	Normal people; quite a concept. It's a new world, my wife, my one, my star circling my sun.
TESS:	And Abdul is your…?
HANDEL:	He is mine not yours. What does it matter what he is? He's a nothing. He wandered in.
TESS:	I want him to model for me.
HANDEL:	No.
TESS:	An hour a day.
HANDEL:	No!
TESS:	You've become a man of few words.
HANDEL:	You have grown distant, Tess. You were once a good wife.

TESS:	You picked me out of the gutter.
HANDEL:	That ridiculous story again. I met you at an exquisite dinner. You spoke English with hardly an accent.
TESS:	I was the whore of your money launderer. How much did you pay?
HANDEL:	The words that come from your mouth, my Tess. Tut, tut. All of a sudden. My point. So frank. As if you have nothing to lose; is that it? A new world. Weighty decisions occupy my mind. I cannot watch the door at all times. You are allowed to sculpt. He will not model for you. And you must not go out. Photographs are forbidden, henceforth; who knows what danger lurks. Who knows who could find your camera with photos of prime sites, homes of the very rich. If you attempt to leave, I will cut you off. And my testicles, Tess, I remind you, are sensitive to your touch. You will find yourself on the street, my pet, penniless, with no one else. Chechnya is not a happy place. So, dear wife, be content. Do your artistic work. We will arrange a show in Soho all gold-leafed, if you behave.

Scene III

(Strauss waltz plays while a table in an expensive restaurant is laid. ABDUL *rolls* HANDEL *in his chair to sit alone at a table covered with a thick white damask cloth; he is nursing a scotch, ice cubes clinking in his glass.* DAVID ABBAS, *a dark, handsome man in his forties, approaches.)*

HANDEL:	Abbas!
DAVID:	Mr. Handel, sir.
HANDEL:	Sit down.
DAVID:	Sir, yes. Thank you for…
HANDEL:	For what?
DAVID:	Well, sir, for…
HANDEL:	What? What! What for, I ask you that.
DAVID:	Inviting me, I'd say…
HANDEL:	Correct. Why ever for?
DAVID:	Sir, really, I haven't a clue.
HANDEL:	I have a daughter.
DAVID:	I've heard.
HANDEL:	Life-blood. Heart ache is real, Abbas. My heart aches every moment of every day. *(He strikes his chest)* Nighttime, lurch awake. Sorrow in the chest. Do you have children?

DAVID:	I've never married, sir.
HANDEL:	Hidden children, then?
DAVID:	None that I know.
HANDEL:	Know more. They can appear. Do a man in.
DAVID:	I'm sure.
HANDEL:	FBI.
DAVID:	I've recently left the Bureau.
HANDEL:	A man of principle.
DAVID:	I have no illusions, sir, that what I do, in any way, might make…
HANDEL:	A bachelor. Not congenital?
DAVID:	I don't think so. I haven't yet met…
HANDEL:	My daughter, Lucia, is very beautiful.
DAVID:	I've been told as much, sir.
HANDEL:	She's late. Not congenitally principled, I suggest?
DAVID:	Well, I suppose I don't know. No one knows, do they, until… I resigned, that's all.
HANDEL:	*(Leans across the table, whispering)* Big fish. This guy you hooked. What's his nom de guerre? Ibn al-Shaykh Al-Libi. In Pakistan. Good work.
DAVID:	*(Surprised)* Thank you, sir.
HANDEL:	Tremendous catch.
DAVID:	An al-Qaeda operative; we know that much.
HANDEL:	Paid for with cash by the barrel. Money talks. Pass the bucks. Is that how that was engineered?
DAVID:	In a manner of speaking, I suppose.
HANDEL:	Where is this Al-Libi now?
DAVID:	Classified, I'm afraid.
HANDEL:	The CIA cut off your balls.
DAVID:	We disrupted the plot in Yemen. Al-Libi talked. Al-Qaeda was going to blow the Yemeni embassy up.
HANDEL:	Fine. Good. Who even knows where Yemen is? Who can find Yemen on the map? Excuse me, but who gives a crap. Our embassy in Yemen is staffed by Yemenis. We see them lying in the rubble for 10 seconds on the news, who cares?
DAVID:	I'm sorry Yemen is so far away. Nevertheless, we saved innocent lives.
HANDEL:	You want Cleveland to be attacked? The Golden Gate?
DAVID:	Of course not.
HANDEL:	My own daughter's fiancé jumped. She miscarried on the spot.
DAVID:	I am sorry, sir. I had heard, of course. My condolences.
HANDEL:	They'll come at us again unless we stop them where they live.

DAVID:	Absolutely, sir, agreed.
HANDEL:	And, so, we need to know. Saddam Hussein was in on 9/11.
DAVID:	That's hardly likely.
HANDEL:	That's what Al-Libi told the CIA.
DAVID:	Al-Libi was talking freely to me; he never said such a thing.
HANDEL:	You stopped too soon.
DAVID:	It's just not credible.
HANDEL:	No one admires a man who quits.
DAVID:	Sir, with all respect, those tactics never work.
HANDEL:	Al-Libi spilled the beans. Bin Laden and Saddam Hussein are allies, friends.
DAVID:	Sir, just to make the pain stop a man will say…
HANDEL:	Powell's got to take the facts to the UN. Do you suggest the President, the Secretary of State repeat false intelligence?
DAVID:	Of course not. Who could think of such a thing?
HANDEL:	Saddam Hussein planned 9/11. Done deal. We invade.
DAVID:	*(Pause)* I see.
HANDEL:	I like you, Abbas. I do. I don't believe the things that people say.
DAVID:	What do people say?
HANDEL:	Come, come. You're an Arab.
DAVID:	Half. My father was born in Syria.
HANDEL:	Syria is friendly with Hezbollah, Hamas.
DAVID:	My father was educated in Britain.
HANDEL:	You know how people talk.
DAVID:	My father was an engineer.
HANDEL:	Explosives. Detonations.
DAVID:	He built bridges.
HANDEL:	Muslim?
DAVID:	By birth.
HANDEL:	Tell me, Abbas, did your father pray?
DAVID:	At Ramadan, on holidays, not five times a day.
HANDEL:	Did your father take you with him to the mosque?
DAVID:	Sometimes, yes; he wanted me to… My mother was Unitarian. Born and raised in Boston. I also went to church with her. I'm an American, sir.
HANDEL:	Through and through…
DAVID:	My father became an American citizen.
HANDEL:	My father, too. We are a nation of immigrants.
DAVID:	Yes, sir. Stronger, better, braver for being a melting pot.
HANDEL:	I dismiss the nasty rumors out of hand.
DAVID:	I'm a trained interrogator, sir. I'm good at what I do.

HANDEL:	They say you're *soft on terror*.
DAVID:	That's ridiculous, sir.
HANDEL:	Al-Libi talked, but not to you.
DAVID:	The CIA rendered Al-Libi to Egypt.
HANDEL:	Correct. What did this sick bastard know? Why else strap him down? Why risk ourselves, our sanity at stake? They hate our way of life. Slap his penis back and forth. Why suffer so? We are shat upon; we shit on others if we're wise. You wish for loftier thoughts. Smear menstrual blood upon his balls. Ask once more. Stick something up his rectum. He gives us what we need.
DAVID:	God forgive.
HANDEL:	Good! I want you at the helm of Deepwater, Abbas. Principles you have. Your hands are squeaky clean. The private sector is the place to be. I want you on the Deepwater team.
DAVID:	Deepwater, sir?
HANDEL:	The pay is high. A million or more a year. You can support a wife on that. Better yet, you'll be in control. Fuck the CIA. Deepwater works directly with the highest office in the land.
DAVID:	Sir!
HANDEL:	Enough. My daughter suffers and it breaks my heart. (HANDEL *sees* LUCIA) She's coming, step away. Appear as if by chance.
	(DAVID *exits to the bar as* LUCIA *enters looking around for her father; she is wearing a particularly exquisite dress, not flashy, yet it should have something metallic, silvery, about it, as if made out of moonshine.* HANDEL *rises, kisses her on both cheeks, gently.*)
	Child, child, child, daughter.
	(*He pats her bottom as she walks by to her chair. She grabs his hand and twists it hard enough to make him wince. They smile at one another.*)
	Exquisite dress.
LUCIA:	You said I should dress.
HANDEL:	Scraggly you got, awful running pants, sneakers, deranged look. Ever since, well, never mind. One year has passed. So, it's enough. Let Geoff rest in his grave, be at peace.
LUCIA:	Geoff has no grave. Not one ounce of Geoff was ever found.
HANDEL:	Tess memorializes with gold leaf.
	(LUCIA *dismisses this.*)
	It costs. Cannibals. Monsters. What kinds of people do such things? The lobster is fleshy and fresh. Raw oysters to begin. Steak. You are over-thin. Delicious to behold, décolletage. Game hen?
LUCIA:	Whatever you want…

HANDEL:	Warm breasts…
	(HANDEL snaps his fingers, waves for the waiter.)
	… of Cornish game hen, oysters, first, some lobster, steak, champagne; he knows what to bring. Now, then…
	(HANDEL reaches across the table and takes LUCIA's hands in his, he leans in.)
	My child, I have suffered watching you. And yet, you must begin again, remake your life. I have done so more than once. My mother ran in front of me and leapt, your mother fell from her horse. We lose them in the air, it's our fate; then Geoff. They fall away from us. We stay. We are tasked with the task of picking up. We must become anew, despite, because. You would have become a mother by now, with Geoff, working hard at some clinic in the South Bronx, living in a roach infested apartment…
LUCIA:	Don't ever speak of Geoff, the child, our life… That is mine. Why did I come?
HANDEL:	Indeed, yes. We would not be having this talk; we would have been no doubt about it, estranged. Your delicious dress would not have been bought. Nor this.
	(He reaches into his jacket pocket and takes out a jewelry box which he opens. Inside is an expensive bracelet which he puts around her wrist, holding tight to her arm once it is fastened. Silence)
LUCIA:	What do I want with this?
HANDEL:	A father's love. Don't break my heart. It's a new world, my child. We took the hit. We answer back. Before, it was possible to live as you imagined, in your scrubs. Not now.
LUCIA:	Please, stop.
HANDEL:	Fascism threatened. We stood up. Forgot Depression. So, now, once more, unbidden. Enjoy the emeralds on your wrist.
LUCIA:	I don't want any part of this. I don't wish anyone else in the world to suffer as I have. What good is revenge?
	(She stands as if to go. HANDEL waves his arms. DAVID approaches the table.)
DAVID:	Sir!
HANDEL:	Fortuitous. Mr. David Abbas.
DAVID:	Amazing to run into you.
HANDEL:	My daughter, Lucia.
DAVID:	Lucia. Enchanté. A beautiful name for a very beautiful woman.
LUCIA:	Please, I was just on my way.
	(HANDEL stands.)

HANDEL:	Sit.
	(Everyone remains standing.)
	David Abbas is about our nation's business. Sit down.
	(DAVID pulls out LUCIA's chair.)
DAVID:	Please.
	(Everyone sits.)
HANDEL:	Now, then, now, then.
	(DAVID admires LUCIA's new jewelry.)
DAVID:	What a lovely bracelet for a lovely…
LUCIA:	Enough.
DAVID:	*(Smiling)* I've made my point.
HANDEL:	A celebration of sorts, a new start, a new life. A new world, Abbas. New job. New life.
	(LUCIA makes as if to get up again.)
LUCIA:	I don't think so.
	(LUCIA leaves the table; DAVID goes after her.)
DAVID:	I wouldn't go. Rather, I'm asking you to stay, just a bit. Please. We've only now met. Don't leave. I understand.
LUCIA:	I don't want to be…
DAVID:	An object. Of course not. Of pity or anything else. Trust me.
HANDEL:	*(Calling from his table)* Lucia's a physician, a healer; she has learned from her father. She has enormous gifts. She should be of use.
	(DAVID takes LUCIA by the arm and moves her further away from HANDEL.)
DAVID:	A doctor. That's wonderful.
LUCIA:	I've not been a doctor for a year.
DAVID:	Then it's time.
LUCIA:	Oh, I tried. I found out something very odd. I can no longer stand the sight of blood.
DAVID:	He didn't tell me.
LUCIA:	He doesn't know. Why would he? An object did you say? To him, I'm a creature made-up, Prospero's Miranda. It's an unsightly trait in a doctor. I was suturing a child. I ran out of the room to wretch and I never went back. I have blood on my hands, that's how it felt. I can't explain.
DAVID:	There's no need to explain. I know. I lost close friends at the Pentagon. We are tainted, you and I. Sometimes, Lucia, I think it's more difficult to survive. But we're here. We're alive. Please stay, you can trust me.
	(He gestures LUCIA back to the table.)

DAVID:	Our work is our salvation, has to be…
HANDEL:	She's the dearest thing to me, Abbas, and, yet, I could not spare her. Helpless I was to save her. Those who attacked us took her joy. Her innocence is gone. My child has suffered more than… *(He is near tears with emotion)* David can speak far better than I.
DAVID:	Look, there's a war in a faraway place. Afghanistan. Very soon there will be an invasion of Iraq. There is nothing any one of us can do about that. We'll take down Saddam and I, for one, say it's about time. The Iraqis will thank us for that. We will crush Al-Qaeda in Afghanistan. There are those who hate us. And, so, there will be prisoners. Trained interrogators are in short supply. I speak Arabic. I know the region. Lucia, I want you to come along. Trained interrogators need trained medical help. No. Don't leave. Don't try to run anymore. Don't say anything at all. Ask yourself if you can be of use. I think your fiancé would want that.
HANDEL:	We are dedicated to the Geneva Convention. Deepwater, that's our name.
DAVID:	Believe me when I tell you private contractors have their place. The CIA can get rough. The FBI is being sidelined. The Military Police can't police themselves. Our best, our most humane chance is with the private sector. We have no axe to grind. I need you, Lucia; it's as simple as that, to keep the Hippocratic Oath. Do no harm. *(He speaks directly to Lucia.)*. Don't speak. Don't tell me now. You won't have to see blood. You'll be with me so blood doesn't flow. *(HANDEL takes her wrist, the one with the bracelet on it.)*
HANDEL:	It's a beautiful thing, is it not? It's belle époque.

Scene IV

(ABDUL is reclining and his upper body, naked, is draped in a loose cloth. His back is to the audience. TESS sits upstage of ABDUL. She is drawing ABDUL, making studies of him for the sculpture.)

TESS:	What do I see when I look at you?
ABDUL:	Let me tell you a story.
TESS:	I am looking inside the living man. That's where I'm trying to look.
ABDUL:	On my breath the inside comes out. Let me speak.
TESS:	What good are words in times like these?
ABDUL:	Words are of no use. Stories, yes.

TESS:	He's at dinner; he'll be back.
ABDUL:	Until then we are free.
TESS:	Locked in.
ABDUL:	Stories take us out.
TESS:	All right, talk, but try not to move.

(As ABDUL *speaks,* TESS *continues to draw. Perhaps, her quick charcoal sketches appears projected on the stage left panel, while on the panel, stage right, Islamic patterns and finally a painting of two lovers, appears. Note: in our production the middle portion of this speech was performed in Arabic.*)

ABDUL: The vizier of the sultan was riding through the market when he came upon a slave-girl auction. The girls were displayed in a semi-circle, gowned in dresses of rich vermilions, azures, burgundies, and emerald greens, each embroidered in golden threads. Their hair and lips were covered but their shapely noses and wide eyes were available to view and the vizier could see that the slave girls came from all races – Turks, Franks, Circassians, Abyssinians, Nubians, Takruris, Rumis, Tartars, Georgians, Chechens, Albanians and others. (*The actor switches into Arabic and begins to move around the stage, telling the story also in gestures.*) Around the slave girls who stood silent with heads slightly bowed so as to avoid catching any buyer's eye, stood a group of leering men, both old and young, comely and hideous to behold, some clearly wealthy and others less well-dressed. The men's eyes were alive with lust as they surveyed the shapely women arrayed before them. This vizier of the sultan was not used to feeling empathy, and did not quite know himself why he reined his shiny bay stallion to a stop, remaining mounted while he overlooked the group. Nevertheless, his presence caused a stir. For the auctioneer, seeing the sultan's vizier had come to the slave girl auction, naturally assumed the vizier had come on order of the sultan in order to purchase the most beautiful and docile girl. It was a Nubian girl the auctioneer fancied would bring the largest price for she appeared beautiful beyond all others: she was the tallest in the group, clothed almost completely in white, unlike the others, white with emerald green stripes around the borders of her robes. Her black hair could be seen to fall in braids down to her waist. Her eyes were large, wide and sparkling dark. The fingers with which she held her robe around her shapely frame were long and thin and lovely to behold. The girl held her head up, her entire demeanor looked fearless and proud. Surely a slave girl like this should go for a small fortune. And so the auctioneer put his hand upon the arm of the Nubian girl and moved her forward into the center of the semi-circle made by slave girls and leering men. As he did so, he spoke to the sultan's own vizier on the bay stallion, 'has one ever seen a slave girl more perfect in every dimension than this? And would not the Sultan himself be honored to have this Nubian girl in his bed?' The girl (whether or not she knew the language of the auctioneer, she heard every word and most certainly his meaning was clear) betrayed not a feeling, nor did she move one part of her beautiful frame.

TESS: Abdul!

ABDUL: *(Sits back on the table and switches to English.)* The vizier from his stallion said nothing. He had been struck speechless, in fact, by his love for the Chechen girl at the edge of the semi-circle. Why this one and not that one, the vizier of course could not tell for when love strikes one is helpless and against all sense. As for himself, the vizier knew his life would be over and unfulfilled, all meaning would depart, and soon after his very will to live, were he not to wed with the Chechen girl whom he promised to treat with great respect all his life.

(Sound of several keys turning several locks and the opening of a heavy door. HANDEL's *voice is heard.)*

HANDEL: My Chechen girl, a stirring in my groin, a good night's work. My heavy heart is grown light. Attend. Attend.

TESS: Where is Lucia?

HANDEL: Secured. My will procured. Closer come; the night is young.

TESS: Why isn't Lucia with you?

HANDEL: Lucia is no longer your concern.

TESS: What have you done with her?

HANDEL: Tess, Tess, is this an inquisition which you run.

TESS: You've done something terrible to her.

HANDEL: Is this an insurrection boiling up? I leave you home alone. No, not alone, with someone, him... where, Mohammed, come.
(He enters.)

TESS: His name is Abdul, Handel.

HANDEL: His name is what I say it is. Nameless in his box; no habeas corpus rights. Appear, my boy, before your judge.

TESS: You've involved Lucia in your schemes.

HANDEL: You hardly know; you cannot think, envision; you're an artist, Tess, a decoration. If not that, what? A whore that I picked up. Come here. Massage my groin.
(ABDUL steps forward, to interrupt.)

ABDUL:	You called.
HANDEL:	I need my groin massaged. Any hand shall do. Enlightened, I allow a choice. Who first?
	(HANDEL *sits in his chair his legs spread.* TESS *freezes.* ABDUL *approaches.*)
TESS:	(*To* ABDUL) No.
	(*She takes a step toward* HANDEL.)
ABDUL:	(*To* TESS) No.
TESS:	Not you.
ABDUL:	But please, I cannot witness such a thing. It is not…
HANDEL:	Not *love,* the word upon your tongue, inside what you call your heart? Or *right?* Of justice dare you speak? So, you two have formed a bond. Well, well. Enough. Mohammad will massage my groin.
	(*He swivels his chair around and, then, in the course of the speech back around.*)
HANDEL:	Open the curtains up so I can see the stars, to cum within the Milky Way, to soar, to be a part of the great enduring cosmic mystery, source of eternal life. Across the sea a land awaits its fate. And, now, again, an epic hand. Primal force. Shock and awe. I'm so full I shall explode.
	(HANDEL *snaps his fingers motioning* ABDUL *toward him. But* TESS *stops him and stands behind his chair, her hands around his neck.*)
TESS:	(*Seductively*) What have you done to Lucia?
HANDEL:	(*Takes her hands away from his neck and twists her wrists*) I am stronger, my dear, than you. Recite the litany you know by heart or, I do fear, the window here is very high. A suicidal female jumped; it's hardly news.
	(*At this,* ABDUL *approaches. He is ready to defend* TESS's *life.* HANDEL *holds her tightly by the arms as if to throw her out the window.*)
HANDEL:	Your choice, my Tess. A choice to make we always have. To be or not to be. What's yours, my pet?
	(*Silence.* TESS *succumbs, but not completely; she motions to* ABDUL *to step a safe distance away; and he does as* TESS *seduces* HANDEL *with her voice, and strokes his head.*)
TESS:	My sun, the center of my life, all good radiates from you, my dear, my husband, my beloved. You are most just, most righteous in intent, liberatory by design; you bring with every breath you draw more goodness to the world. Source of abundance, enduring peace, source of might.
	(HANDEL *climaxes with deep satisfaction.*)
HANDEL:	Yes, yes, yes. We dare. Invade. Invade.

Scene V

(A black site prison, a hidden part of Bagram Air Force Base, Afghanistan. Outside the door to an interrogation room, DAVID ABBAS, *in civilian clothes, and* LUCIA, *in white medical coat, stethoscope, with a clipboard.* DAVID, *cell phone in hand, is looking through a small observation window.)*

DAVID:	*(Excited)* This guy's a big fish.
LUCIA:	Have you read his diary?
DAVID:	This guy's the biggest of the big fish. A whale, not white. A big dark whale.
	(He speaks into his earphone to Washington.)
	Yes, sir, Abu Zubaydah has just entered the Bagram Air Force Base interrogation room here in Afghanistan. *(He looks through the window into the interrogation room.)* He's well... They're starting right now. Yes, sir, I'll stay on the line.
LUCIA:	*(Consulting the medical records)* He's recently had major surgery.
DAVID:	We saved his life. The guy was sitting at a kitchen table in the middle of making a bomb. Jumped out the window to escape. He was shot in the gut and lower down. We flew a surgeon in all the way from Johns Hopkins Hospital.
LUCIA:	*(Consulting her clipboard)* He's got edema, swelling of the ankles, the legs, open suppurating sores. *(To* DAVID*)* None of this is consistent with his initial injuries.
DAVID:	You're here to monitor his treatment. This one is full of information. Believe me.
LUCIA:	I suggest you give his diary a read.
DAVID:	*(Into phone)* Yes, sir. Right. The interrogation is currently beginning, as planned.
LUCIA:	Why are his legs swollen like that?
DAVID:	This guy knows stuff that can save innocent lives. *(A groan is heard from inside the room.* DAVID *looks through the window.)* Man oh man. That's rough. *(He speaks to the interrogators inside the room)* Listen up. Ease up. Take him, nice and easy. Right. *(Pause)* Okay, okay, he's back. No need for you to go in. *(Into phone)* No, sir, silent as the night. Yes, sir. He's a tough bastard, all right.
LUCIA:	What are they doing to him?
DAVID:	Talking. Want to look?
LUCIA:	No. I do not.
DAVID:	*(He returns to the window)* Shit, he's fainted. You don't want to look. Just go in. Check his vitals. Tell them if it's safe to continue. *(The door opens just enough for* LUCIA *to squeeze through.)*

DAVID:	I'll be right here, Lucia.
	(LUCIA *goes inside.* DAVID *lights a cigarette and takes out his phone.*) Yes, sir, right. He's holding his own. Medical is with him now. *(Silence)* Thank you, sir. Yes, sir, I do understand. *(Pause)* Yes, sir, I am with you one hundred percent. He knows stuff, for sure. We know that much. I'm with you. Yes, sir. American lives are at stake. (LUCIA *exits the room.*)
	How is he?
LUCIA:	He'll live.
DAVID:	Okay. *(He signals thumbs up through the door but also speaks into his phone.)* We just got medical clearance. Right, sir. *(Into the room)* We've got orders from the chief. Ramp it up.
LUCIA:	Stop. He's naked and freezing. He's got suppurating open sores on his arms, legs. His blood pressure is high. His heartbeat is irregular. He could have a stroke. I told them to stop, David.
DAVID:	Too late.
LUCIA:	I'm the medical officer. I told them to lay off.
DAVID:	I just got clearance. *(A loud bashing sound is heard, a terrible groan.)* Poor son-of-a-bitch. I'll turn the speaker off.
LUCIA:	He's hypothermic, blue.
DAVID:	Look, I'm talking to Washington on the phone; we've got clearance from the chief, no stopping, now.
LUCIA:	Washington can't see. I can.
DAVID:	Listen, this guy begged to be killed. He asked to be smothered with a pillow.
	(He stares through the window.) Oh, oh, oh, man, oh man, that *was* rough. He's down. Shit. Why can't they take it easy?
LUCIA:	I'm going in.
DAVID:	No, no. It's all right. He's up; they've got him up. Tied up. He's not going to be able to stand…
LUCIA:	Let me past…
DAVID:	I tell you, we're not going to lose him. Not on my watch. I'm on your side, Lucia. Trust. *(Into his phone)* Nothing yet. They're on it, sir, you bet.
	(LUCIA *slides down to the floor and puts her head in her hands. He gets down next to her.*)
	Hey, there, come on. Chin up, you know, all the rest. Stiff upper lip. This guy's a bona fide, dyed in the wool, terrorist fuck. He was building a bomb for Christ's sake.
LUCIA:	Perhaps. Maybe I'm a physician.

DAVID:	You're a doctor; a compassionate, feelingful, woman. And Abu Zubayda is a fucking terrorist pig who would kill you soon as look at you. Throw acid into your lovely face. He's got the resume, let me tell you: First off, the guy's a Palestinian; his parents are from the Gaza Strip. He was born in Riyadh, Saudi Arabia, home to Osama. He fought jihad against the Russians in Afghanistan on our dime. After that, he ran logistics and *recruitment* for his pal Bin Laden. I know these people, Lucia. I know how they think. I tell you this guy wants to kill every American.
LUCIA:	My orders are to keep him well enough to tell you what you want to know. I'm telling you to stop them from torturing…
DAVID:	Ramping up.
LUCIA:	Tell them to stop. You'll have a corpse on your hands, on all our hands, if you don't.
DAVID:	Okay, okay. *(They both get up.)* *(Looking through the window)* Wow. It's happening. Thank God. The fucker's finally talking. I can see his jaw moving. He's tied up and he's babbling. I'm going to turn this on. *(He flicks on the switch; in accented English we hear:* *'Parking malls, shopping malls, parking lots, big cities all over your country. You want to know. Everywhere. No one is safe.')* Shopping malls, shit. See, if we had stopped… you can stop too soon. Believe me, you can. You let them off the hook and then, your job, your reputation, far more important, lives, innocent lives, you can't have… I can't afford to have that on my conscience … *(Into his phone)* You heard right, sir. Parking lots. Shopping malls. Shit, he fainted.
LUCIA:	Get out of my way. *(She pushes past him inside the interrogation room.)*
DAVID:	*(Back and forth between his phone and the window)* Sorry, sir. The son-of-a-bitch is hanging from his arms, dangling in mid-air, naked as the day he was born. He fainted. That's all. Yeah, medical is with him now. They're taking him down. Yeah, she's giving him a shot. Yeah, he's coming 'round. No, sir, we can't go on. Yes, sir, we use what we've got. You heard the fucker say it himself. Parking lots, shopping malls, families at K-Mart, at Wal-Mart at Target are targets, my God. Where? How the fuck are we supposed to know that? The guy's completely out. I told them to go easy, but… Yes, sir, it's a terrorist plot. Everywhere. No one is safe. *(LUCIA comes out.)*

LUCIA:	He's going back to his cell. I ordered a blanket. Clothing. Pain medication.
DAVID:	You did the right thing. But, when…
LUCIA:	Not until he's had sleep.
DAVID:	Look, we've got critical, time-sensitive actionable intelligence right this minute, right now.
LUCIA:	Shopping malls?
DAVID:	That's why we've got to get the specifics. We stop now… there are mothers with babies in their arms, Lucia.
LUCIA:	What makes you think he wasn't making it up? Babbling to get them to stop slapping him in the gut.
DAVID:	Because, we can't think like that. It's too dangerous.
LUCIA:	David, do you want to kill him in that room?
DAVID:	Of course not. We're not even supposed to leave marks.
LUCIA:	Then, listen to sound medical advice.
DAVID:	I am not making these decisions, Lucia; they come from higher up. I'm a cog in the wheel. So are you. There's a limit to what any one of us can do.
LUCIA:	I'm telling you, you can cause irreversible damage to his system if you don't stop.
DAVID:	Okay. Look, they're dragging him out. You want to see.
LUCIA:	*(Peering through the window)* Tell them to use a stretcher, for God's sake.
	(DAVID goes into the room.)
DAVID:	*(His voice)* Twenty-minutes. No more. I've got Washington hanging on; they're waiting to send SWAT teams into shopping malls. We need location, location, location. Strap him into a chair. Slap him until he holds his head up. *(Into his phone)* Yes, sir, the interrogation is proceeding. He's giving us actionable intelligence right now. Shopping malls. It's a big country. I *do* know that, sir.
GEOFF'S VOICE:	Hey, Luce; what's going on with you.
LUCIA:	Stop it, Geoff; go away.
	(GEOFF enters.)
GEOFF:	Come on, kiddo, let me in.
LUCIA:	Really, I can't. I'm on duty. On call. Leave me alone. You have. You will.
	(He takes her head in his hands, looks lovingly into her eyes.)
GEOFF:	Hey, you've gone back to work. That's wonderful. Great. St. Vincent's?
LUCIA:	I'm a cog in the wheel of the Global War Against Terror.
GEOFF:	What's that?

LUCIA:	*(Laughs)* And it's all your fault. If you hadn't jumped. If you hadn't been in that building that day. If you had met me at Starbucks, like you promised, it wouldn't, I wouldn't be… none of this…
GEOFF:	Lucia, you're not making sense.
LUCIA:	Look, Geoff, listen to me; it's another world. It's not the life you and I had. And I can't talk to you anymore. I've got high security clearance. I can't talk to anyone. I can't even hear your voice.
GEOFF:	Lucia, I don't understand one word you are…
LUCIA:	I can't hear you, Geoff. Go away.

(GEOFF vanishes. DAVID comes out of the interrogation room.)

DAVID:	Listen. The bastard's stopped talking again. *(Into the room)* Slap the fucking son-of-a-bitch awake. *(Into the phone)* Yes, sir. He's on the verge of giving us locations, streets. Chicago? St. Louis? L.A.? Teaneck, New Jersey? *(Into the room)* Show him a map. Tell him to point. Fuck, he's bleeding. He's bleeding all over the fucking map. He's bleeding all over the floor. Clean that blood up. *(He opens the door)* Go on in, doc.

(LUCIA pushes past DAVID and enters the room.)

(Into the phone) Yes, sir, of course; of course, we showed him the map. It looked like the Midwest or the Southwest. Yes, yes, he was talking all right, spilling the beans; these guys will stop at nothing. Shopping malls. Who could imagine. He lost consciousness. No, no, the medical officer is with him now. He'll come around. These guys are tough like barbed wire. You can't shut them down. I know we don't want a high visibility corpse on our hands. I'm totally with you, sir, on that.

(LUCIA comes out of the room; her white coat is covered in blood. She has blood on her face; she is in a dissociated state.)

LUCIA:	Geoff, look; I've gone back to work. Remember how you used to say, I was happiest covered in blood. Remember the day you surprised me in the emergency room. You complained of a chest pain just so they'd check you in. I had just staunched a gunshot wound. I was covered in blood. I had a big, dopey smile on my face. That's what you said. 'You have a big dopey smile on your face.' I was so happy because my patient was going to live. Geoff? Please, look, talk back. You're never here when I need you.
DAVID:	Hey, Lucia, it's me, David. Hey. *(He slaps her gently on her cheek)* Come on, come on. What happened in there? Is the fucking bastard alive?

LUCIA:	I don't know. I fell. I slipped in his blood, from his nose, from his rectum. Transfusion. Blanket. Someone had better call someone. Obviously I... I obviously... it's obvious, isn't it... I am going to be sick. I am quite, quite sick.
DAVID:	Fuck. I've got to go in. *(Into phone)* Yes, sir, calm down. Tell the Secretary to calm down. I'm going in. Trust me. I'll get the son-of-a-bitch to tell me exactly.
	(He goes into the room. She slides down the wall. GEOFF *enters.)*
GEOFF:	Luce, for god's sake, here I am. What's wrong? You weren't like this before.
LUCIA:	Before. No.
GEOFF:	When we were together you were brave. You were strong. If someone behind that door needs you, Luce, you go in. You never give up. You give CPR way too long. You beat on his heart. Even if he's homeless. Even if he's an addict with HIV, an ex-con who has nothing to live for, you, Lucia, bring back from the dead. You smile at him and you hold his hand. It's not in you, Luce, to stop. Every life is worth... you used to say that 'each life is worth the whole world.'
LUCIA:	Do you know how many shopping malls there are in America? Do you have any idea? The guy's babbling. He's out of his mind. Look, Goeff, here, they gave me a copy of his diary. He writes in three voices: Hani 1, Hani 2, Hani 3; he writes obsessively. 'My left thumb is dirty and it has a scratch,' says Hani 1. Hani 3 says: 'No, no, no, I want to pick my nose and get inside her blouse.' Hani 2: 'Everybody is looking funny at me.' This is the man we are torturing to get the truth.
GEOFF:	I hear you, Luce, I hear every word you say, believe me, but you are not making any sense.
	*(*DAVID *enters from the interrogation room door.)*
DAVID:	*(Into phone)* Yes, sir. Shopping malls, that's what he said. I don't know where. Everywhere for all I know. Orange alert. Nationwide. National Guard. Armed. In every shopping mall. These motherfuckers will stop at nothing. Of course, people shouldn't stop shopping. But they'd better be on the alert. If they see anyone suspicious. Muslim, yes. Non-white. With backpacks. *(He takes the ear piece out of his ear.)* My God. I was against all this. I promised myself I never would... You think I don't know what a man can become? You think I wanted to beat him to a pulp? You think I want them to blow us up?

Scene VI

	(HANDEL *sits in his chair.*)
HANDEL:	(*Snaps his fingers*) Boy.
	(*In shuffles* ABDUL. *He is a relic of his former self, meaning, he's been tortured. He stands, shoulders hunched, head bent; he has a laptop computer in his hand.*)
ABDUL:	Master.
HANDEL:	Master of the Universe, hosanna, master builder, master of, the wish, intention to, the well-intentioned everywhere on earth. Alas, not all can ascertain, ascend to, self-mastery, and, thus, from this deficiency, we arrive at master-slave. To grim necessity we bow. You think such power over you does not try my soul? Monologist I have become. I speak for me and you and those who ever will exist. I speak of consciousness, unconscious wish, dream-life. All tweets, blogs, all airways, I shall own. I have peered inside. I see the vastness of the human mind. Inner space belongs to me. Closer come.

(ABDUL *approaches, cautiously.* HANDEL *strikes him on his head.*)
Head down. (HANDEL *strikes* ABDUL *again*) Head down. Evil one. Head keeps bouncing up. Proof. The terrorist inside thee lurks. The plot inside your disobedient brain, I am forced to pre-empt strike. *(He hits* ABDUL's *head again)* Otherwise, I am not. You are. Not me.

ABDUL:	Yes, Lord.
HANDEL:	Lord, yes. And, well, why not? The power's mine thus I am. Write thus, this, now; transcribe my inner thoughts. Take down: conceive, contort, conquer, and convert. Take notes. (ABDUL *begins to open the laptop*) I improvise: desire first, contort the facts, believe the lies you speak; conceive the strike, convert the infidels. Have I the order right? Reread me now.
ABDUL:	(*Rewriting* HANDEL) Contort the facts that you believe are lies, conceive the lies you speak, convert yourself into belief of lies that you desire to be truth. Have I the order right?
HANDEL:	That was it, is it, was it, that? No word misplaced. Be precise. Take note. Now I continue. Faith. (*Pause*) Have it in you?
ABDUL:	Have it in you?
HANDEL:	Faith.
ABDUL:	Faith.
HANDEL:	Faith, fool.
ABDUL:	Faith, fool. I read back.

HANDEL:	Do you have it in you?
ABDUL:	Do you have it…
HANDEL:	Stop! In you? In you?
ABDUL:	In you?
HANDEL:	Fool! In you. Not I. In you, faith, do you? Read this back: In me; do I have faith? Answer that.
ABDUL:	There is no God but God.
HANDEL:	Palaver. Useless tool. Pick up your tool and transcribe. Faith not yours to have, is mine, all mine. Boot up or I boot you. My thoughts will run amuck; they must be caught, contained *(ABDUL transcribes on the laptop)*. So, we shall begin again. Today's lesson to be released by you upon my blog into the eternal blogosphere, where millions turn their eyes to glean self-help as Handel speaks. The network news will later quote. Our topic for the day is Common Feeling. What? You say.
ABDUL:	What?
HANDEL:	A feeling, common feeling is… once was, common, no longer is. And now you must ask of me?
ABDUL:	*(Sardonic)* Why, indeed?
HANDEL:	Don't roll your eyes, snail, wart, insect brain. Attend. Why this turn away from common fellow-feeling which in the past delivered up so much: public schools, libraries, emergency rooms, bridges over troubled waters?
ABDUL:	A question most well put.
HANDEL:	Of course. And, I must now ask: What has transpired to tear us so apart? To render us single, individual, one of a kind, myself? *(Pause)* Speak. Lout.
ABDUL:	Myself, my sire, stopped me cold.
HANDEL:	Self! Selfless your self is, was, will be, unto eternity. Bend down. Eternal glory come to those most meek. You comprehend?
ABDUL:	Duck. Lie-low. Yet there's more inside your febrile brain.
HANDEL:	Fertile, fool. More wisdom you expect?
ABDUL:	A fount. You have not plumbed your depths.
HANDEL:	Correct, yet, I must admit: If I turn myself away from even lowly you even I am wounded, diminished and made less. I suffer if I blind my eyes to suffering beneath. You masses are not I. I, Handel never fall so low. I stand upon the promontory. Great height. Desire to be, become, remake, propels above all else. Selfless ones with rheumy eyes entreat. I dare not turn from them. Here is Common Feeling. Common Feeling reigns. From the top look down with empathy. *(Pause)* What word? What word did I say? Repeat.

ABDUL:	Empathy, as clear as day, you said.
HANDEL:	Strike that. Strike again. (HANDEL *strikes* ABDUL's *head again*) True empathy is pain. Feeling for someone else. Is terror. I go too far, to feel the sorrow of another. Stop! Such feelings would take over. Can't. Bring Tess. I want my wife.

(The only sound is the keyboard as ABDUL *finishes typing.)*
Hit save. Slave. Save. Slave. Save. Hit send. Release into the strato-blogosphere. Relief. Tess, now.
*(*ABDUL *exits.)*
Alone, at last, all by myself, alone, I can confess: I have never actually felt for someone else. What brand of loneliness is that? Profound discontent.
(Silence)
It is my parents' fault. No doubt. Deprived from birth. They never picked me up.
(Silence)
(Sound of chains. ABDUL *enters leading* TESS *by her chains. She is clothed in an orange jump suit. Her legs are shackled together and her arms are shackled to chains around her waist. She wears goggles.)*
Tess. Unshackle her at once. My Tess. Unbind. Unblind. Goggles off. You see me, now. Rechain, arms behind her back.
*(*ABDUL *unchains her arms and rechains them behind her back.)*
Dear, dear, Tess. Down upon your knees. Head here upon my lap.
*(*ABDUL *guides* TESS *to* HANDEL, *pushes her gently down on her knees and takes her head in his hands arranging her so that her head is in* HANDEL's *lap.)*

Scene VII

(Baghdad, a hotel housing internationals, 2004. LUCIA, *in a smart black dress, and* DAVID, *in more casual civilian clothes.)*

DAVID:	I didn't think I'd ever see you again.
LUCIA:	Or I, you.
DAVID:	Then, all of a sudden, there you were this afternoon on the Red Cross tour, with your clipboard, as usual, only in Baghdad, not Afghanistan.
LUCIA:	I prefer the ICRC to my father.
DAVID:	I also resigned, immediately after...

LUCIA:	A man of principle.
DAVID:	It is possible to run a humane facility.
LUCIA:	Is it really?
DAVID:	My part; where I call the shots.
LUCIA:	Here, in Baghdad not Afghanistan?
DAVID:	You saw me at my worst.
LUCIA:	You don't have to explain.
DAVID:	You don't often see *(referring to her dress)*…
LUCIA:	No.
DAVID:	We're all on the run.
LUCIA:	Sure, why does anyone come over here?
DAVID:	Round up the desperate ones, give them a purpose.
LUCIA:	You were quite purposeful; that is one way to say it.
DAVID:	Look, I thought, truly… you have no idea the pressure I was under.
LUCIA:	Thank you for shielding me.
DAVID:	Actually, I would like to.
LUCIA:	Nurture and protect.
DAVID:	Why not.
LUCIA:	The torturer comes home; we find out he's a good family man.
DAVID:	I am not what you think.
LUCIA:	I was there.
DAVID:	We both were there, doing our thing.
LUCIA:	I'm aware.
	(She turns from him. Silence)
DAVID:	Look, we need to speak about today.
LUCIA:	Where I went?
DAVID:	Things like that.
LUCIA:	I'm not altogether certain I am going to tell you.
DAVID:	Let's have a drink, then.
LUCIA:	A drink?
DAVID:	You're wearing a cocktail dress. In my room. Only bourbon, I'm afraid, but very fine.
LUCIA:	Is that what happens now?
DAVID:	Usually, yes.
LUCIA:	Bourbon and then sex.
DAVID:	Then forget.
LUCIA:	I don't drink.
DAVID:	Lime juice, here, on the hotel terrace, in full view.
LUCIA:	I do do sex.
DAVID:	Thank God.

LUCIA:	Not necessarily here, now.
DAVID:	Not required.
LUCIA:	Used to.
DAVID:	That's something else we have in common.
LUCIA:	If I could forget.
DAVID:	Believe me. It's best.
LUCIA:	I suppose.
DAVID:	I expected you to disagree.
LUCIA:	Oh, no, drinking, fucking… universal, I believe. Oblivion.
DAVID:	It's the in between that gets one down. The spaces where memory comes.
LUCIA:	A bit of a poet.
DAVID:	In my youth.
LUCIA:	No money in that.
DAVID:	True enough.
	(Silence)
	Look, those of us who've been here before… you already know, this is the sort of stuff that goes on. It may not be nice. We should talk.
LUCIA:	What can we talk about?
DAVID:	Feelings, I suppose; we've both been…
LUCIA:	Talking helps?
DAVID:	Might.
LUCIA:	How about bourbon and sex?
DAVID:	Completely reliable, yes.
LUCIA:	You can tell me; actually, I'd like to know.
DAVID:	Tell you what?
LUCIA:	How was *your* day?
DAVID:	Ah, yes.
LUCIA:	We lost sight.
DAVID:	You were at my side; then you weren't anymore.
LUCIA:	I turned down a hall.
DAVID:	It was an official tour; your group was supposed to stay…
LUCIA:	I was wearing a white coat, stethoscope. I find I can go anywhere.
DAVID:	Where did you go?
LUCIA:	You were going to tell me.
DAVID:	Lunch time, you see. Trays of hot Halal food. Spotless floors. The men had beards. Some had lenses in their glasses, even.
LUCIA:	Do you ever look at their backs? At any of the exposed flesh?
DAVID:	No bruises. I was your decoy, in case you didn't know. I let you slip away. Now, you tell me.

LUCIA:	I see.
DAVID:	Yes, that's right. Bourbon in my room or lime juice on the terrace, you decide, as long as we're not overheard.
LUCIA:	I was saluted by a skinny and rather frightened looking 19-year-old. 'Major,' he said. 'Go right in.'
DAVID:	Makes you think.
LUCIA:	Indeed, it does.
DAVID:	He didn't see your Red Cross badge?
LUCIA:	I had tucked it in.
DAVID:	Smart.
LUCIA:	'In' is the operative word. I was let in. He must have thought I was a physician.
DAVID:	As you are.
LUCIA:	Was.
DAVID:	No deception there.
LUCIA:	None.
DAVID:	It's important when you make your report.
LUCIA:	That I not deceive them?
DAVID:	Quite. The cell block you found officially does not exist.
LUCIA:	I think I would like that drink. I would also like sex.
	(They go to DAVID's *room. Lights dim as they get into bed.)*

Scene VIII

*(*ABDUL *has fallen asleep on the floor;* TESS *has dropped asleep on* HANDEL's *lap.* HANDEL *wakes and pushes* TESS *to the floor.* HANDEL *is wearing black gloves.)*

HANDEL:	Why torture me? Why make me suffer so? Shake her till she frankly speak of love, till she spill the beans about devotion; cough up proof of her compassion. Confess once more with feeling. *(*HANDEL *jerks the chains behind her back.* TESS *is silent.* ABDUL *cries in pain.)*
TESS:	I love you, only you.
HANDEL:	*(Relieved)* Ah, Tess, the limits of the female brain. Just me you can conceive while I all humankind. *(He jerks her chains.* ABDUL *is squatting, looking.)*
TESS:	I love you. You.
ABDUL:	Please, don't.
HANDEL:	*(Threatening* ABDUL*)* A hose up your ass. Ensure Plus down your throat. A bucket for your shit. No water to wash.

TESS:	I love you, Handel; you know that, from the first moment I saw you, I knew I thought, I could be protected, helped. You took me from my life.
HANDEL:	Whore. Russian Harlot, worse, from Chechnya escaped.
TESS:	You gave me diamonds, dresses, my own car, yoga lessons, a charge card at Bergdorfs in my name, a Jacuzzi, Botox.
HANDEL:	All a woman could want and more.
TESS:	A camera I picked up. I began to see; I saw.
HANDEL:	Whom do you love?
TESS:	What I saw, I loved.
HANDEL:	What else, Tess, could your reason to be be? You see so purely into me.
ABDUL:	Stop, let me speak to you of wondrous, magical events…
HANDEL:	Cur. One story do I wish to hear. Myself. Me. I. Nothing more. *(HANDEL swats at ABDUL who ducks.)*
TESS:	You are… I do not know… English is not my first… inside you have, I sometimes thought, in the past, I wondered if there was and I would think there must, of course, each person has, a, a, some part all their own. A piece, some part of their soul that lives despite all what, a pure place deep down that has not been destroyed. I used to think: he has a child, a little girl; he brought me here for her, also. It must be good. So I…
HANDEL:	Tell me what you know. The truth. *(He jerks her chains again.)*
ABDUL:	There was a Sultan's servant, a vizier, who riding one day… *(HANDEL jerks her chains. This time, she cries out. HANDEL roughly pushes TESS off his lap.)*
HANDEL:	Look me in the eyes, my pet.
TESS:	Truth is, I would shut my eyes and spread my legs and… I tried hard to believe…
ABDUL:	A slave girl lovely enough to be the Sultan's wife…
HANDEL:	When did things go wrong between us, Tess? Why this tension; why this hurt? Why can't you just accept? Enough. I become tired from all this. No one loves to full capacity, it's true. Even so, I tried to get from her… I never had. I hoped. I thought. The greatest disappointment of my life. Reshackle! Take her back. Lock her in her box. *(ABDUL goes to TESS and very gently helps her up. ABDUL takes off the chains holding TESS's hands behind her back and reattaches them to her front belt.)*

Not food. Not water. No. Not light. Nothing will she have until she learns whom she must love.

(ABDUL *leads* TESS *off; as he does he speaks softly to her.*)

ABDUL: There is no God but God.

Scene IX

(*Lights up on the hotel room in Baghdad.* LUCIA *and* DAVID *in bed after sex.*)

DAVID: Sex helps.

LUCIA: Oh, yes, that and a good cry. Thanks, very much.
          (*He kisses her head. He gets up.*)

DAVID: But, now, I think, you should tell me what you saw.
          (*She sits up, pulling the sheet to cover her naked breasts.*)

LUCIA: People in cages. Dozens of them. The stench of bodies in fear. A voice, I was barely able to hear. 'Stop, please. Help.'

DAVID: Here he was, then, in a corner.

LUCIA: How do you know?

DAVID: Where would I be in similar circumstances?

LUCIA: Of course.

DAVID: Crouched.
          (*He turns his back to her.*)

LUCIA: He was without clothes. His hands were chained behind his legs. His position was permanently bent. He could not stand up. He tried to cover his private parts with his arms, but that was not entirely possible. His entire body was covered in bruises. He said he could not stand up anymore. He said a doctor would come each day to listen to his heart. Then, the torture would start. He said he had no idea why. He had not done anything. He had nothing to tell anyone. He said an American interrogator came every day. He asked me 'Why am I in Guantanmo' I told him, 'You are still in Iraq. You are in Abu Ghraib prison outside of Baghdad.' He was relieved. 'Will they let me go?' I told him I was with the ICRC, the International Red Cross. I gave him a card with a prisoner number on it. I said I would take a message to his family. I would tell them he was alive and still in Iraq. He told me:
          (LUCIA *crouches on the bed in the position of Al-Janabi.*)
          'My name is Emad Khydayir Shahuth Al-Janabi. I was picked up at home without warning by persons dressed in American

185

military uniforms and, also, in civilian clothing. I was beaten in front of my wife and children. I was forced from my house. I was dressed only in my shorts. I was hooded. My hands were tied. I was taken in the back of a truck to a military base and forced inside a wooden crate. I was interrogated. An American interrogator said he would claw out my eyes. Look. You can see the scars. I was slammed by three persons into a wall. When I woke, I was still hooded, still dressed only in shorts, I was dragged across stones and dirt. I was told I would be executed. I heard two gunshots. I believed I was going to die. I began to pray. I heard a helicopter overhead. An interrogator told me to talk or I would be crushed by the helicopter. I heard other prisoners screaming for mercy. After the helicopter left, I was told I would be run over by a tank. I heard it coming toward me. I was taken to a building. I was stripped and threatened with rape. I passed out. When I woke up, I was brought to an interrogation room. The American interrogator said, "Welcome to Guantanamo." The interrogator told me I had been sentenced to execution. The interrogator told me that if I cooperated my wife would be given a stipend after my execution. I said: I know nothing. I know nothing to say. I have done nothing.'
(Silence. She comes back to herself.)

LUCIA: Are you still working for Deepwater, David?
DAVID: I quit. I told you that.
LUCIA: If you kill me now, no one will ever know.
(Silence. He goes to her.)
DAVID: Stop, Lucia.
LUCIA: Go, ahead, ring my neck. Please.
DAVID: Don't get involved. Don't involve yourself emotionally. The Red Cross is neutral.
LUCIA: You mean useless, the Red Cross.
DAVID: There's nothing else.
LUCIA: Mr. Al-Janabi is innocent.
DAVID: You're the humanitarian force. You are allowed to tell Mr. Al-Janabi's family that he is alive and in custody.
LUCIA: Kill me now.
(GEOFF appears.)
DAVID: I'm not a murderer, Lucia.
LUCIA: Not of Americans, no.
DAVID: To whom else do I owe my allegiance?
LUCIA: Those innocent men, innocent women, inside those cells.

DAVID: I'm the one who let you slip away. That part of the prison is strictly off-limits to the Red Cross, or was, until today. You can make a report. We come back to the hotel and get drunk. We have sex.

LUCIA: That's it?

(LUCIA gets out of bed. She takes a step toward GEOFF.)

DAVID: Do not become a whistle blower, Lucia. Do your job or quit. Either way, shut up. Al-Janabi is innocent. We suppose. You make your report to the Red Cross and you never again think of him. None of us is clean. So what? We do what we've been called upon to do. We're the sacrificial lambs. These are the times in which we live. I'm telling you, you drink and you forget if you don't want to destroy yourself.

(She turns away from GEOFF.)

LUCIA: No, no, no. It's there when I close my eyes. Bent backs, blank looks. Go to war and forget; do your work and shut up. There are women inside Abu Ghraib begging to be killed, just like me; only in their case because they were raped, not because they were a doctor, although, they might have been doctors; there were women doctors. Iraq had the best medical system in the Middle East. They were teachers, lawyers; they had lives. They drove cars. They've replaced Geoff in my head. I no longer hear his voice. I've lost him for good.

(GEOFF disappears.)

Scene X

(HANDEL and ABDUL, dressed only in underpants, sits at the desk with the laptop.)

HANDEL: Our daily discourse for my stratospheric blogoblast concerns eternal life. The promise made to each by our god of choice. Such is the weighty topic of my universal news feed hourly on Fox, my blog, mandatory now for all, bleeped straight into all heads. *(He puts a pair of women's underpants on ABDUL's head)* Write, lout.

ABDUL: I cannot see.

HANDEL: See. See! Commit to memory. I speak about eternal life. The promise made to each by our god of choice.

ABDUL: One man, afraid, I fear, of death…

HANDEL: Fear, fear of what? Strike that. I do not speak of fear. I fear not.

ABDUL: I think of fear. I know not why.

HANDEL:	Not I. I speak of eternal life. You dare throw fear into my face. Why entertain your mealy thoughts. Why tolerate you at all.
ABDUL:	Easy, sire. Let me go.
HANDEL:	Go? Go where? Where is a place for one like you? Look how you are dressed.
ABDUL:	Give me back my clothes.
HANDEL:	Off topic, now. I understand the tactic you impose, distraction. Deadly decidedly unmanly. What use are you?
ABDUL:	To me?
HANDEL:	To me, fool, me, what use are you to me?
ABDUL:	I've never fully understood.
HANDEL:	How well you've learned to speak. Distract me. Tell me something to take my mind away.
ABDUL:	The vizier of the sultan,
HANDEL:	I am beset by morbid thoughts today.
ABDUL:	… besotted with love for his lovely Chechen…
HANDEL:	Besieged by mortality, I feel.
ABDUL:	… led her and the tall, proud Nubian across the green and golden tiles.
HANDEL:	Tell me, Abdul, what's my drift? Where Handel wanders in his head? *(Pause, then)* You know me, don't you, Abdul. Love me. You forgive. Forgiveness, lout, is blessed. Those who suffer and forgive, they show us grace on earth. Bring Tess. *(ABDUL shuffles off.)* I am a lonely man, a man alone; for all that I have done and have. I sit in a chair alone and stare at death. *(ABDUL pushes a small, rough wooden box which is on wheels, through the iron mesh, TESS is visible, folded in cramped position to fit.)*
ABDUL:	The most beautiful slave girl of all, the one the Sultan's vizier knew he had to buy and then set free and hold and adore forevermore …
HANDEL:	Louder, cur. Louder, say I. My hearing dims with age. I want to, wish to know what the hopeless, helpless say. *(ABDUL speaks to TESS in the box.)*
ABDUL:	Just at that moment, came a djin, bearing a pot filled with sparkling gems.
HANDEL:	Hear. I want to hear.
ABDUL:	You cannot hear what the wretched think.
HANDEL:	I will.
ABDUL:	Your head cannot hear the words inside our heads.
HANDEL:	I can and do. I put them there.

ABDUL:	You want the ways I speak inside my cell? The stories I tell to get me through the night. While the loud music blares and the white lights. While my heart breaks.
HANDEL:	I've broken you like a bird whose back I snap against my thighs. You cannot fly. You're will-less, wordless but for I.
ABDUL:	Yes, sire.
HANDEL:	Take her back. I cannot look at her like this. Poor Tess. How did this come to pass? But a ruination and a wreck. She might have been; she might have had, Armani, Lacoste, Channel, she might have done, she did do once... all... I... said... the rest... the rest ... is... ought... naught... I... I... I...
	(HANDEL's *head rolls on his neck. He has had a stroke.*)
ABDUL:	He's done.
TESS:	He's dead?
	(ABDUL *takes his pulse.*)
ABDUL:	Not yet.
TESS:	I'll put my chains around his neck and pull.
ABDUL:	We take the keys. I let you go. We leave.
TESS:	The keys are underneath his balls.
ABDUL:	His wife must do. Please.
TESS:	My hands are tied. Cut them off, his balls. Let him bleed to death from there.
ABDUL:	Please. I will retch. Let me reach.
	(ABDUL *goes to* HANDEL's *chair and searches between his legs for the keys.*)
	Nothing here.
TESS:	Inside his pants. You must unbutton his trousers, between his testicles you will find them. Old sot.
ABDUL:	(*As if praying*) In rivers of blood we woke to ourselves. In dark holes where we were lost we groped. In sorrows we stood breathing pain, exhaling hurt, breathing again. In a nightmare of what had been done, we had become, we stumbled and fell and stumbled once more on our way. And yet we held onto, each one remembered, the warmth of the beloved. Bestow on me grace.
TESS:	Abdul, the keys to the chains, to the door, to our lives are right there tucked between his balls. You go inside his pants. Then, you recite.
	(ABDUL *turns away from her.*)
	Look, they are hairy old, wrinkled, wizened things, like the faces of old monkeys. Right between them, he has put the keys. They won't even be cold to the touch.

ABDUL:	Please, Madame.
TESS:	Tess.
ABDUL:	Tess, Tess. My slave girl. My love.
TESS:	Abdul, you must. I don't care about your religion. Your sense of decorum. It's rot.
ABDUL:	Please, don't…
TESS:	Get the keys. Get us out. Then, speak to me of love. *(Nothing happens.)* *(HANDEL wakes. He looks at ABDUL.)*
HANDEL:	What is this? What is it that I see, I saw upon your head? Give. I have had a rare vision and a dream. To tell. But first, to show, to do. To me that item, delicate, most personal; they belonged to my dear wife Tess. They bear her scent. I must… *(HANDEL lurches from his chair. He grabs the women's underwear from ABDUL's head and places them on his own.)* Now, Handel, Be. Yes, Be, no longer not. Finally at last. The sight of one's fellow man, person, I amend, is, is, is. I lack the words to say what my dream was. I shall write a song and sing. I see you, Abdul, best to use a name. I see you, Abdul and I, Handel, am. I, Handel, and you, Abdul, are. Only now I see. I will yet be. I live. At long last, Handel is… *(HANDEL falls back into his chair and dies. ABDUL approaches and lays his head against HANDEL's chest. He shakes his head.)*
ABDUL:	He's gone.
TESS:	Not a moment too soon. You notice he didn't apologize to me.
ABDUL:	There is no God but God.
TESS:	Now, for god's sake, Abdul, please, get the keys. *(They do not move. Pause. Then, HANDEL, dead, stands. His keys clatter to the ground, like bells. The dead HANDEL walks toward GEOFF, who appears. ABDUL picks up the keys, opens the box. He helps TESS out. The bells continue as the two leave.)* *(The afterlife. GEOFF appears on the table, gesturing, and a ladder flies down from the sky.)*
GEOFF:	Mr. Handel, this way out.
HANDEL:	My boy, Geoff, my son. *(HANDEL goes toward the ladder.)* How odd the fear of death now seems.
GEOFF:	All is benign; all is. *(They laugh. Bells)*
HANDEL:	How good to merge with you, my son.

(HANDEL *reaches for the ladder, but it rises without him, as he staggers toward hell.* GEOFF *disappears.*)

(LUCIA *enters in a harsh white spot light. She is testifying before a Congressional committee called to investigate the leaking of the Red Cross report.*)

LUCIA: Yes. After I left the private sector, my late father's company, Deepwater, I joined the Red Cross. I thought that there... yes ... at the ICRC I could be of use. But it was while working for the ICRC that I learned even more. There are black sites within prisons where torture... Yes, I understand. The ICRC works in accordance to strict confidentiality rules with governments. Yes, I released to the press the confidential Red Cross report detailing the systematic and rampant torture and/or cruel and inhumane treatment of innocent prisoners in Abu Ghraib. Yes, I knew that I was contravening the agreement between the ICRC and the participating government, the United States. I released these documents to the press because it was my patriotic duty to do so. Yes, patriotic, I said. I am supposed to be a doctor. I was supposed to be helping people, not... But more than that: I believe we are a nation that stands for something. That our country is founded upon laws. I felt the truth matters – that the truth does matter. What we did... what I did... what our government has done, is doing, was wrong, is wrong, that we are committing atrocities. Yes, that is my word. Yes, my fiancé was killed in the World Trade Center attack. No, I do not believe that war and torture in any way have made us safer. Yes, some of the prisoners may have been guilty of plotting or even of carrying out attacks against our soldiers who, after all, are occupying their country. But the great majority of prisoners I encountered are completely innocent of any wrongdoing whatsoever. And whether innocent or guilty, many of the prisoners would confess to anything just to make the pain stop. Wouldn't you? No, I knew no other course of action to take. I did what I had to do.

END

What She Makes Us See

Rebecca Gordon

[Torture.] The word itself has something repulsive and dangerous about it [...]. Both social conventions and the restrictions imposed on language by good manners make it difficult to speak of things as they really are. Torture is dirty and the language or writing used to describe it should also be dirty. If not, the screaming and the pain will always be missing [...].

Comisión Nacional contra la Tortura (Chile) and Yáñez 1999: 8 [author's translation]

Once a semester I talk to my Ethics students about torture. On that day I take advantage of the professor's prerogative to do something unusual for my fairly democratic classroom: I give a lecture. It is important, I think, that if we are going to discuss the ethics of torture, students know a little bit about the subject. Part of knowing is seeing, so on that day I do something else that breaks with my usual pedagogical style. I use PowerPoint. Students are asked to look at the photographs that soldiers took of their victims at Abu Ghraib prison in Iraq.

Part of knowing is seeing. There is something about our visual sense, the way it helps us locate things in time and space, assigning them prominence and significance and locking them in memory, or consigning them to oblivion. Even blind English speakers use the expression 'I see,' to mean 'I understand.' When we look, we assign values. We decide what to pay attention to, and what to ignore. Looking and seeing are, in this sense, moral choices we make every day.

When you work in a classroom you never entirely know who is there with you. You probably don't know who's been beaten or raped; who've watched their mother commit suicide; whose father was tortured in Lebanon during the civil war there. If there are veterans in your class, you probably don't know what they have seen and done in Iraq or Afghanistan. You don't know what seeing pictures of pain and blood will do to any of these people. If choosing where to look has moral valence, then so does using one's power to direct other people's visual attention in a particular direction. Teachers know this. So do playwrights.

Before I show the photos, I tell students they're welcome to close their eyes, or even to leave the room, if they need to. Usually nobody does. I also tell them this: 'You may be surprised by the way you react when you see these pictures. Some people get chills. Some feel sick to their stomachs. Some people laugh, perhaps because they're nervous. Some people even get turned on. You are not responsible for how your body reacts. What you are responsible for is how you act once you know what torture really is. Once you know that the United States has been, and continues to be, involved in torture.'

The odd thing about the Abu Ghraib pictures is that in most of them, you can't really see the pain. The most famous of them, the one that has passed into iconic status, depicts a hooded man draped in some kind of poncho. His arms are outstretched, and he's standing on a narrow wooden box set on a concrete floor. Wires attached to his hands and running up under the poncho extend beyond the frame of the photo. But the picture doesn't tell the whole story. You only know this is torture when you learn what the man has been told – that the floor is covered with water and that if he falls, he will be electrocuted. This is a mock execution. It is expressly forbidden in the Geneva Conventions, and falls under the general definition of torture as 'severe pain or suffering, whether physical or mental,' outlawed under the UN Convention Against Torture and Other Cruel, Inhuman, or Degrading Treatment. The United States has signed and ratified both these conventions.

Another Abu Ghraib picture shows a skinny man standing with his back against a bunk bed. His arms are spread wide and cuffed to the wire mattress frame behind him. It doesn't look particularly painful. We can't tell how he feels about it, however, because his head is covered by a pair of women's underpants. We don't know what his face reflects.

Pictures like these require a verbal gloss to make their meaning plain. 'Stress positions,' I say, 'don't sound terribly painful. This one looks like a nice stretch, doesn't it? What's so difficult about standing still for a few hours?'. Donald Rumsfeld signed off on a memo permitting a set of frankly illegal 'interrogation techniques' at the US detention center in Guantánamo. In his own handwriting, he famously annotated the memo this way: 'I stand for 8–10 hours a day. Why is standing limited to 4 hours?'

But here's the difference: Donald Rumsfeld can move when he wants to. You can move when you want to. You're all sitting comfortably in your chairs now. And you'll probably still be comfortable 45 minutes from now. That's because you're actually moving all the time. As one muscle, ligament, or tendon gets fatigued, without even noticing, you unconsciously shift your weight and ease that discomfort. But when you can't do that, when you have to remain immobile, the pain quickly becomes excruciating. As the philosopher Elaine Scarry says, 'Standing rigidly for eleven hours can produce as violent muscle and spine pain as can injury from elaborate equipment and apparatus' (1985: 45). And it doesn't leave a mark.

Not leaving a mark matters, because it lends credence to the modern torturer's strategic insistence that – whatever it is he's doing – it isn't torture. The detention center run by the Joint Special Operations Command in Iraq took this approach, as demonstrated by the sardonic slogan posted around the place: 'No blood, no foul.' The JSOC center is less famous than Abu Ghraib, although it's likely that much worse abuses took place there. No photos have leaked into public view. Known by the acronym Camp NAMA (for Nasty-Assed Military Area), its activities were so secret that even General Geoffrey Miller, who was in charge of all the US-run prisons in Iraq, needed special permission to enter. Such 'rhetoric of denial,' as Talal Assad has called it, is primarily a feature of contemporary liberal states. Most pre-modern nations were unashamed of employing torture as an essential method of determining the truth of any human situation (Assad 2003: 105).

On that day each semester when I talk to my students about torture, I use my authority to make them do something most people in this country can choose not to do – to look (in both a literal and a metaphorical way) at the price we've been told we must pay, the sacrifice we've heard we must make, to guarantee our security. This is exactly what Karen Malpede uses the playwright's authority to do in *Another Life*, her deft exploration of life after the attacks of September 11, 2001. Once we've bought our tickets and taken our seats, we have to encounter what we've paid to see.

In Handel, the character who dominates the stage and the action, we see embodied both the arrogance of violent physical and economic power, and, curdling underneath it, the fears and resentments of a child. Handel's childishness reminds me of my own favorite metaphor for my country's military stance – we're like an angry giant two-year-old, stomping around the world waving missiles and smashing entire nations with our outsized feet. Reading *Another Life* I could not help but be reminded time and again of the 'Handel' who's currently stomping around the stage that is the US Presidency: Donald J. Trump. It's all there: the self-involvement, the taste for lurid luxuries, the rapacious sexuality, the gleeful eagerness to bring back waterboarding 'and a whole lot worse.'

But Handel is not the only person *Another Life* indicts. Malpede doesn't let ordinary citizens off the hook either. We aren't permitted to blame Handel for torture, for the CIA black sites, for Abu Ghraib. In the former FBI agent David Abbas and Handel's adopted daughter Lucia, a doctor, we watch the country's slide into accepting torture as the necessary and inevitable response to terrorist attacks. David ends up as a private contractor at a CIA dark site, accompanied by his lover Lucia, whose ostensible job is to keep the 'interrogators' from killing their captives.

In a pivotal moment, Lucia hears what is going on in the locked room behind her. She hears, but she doesn't yet see. 'Want to look?' asks David.

'No,' says Lucia, 'I do not.'

A few lines later, we're told that the detainee has fainted. It's Lucia's job to 'monitor' his health, so David cajoles her to enter the cell. 'You don't want to look,' he warns her. 'Just go in. Check his vitals. Tell them if it's safe to continue.' But of course there's no way to 'check his vitals' without looking. David's on the phone to Washington, updating his employers on the interrogation's progress. After a few exchanges, he offers to turn off the speaker so they can't hear what's going on inside the cell. Lucia is worried, though. The detainee is turning blue from hypothermia.

'Look,' says David, 'I'm talking to Washington on the phone; we've got clearance from the chief, no stopping now.'

'Washington can't see. I can.' Exactly. Lucia can see.

The man who's being tortured in the play is a real human being. His name is Zayn al-Abidin Muhammad Husayn, but he is better known by his Arabic nickname, Abu Zubaydah. He had the dubious luck to be the subject of a number of CIA 'firsts': the first post-9/11 prisoner to be waterboarded; the first to be experimented on by the psychologists James Mitchell and Bruce Jessen who were working as CIA contractors; one of the first of the Agency's 'ghost prisoners'(detainees hidden from the entire world, including from the International Committee of the Red Cross); and one of the first prisoners to be cited in a memo written by Justice department employee Jay Bybee for the Bush administration covering what the CIA could 'legally' do to a detainee, supposedly without violating US federal laws against torture.

Abu Zubaydah became Exhibit A to justify the whole torture program – the proof that, sad as it might be, our security demanded such extreme measures. The allegations against the man were serious indeed.

*Donald Rumsfeld said he was 'if not the number two, very close to the number two person.'

*The Central Intelligence Agency informed Assistant Attorney General Jay Bybee that he had 'served as Usama [sic] Bin Laden's senior lieutenant. In that capacity, he has managed a network of training camps […] He also acted as Al-Qaeda's coordinator of external contacts and foreign communications' (Central Intelligence Agency cited in Gordon 2016).

*CIA Director Michael Hayden would tell the press in 2008 that 25 percent of all the information his agency had gathered about al-Qaeda from human sources 'originated' with one other detainee and him.

*George W. Bush claimed that 'he had run a terrorist camp in Afghanistan where some of the 9/11 hijackers trained' and that 'he helped smuggle al-Qaeda leaders out of Afghanistan' so they would not be captured by US military forces (cited in Gordon 2016).

None of it was true. In 2010, the Justice department quietly withdrew all the claims they'd made against Abu Zubaydah. In a brief filed by the Obama administration opposing Abu Zubaydah's habeas corpus petition, government lawyers claimed that the Bush administration had never 'contended that [Abu Zubaydah] had any personal involvement in planning or executing either the 1998 embassy bombings in Nairobi, Kenya, and Dar-es-Salaam, Tanzania, or the attacks of September 11, 2001,' although they had claimed both these things (cited in Gordon 2016). They added that 'the Government also has not contended in this proceeding that at the time of his capture, [Abu Zubaydah] had knowledge of any specific impending terrorist operations' – an especially curious claim since the prevention of such future attacks was how the CIA justified its torture of Abu Zubaydah in the first place. Far from believing, the brief continued, that he was 'if not the number two, very close to the number two person in' Al-Qaeda, as Secretary of Defense Donald Rumsfeld had once claimed, 'the Government has not contended in this proceeding that [Abu Zubaydah] was a member of al-Qaida or otherwise formally identified with al-Qaida.'

And what did they want from Abu Zubaydah? In the play, he's made to talk vaguely about future attacks on US shopping malls. But what they really wanted was for him to say that there was a connection between Al Qaeda and Saddam Hussein, to justify the US invasion of Iraq. Writing in *Vanity Fair*, journalist David Rose describes his conversation with an anonymous Pentagon analyst, who said:

> There was a lot of stuff about the nuts and bolts of al-Qaeda's supposed relationship with the Iraqi Intelligence Service. The intelligence community was lapping this up, and so was the administration, obviously. Abu Zubaydah was saying Iraq and al-Qaeda had an operational relationship. It was everything the administration hoped it would be.
>
> (2008)

None of it was true, but Abu Zubaydah's 'testimony' became key support for the greatest crime of the George W. Bush administration, the illegal, unprovoked invasion of Iraq – a crime that directly and indirectly led to hundreds of thousands of deaths, millions of people made refugees and the almost-complete destruction of a modern industrialized state.

Today Abu Zubaydah lives in solitary confinement at Guantánamo. According to the Senate Intelligence Committee report, CIA headquarters assured those who were interrogating him that he would 'never be placed in a situation where he has any significant contact with others and/or has the opportunity to be released.' In fact, 'all major players are in concurrence,' stated the agency, that he 'should remain incommunicado for the remainder of his life' (Senate Select Committee on Intelligence 2015).

When Abu Zubaydah finally starts 'talking' in *Another Life*, David says he's revealing 'stuff that can save innocent lives.' And, despite everything we know – if we want to look – we continue to believe this, because we want to believe that something can save our innocent lives. It's as if we've been offered a promise of immortality. 'You let us do whatever we have to do over here "on the dark side," whatever we have to do once, as National Security chief Cofer Black told Congress, "after 9/11, the gloves come off," let us do it all, and in return we promise that we will always keep you secure.'

Of course it's a false bargain. There is no such thing as complete security. All the torture in the world can't stop an angry man from buying a gun and shooting up a gay dance club in Orlando, Florida. It won't stop a disaffected pair of brothers from blowing up the finish of the Boston Marathon. The truth that we don't want to look at, the truth that Malpede insists we see, is that every one of us is going to die. The only real question is about how we spend the meantime. Are we willing to live with our eyes open?

Author's note: Some portions of this essay appeared in an article for TomDispatch.com called 'Tomgram: Rebecca Gordon, exhibit one in any future American war crimes trial' – 'The Al-Qaeda leader who wasn't', 24 April, http://www.tomdispatch.com/blog/176132/tomgram%3A_rebecca_gordon,_exhibit_one_in_any_future_american_war_crimes_trial.

References

Assad, Talal (2003), *Formations of the Secular: Christianity, Islam, Modernity,* Stanford: Stanford University Press.

Comisión Nacional contra la Tortura (Chile) and Yáñez, Pedro C. (1999), *Memoria, 1983–1990: Una Parte De La Historia De Chile,* Santiago?: La Comisión.

Gordon, R. (2016), 'Tomgram: Rebecca Gordon, exhibit one in any future American war crimes trial', TomDispatch.com, 24 April, http://www.tomdispatch.com/blog/176132/tomgram%3A_rebecca_gordon,_exhibit_one_in_any_future_american_war_crimes_trial.

Rose, David (2008), 'Tortured Reasoning', *Vanity Fair,* December 16.

Scarry, Elaine (1985), *The Body in Pain: The Making and Unmaking of the World,* New York: Oxford University Press.

Senate Select Committee on Intelligence (2015), *The Senate Intelligence Committee Report on Torture, Committee Study of the Central Intelligence Agency's Detention and Interrogation Program,* Brooklyn: Melville House.

Part IV

Extreme Whether

For Carrie Sophia, Greg and Abel; for the next seven generations.

Note on the text: *In my play* Extreme Whether *(W-H-E-T-H-E-R) I am, again, using current research, not only about the science of global warming and climate change that, in and of itself, is enough to stand one's hair on end, but about the ways in which that science has been censored and is being willfully misunderstood by the so-called climate change deniers, those with financial ties to the coal, oil and natural gas industries. This well-funded campaign against scientific truth may well prove the most consequential blockade of human knowledge in human history.*

The play is based on the life and work of American scientists, most particularly James Hansen, Michael Mann and Jennifer Francis, plus the research of biologist Tyrone Hayes into the effects on amphibians of the herbicide atrazine; these scientists have been attacked and vilified for their groundbreaking research.

I came to view climate scientists as visionaries and altruists, flawed and flummoxed like all such people who are suddenly called by forces outside themselves to excel themselves, fighting not just their own reluctance to become publically involved, and their own ill-adaption to public and activist lives, but, ultimately, fighting for the truth in the face of falsehood, not just because truth matters in some abstract or even in moral terms, but because the fate of the Earth itself, and all who live here, is ever more obviously at stake. I set the play as a family drama because we are an American family; what happens to the least of us, a frog in this case, is likely to happen to us all.

Extreme Whether, *whose title is a pun that is also a dare, is built on pairs and opposites. The scientists, John and Rebecca, struggle with the implications of their knowledge, one supports and encourages the other when the other loses strength or hope; the publicist and lobbyist, Jeanne and Frank, plot and plan their misinformation campaign and the exploitation of the family land; and the wise old environmentalist Uncle and young, motherless, intersex, Annie, bond across generations and through a shared commitment to protect Earth and Earth's creatures.*

Throughout the play I am also juxtaposing the styles of what might be called psychological and magical realism.

In Extreme Whether *I want people to re-experience those moments of absolute wonder, utter peace and sudden insight we have all experienced alone in the natural world. Through the oracular voices of Uncle and Annie and the juxtaposition of lyric and realist stylistic modes, I try to create a poetry of the theater that frees the imagination and allows us quite literally to come to our senses.*

KM, Brooklyn, 2013

Extreme Whether, staged readings: Theater for the New City, The Cherry Lane Theater, 2013; the play premiered in 2014, Theater for the New City, directed by Karen Malpede. Lights: Tony Giovannetti. Costumes: Carisa Kelly and Sally Ann Parsons. Video projections: Luba Lukova. Music: Arthur Rosen. Set: Michaelangelo De Serio. Cast: George Bartenieff played Uncle; Di Zhu played Rebecca; Kathleen Purcell played Annie; Jeff McCarthy, John Bjornson; Ellen Fiske, Jeanne; Alex Tavis, Frank. The play was given three staged readings as part of ARTCOP21, Paris, 2015, during the COP21 Climate Conference at the Fondation des Etats Unis and Bilingual Acting Workshop, Paris. Directed by Karen Malpede and Nathalie Sandoz. Lights: Tony Giovannetti. Music: Arthur Rosen. Cast: Claude Aufaure and May Royer, French-speaking Uncle and Annie; George Bartenieff and Kathleen Purcell, English-speaking Uncle and Annie; Benjamin Knobil, John Bjornson; Nathalie Sandoz, Rebecca; Dominique Hollier, Jeanne; Julien Muller, Frank.

Characters

Uncle, elderly steward of the land

Annie, in her early teens, John's daughter, she has Asperger's syndrome, some say

Rebecca, thirties, a climatologist specializing in Arctic ice, later, John's lover

John, 60, an esteemed climate scientist, works for NASA

Jeanne, 60, John's twin sister, a public relations specialist

Frank, forties, Jeanne's husband, a lobbyist

Setting

Prologue and Act I are set in the summer of 2004; Act II takes place in the summer of 2012. The Epilogue is set in the near future. Yet, it's as if no time has passed between the two acts.

A tract of wilderness land, somewhere on the northeast coast, that has been in the Bjornson family for several generations and which is now held in trust by the twin heirs John and Jeanne. On this land there is a simple, rustic house, surrounded by meadows and trees and a hill from which you can see the sea. The house should have a transparent quality about it as it is necessary to move fluidly from inside to outdoor scenes.

Prologue

(A hill top, below is a pine forest, to the west a waterfall and a pond, to the east, a view all the way to the sea. UNCLE, *in a wheel chair, pushed from behind, bursts into the space.)*

UNCLE: *(To someone off-stage)* Every story is a miracle.
                                    (A young girl enters, dancing around.)

ANNIE:	Suspend disbelief. Yes, yes, yes.
	(Panting from the effort of having rolled UNCLE *in his wheel chair up the hill,* REBECCA, *throws herself on the ground.)*
REBECCA:	It's hardly a hill.
ANNIE:	It's the top of the world.
	*(*UNCLE *spins himself around in his chair.)*
UNCLE:	Forests, the sky, waterfall, meadows down to the shore. Fish jumping, clouds dipping; this is the center of creation.
	*(*REBECCA *still on her back.)*
REBECCA:	*(She sits up)* A mile or more, pushing you straight up; Uncle, you might have told me.
UNCLE:	Would you have come if I'd warned you? If we saw what is to be asked, we would be frozen in place.
	*(*JOHN *and* JEANNE *exit from the house, and walk across the road toward the path up the hill.)*
JEANNE:	The dear, old house is shabby, John; it should really be torn down, rebuilt.
JOHN:	I like the house.
JEANNE:	With your considerable reputation, surely you should live…
JOHN:	I've decided to take a salary cut.
JEANNE:	Dear me. I had no idea things had gone that far.
JOHN:	What things?
JEANNE:	Never mind. I have just the antidote.
JOHN:	I've not been poisoned, yet. *(They exit.)*
	(On the hill.)
REBECCA:	Where is Annie?
UNCLE:	This is where you will bury me.
REBECCA:	Don't say such things.
UNCLE:	I'll be dead weight. You'll complain lugging me up.
REBECCA:	Uncle, stop. We could not live here without you. You do know that.
UNCLE:	I finished the work. The last solar panel firmly in place, I slipped.
	*(*ANNIE *returns.)*
ANNIE:	The pond is there, Uncle, just as we left it. And *(climbs into his lap, whispers).*
UNCLE:	You don't say.
ANNIE:	I'm sure that it's him. He was just a tadpole last year, but I do think he recognized me.
UNCLE:	I'm certain he did.
REBECCA:	*(She smiles)* The air is so clear.
	*(*JEANNE *and* JOHN *arrive on the hill top.)*

JEANNE:	Suddenly, I am positioned to be able to look out for you. I would like to. I'm one whole minute older, don't forget. Read this paper with an open mind. *(She hands him a paper; he glances at it.)*
JOHN:	'True Science'? Is there another kind? *(He folds it and puts in his pocket.)*
JEANNE:	*(She laughs)* Not that I know. It's so good to be home. I've always thought this the most beautiful place in all the world.
ANNIE:	Papa, what are you doing here?
JEANNE:	(To ANNIE) Say hello to your Auntie Jeanne.
JOHN:	We used to nearly live up here in the summer as children.
JEANNE:	Run downhill to the ocean to swim.
JOHN:	Pick mushrooms and berries in the woods.
JEANNE:	Bathe in the waterfall, torture frogs in the pond.
ANNIE:	No!
JOHN:	She exaggerates.
ANNIE:	How did you know about the pond? It's secret. Uncle said no one but us. *(She starts to cry.)*
JOHN:	When we were children, Uncle told us the very same thing. The pond's secret for everyone but Uncle's small friends.
ANNIE:	Uncle, how dare you be so entirely duplicitous!
UNCLE:	These two ensnared me once in their spell, just as you do, now; they were nearly, but not quite, as smart and they cajoled the truth of the secret pond from my mouth. I know it's impossible to imagine when you look at them, now, beginning to go to ground.
JEANNE:	Uncle, dear, dear Uncle. How terrible to see you like this.
UNCLE:	Soon I shall loft. I've utter freedom to look forward to.
JEANNE:	Right here I introduced John to Beth. You were smitten, John.
REBECCA:	How good to meet you, at last.
JEANNE:	This must be Rebecca West. *(They shake hands.)* Thank you, my dear, I'm sure you've been a great help with Annie, ever since…
REBECCA:	I do hope so.
JOHN:	Rebecca has her own work, as well.
JEANNE:	Father, first, then poor, dear Beth, gone already five years. All of a sudden, my Frank. No one was at my side. I received a phone call. He had a huge shark on his line. It jerked free, line, pole and all, slapping the waves. Massive heart attack. I stared straight at the abyss. My own heart stopped.
UNCLE:	They say the fish let out a huge yell…
ANNIE:	Yippee, I'm saved.
JEANNE:	It is a great gift to love as Frank and I do.
UNCLE:	… the day the oceans were born.

JEANNE:	I felt my own heart was able to live.
UNCLE:	Fish can be single or plural, multiple, manifold.
JEANNE:	Uncle is the same. Speaking in riddles. Are you mad or sane, dear Uncle. 'I could not steward this land without Uncle,' father always said. And here you are, poor dear, crippled. But the land is as beautiful as the day it was made. *(To* ANNIE*)* Come; give your auntie a hug.
ANNIE:	Uggh. *(*ANNIE *runs off.)*
REBECCA:	You mustn't mind her.
JEANNE:	She's always been a bit strange.
JOHN:	Annie barely knows who you are.
JEANNE:	Wasn't there talk of autism?
JOHN:	Asperger's. We ruled it out.
JEANNE:	Whatever is the difference?
REBECCA:	Asperger's children are usually brilliant.
JEANNE:	But you ruled it out.
JOHN:	All, but the brilliant part.
JEANNE:	Well, but of course, she is your daughter, isn't she John, and poor, dear Beth actually had quite a fine brain.
JOHN:	Why do you always use those words?
JEANNE:	What words?
JOHN:	'Poor, dear' when you speak about my late wife?
JEANNE:	Do I?
JOHN:	Beth had a vibrant inner life.
JEANNE:	She worshipped you.
JOHN:	I loved her.
JEANNE:	She looked upon you as her savior.
JOHN:	I failed in that regard.
JEANNE:	We were so very lucky, Frank and I. The heart can be fixed. They know ever so much about the heart. There he was, in intensive care, still ruddy from the sun, tubes everywhere, looking so handsome and strong. Where is Beth, by the way? *(Silence, as if they don't understand, then.)*
UNCLE:	There is no death without life.
JOHN:	Of course.
UNCLE:	No eternity without memory.
REBECCA:	That's exactly what I've always thought.
JEANNE:	I meant where is Beth buried? *(*ANNIE *comes in, holding something in her hands. Her face is streaked with red, like war paint. She dances in a circle around them.)*

ANNIE:	The earth is our Mother/we must take care of her. Every step we walk/every breath we take.
JEANNE:	Whatever is on her face?
JOHN:	It's the iron in the soil. We used to paint ourselves like Indians, too. What have you got there, Annie?
ANNIE:	Nothing.
JOHN:	Well, kiss it and put it back.
ANNIE:	I'm going home.
JOHN:	Why don't you take Aunt Jeanne down?
ANNIE:	No way. *(ANNIE runs downhill.)*
REBECCA:	Be careful, Annie.
JOHN:	She's as sure-footed as a goat.
JEANNE:	'Kiss it,' really John, what if it's a toad.
JOHN:	We'll have a new prince in the woods.
REBECCA:	She's not going to put it back.
JOHN:	A prince in her bed.
REBECCA:	Devoutly to be hoped, but not just yet.
JEANNE:	How happy we all used to be. *(Pause)* There! For just an instant, I could hear our laughter. This part of the hill will never be touched. I can promise us that.
JOHN:	The entire estate is a land trust. Come, it's getting dark. We best go back.
JEANNE:	How sad I feel all of sudden. As if our whole lives had slipped past and I only now noticed.
REBECCA:	The life you had here is not gone. We work very hard. We live as simply as we can.
JOHN:	Our life has a natural rhythm that suits.
JEANNE:	How nice that Rebecca is willing to stay on.
	(Silence)
REBECCA:	We have made a sort of a family.
JOHN:	We're colleagues. Rebecca is in ice.
JEANNE:	How quaint. A beautiful ice lady lives in your house.
REBECCA:	Ice melt. Uncle has fallen asleep. You must help me, John, with the way down.
UNCLE:	*(Wakes)* One big push; gravity will do the rest.
REBECCA:	Don't be silly, Uncle. You'd hit a rock, be pitched out on your face.
UNCLE:	I was dreaming of death. Such bliss.
JEANNE:	Surely, there is life after death. We meet again.
JOHN:	Are there breaks on this thing?
UNCLE:	Brakes? It's a racing chair.
JEANNE:	And you, John, when Beth died, what did you think?

JOHN:	Think?
JEANNE:	You are a scientist, after all.
JOHN:	I came up here. Annie, Uncle and I. I suppose I thought, as you do, this is the most beautiful spot in the entire world. Help me, Rebecca.
REBECCA:	Look, there's a full moon.
	(They all look up. Silence)
JEANNE:	And what does Beth think, looking down on all of us?
JOHN:	Beth was not a thinker, Jeanne; I'd be surprised if she started now. *(They each grab one handle of the chair. JEANNE walks behind. They go off.)*
UNCLE:	Don't bother to hang on. Let 'er rip.
REBECCA:	Nonsense, Uncle.
UNCLE:	Atomized, I tell you, that's what it's like. Orgasmic union with all that is.
	(Musical interlude)

Act I

(The house: a rustic main room in good taste. Nature is all around; almost as if the wooden walls of the house are part of the natural world. On stage left, ANNIE begins to construct the frog pond. In the house, stage right, JOHN sits in the large chair, reading REBECCA's lecture. REBECCA is in the kitchen finishing the dishes.)

REBECCA:	It was cornstarch.
JOHN:	What if you had a weak heart?
REBECCA:	*(Enters, dish towel in hand)* I don't have a weak heart.
JOHN:	*(REBECCA exits)* White powder in a strange envelop.
REBECCA:	*(Enters without dishtowel)* Actually, it was an ordinary, yellow campus mail envelop, smudged with a thousand fingerprints.
JOHN:	It was a threat.
REBECCA:	This is what I get for lecturing about this summer's ice-melt statistics –
JOHN:	What did the police say?
REBECCA:	'Is there anyone who might have it in for you, ma'am?'
JOHN:	What did you tell them?
REBECCA:	How do you tell them?
JOHN:	Someone is attacking you for what you say in the classroom.
REBECCA:	That's what the police don't quite get.
JOHN:	Someone on our faculty. Make them write that down.

REBECCA:	Someone, that's the point. It is time you made your voice heard again. We need you, John.
JOHN:	I promised Beth when we moved here; I would devote myself to pure research, to Annie and her.
REBECCA:	You mustn't let one defeat…
JOHN:	My finest moment, so I thought. The man who first uttered the words 'global warming' to Congress. It was a blistery hot, humid day. CO_2 was at 350 parts per million in 1988. I told them that it was absolutely the uppermost safety limit before we began to see a significant warming affect. But today, in 2004, we are at 370 parts per million and by 2013, we should hit 400, if we do nothing. I wake up in the middle of the night, sweating.
REBECCA:	They should have listened to you.
JOHN:	Well, but, of course.
REBECCA:	Your models were correct. All the significant projections had been made by you, John, then. I was so thrilled in sixth grade when I learned that climate models can actually see into the future; I decided to become a scientist on the spot.
JOHN:	Sixth grade?
REBECCA:	I'm sorry.
JOHN:	I am sorry. There was just one glaring methodological mistake. Beth used to say, 'John, you cannot expect everyone to think as you do.'
REBECCA:	You could expect them to listen to facts.
JOHN:	Quite. I was absolutely convinced everyone would understand my graphs. I picked up my pointer and I started to speak. I saw their eyes glaze. There were yawns. I began piling on facts. They called me an 'alarmist' for all that. You tell responsible men that greenhouse gas emissions will destroy the planet on which they live, but government policy can save us, just in time. They blow their noses. They pick at their ears. *(He goes out into the garden)* I never spoke in public again. We have a sacred duty, Beth said, to make life even in the face of death. Annie was born. She was not 'poor, dear, Beth'; she had a fine, a noble spirit.
REBECCA:	I wish I had known her.
JOHN:	She would have approved your fire. *(He comes back into the house.)* *(Silence)*
REBECCA:	Have you read my cornstarch lecture, John?
JOHN:	What we could not, then, predict was the effect increasing greenhouse gas emissions would have on the Arctic ice sheets that cool the seas.

REBECCA:	That's the thing: the Arctic sea ice is melting at a faster rate than any of us thought. Is this a singular, once in a life-time event, or a trend?
JOHN:	Your lecture is quite clear on that.
REBECCA:	You believe I'm correct?
JOHN:	I'm afraid I believe that you are. Get your notes into publishable form. We need every shred of proof.
REBECCA:	It's good?
JOHN:	Why else would you get white powder in your mail box?
REBECCA:	After all you've gone through, I felt rather honored. I did.
JOHN:	You've proven yourself Rebecca, with this. *(He waves the lecture; she takes it from him, smoothes it out, laughing.)*
REBECCA:	Thank you.
JOHN:	You are vital, Rebecca. Indomitable, I think. Fearless. And I need that, now.
REBECCA:	Then you have what you need.
JOHN:	Recently, I was approached to give a major speech at a Democratic fund-raising event.
REBECCA:	But that's wonderful.
JOHN:	Naturally I had to refuse. I'm a government employee: I cannot afford to be associated with one political party. *(They go out to the porch.)*
REBECCA:	Surely, John, you can find a way.
JOHN:	The National Council on Freedom is completely non-partisan. I have been asked to give their annual lecture, in Washington on October 4.
REBECCA:	And you've said yes?
JOHN:	No.
REBECCA:	John!
JOHN:	I asked for a few days to think it over.
REBECCA:	You will say yes.
JOHN:	I did not know if I dared, not until this very moment. Yes. *(They laugh.)*
JOHN and REBECCA:	*(Together)* Yes.
JOHN:	They've promised me major press coverage. From that podium, I swear to you I shall call attention to greenhouse gas emissions *and* to the way the science is being denigrated by the current administration. *(UNCLE and ANNIE enter stage right with plants for the frog pond; they work on the pond. ANNIE has Sniffley with her in a bowl.)*
REBECCA:	You could affect the outcome of the election.

JOHN:	These people must be voted out and sane energy policy voted in.
REBECCA:	I will work day and night with you.
	(JOHN impulsively kisses her.)
JOHN:	Well, well, excuse me. I'm sorry. *(He walks past her, back into the house.)*
REBECCA:	Don't be.
JOHN:	I was overcome. Congratulations on your research, again.
REBECCA:	Do you normally kiss your colleagues? When they please you, I mean.
JOHN:	I do not normally kiss anyone.
REBECCA:	Perhaps you should try it more often. You are quite good.
	(The screen door slams. UNCLE *listens from his wheel chair outside the house.)*
ANNIE:	It's Sniffley, Papa.
JOHN:	Shut the door, do not let it slam.
ANNIE:	I know, but Papa, look; it is Sniffley. Uncle agrees. He's become a six-legged frog. Poor Sniffley. Something happened to him growing up.
JOHN:	What is he doing here, in the house?
ANNIE:	I've brought him in from the wild. I'm afraid for the life of the pond. Sniffley is now a protected species. Sniffley has been adversely affected by environmental pollutants, Uncle and I believe; therefore, I am creating a frog pond in our backyard, where I can effectively monitor water purity.
JOHN:	Are you telling me this frog came from the pond near the waterfall.
ANNIE:	I am, Papa; it's true.
JOHN:	That the water up there is polluted?
ANNIE:	I shall take samples and let you know. Sniffley remains in my care. Other frogs will find their way to keep him company, once the pond is set up. Uncle is supervising my dig.
REBECCA:	Can I see?
	(ANNIE does not show the frog; she speaks quickly with great seriousness, like her father.)
ANNIE:	Sniffley is a most unusual amphibian. He has six legs of uneven length. Sniffley has been subject to unnatural forces. But, then, I qualify: he is differently abled. With six legs of different lengths, I have measured them and could be exact, but for current purpose suffice to say, Sniffley has trouble hopping and landing straight. This makes him an unusually contemplative amphibian and it means he has over-developed his voice. Sniffley's songs are the

214

best. You will love waking up and going to sleep with Sniffley close to the house.

(ANNIE *leaves; the screen door slams again.*)

REBECCA: (*Laughs*) Yes, you'll be working, and I shall, too, through the nights. Sniffley will be singing to us. John, I am proud of you.

JOHN: Well, now, you must go write-up your ice melt lecture. And I must get to work.

(JEANNE *walks through the room, fiddling with her cell phone.*)

JEANNE: Excuse me. I'm trying to find a connection. 'Hello, darling. Wait till I get...'

(*She slams the door.*)

REBECCA: We really must get that door fixed.

JOHN: Yes, yes, after everything else.

REBECCA: With Uncle indisposed, it's so hard to keep up. The garden is overgrown.

JOHN: We must focus on the real work; the science and getting it out, in simple, clear language. We'll go straight to the people. Then, surely, once people know...

REBECCA: Assuming people are rational.

JOHN: Of course, people are rational. What else have we got but our minds? Why were we put here at all, if not to know, and understand?

(JEANNE *is outside in the dark, under the night sky.*)

JEANNE: Frank, my dear, finally; I can hear your sweet voice. How are you, my love? No, I am to be ignored as usual. He's in the house, storming about with that young woman of his. Yes, dear...

(*Silence.* JEANNE *walks closer to* UNCLE *who is lost in a reverie, he grabs her arm, thinking it is* REBECCA.)

UNCLE: What a magnificent woman!

JEANNE: Uncle!

UNCLE: (*Disappointed*) Jeanne?

JEANNE: I can't talk. I bumped into Uncle in the dark.

UNCLE: I must have been dreaming.

JEANNE: I can't see a thing.

UNCLE: Dark, you call this dark; look up: I wasn't dreaming at all, I was running around in the sky, lost in a riot of stars. A racket of joy in my head. There's Venus. There's Mars. Everyone, outside!

(*Frogs croak in the night; night music of the stars.*)

ANNIE: It's Sniffley; he's found a friend. A new frog has arrived. 'Oh, Sniffley I do not mind if you have six legs; you are profound.' I do intuit what they say.

215

UNCLE:	There's a wilding inside. Rebecca! John!
JEANNE:	Dear Frank, I have to hang up; it's a madhouse.
UNCLE:	A wilding inside that wills to connect to the wilding up there.
	(The door slams.)
ANNIE:	Papa! Rebecca!
JOHN:	Whatever is it?
ANNIE:	It is the heavens on fire.
	(She pulls JOHN *outside. More frog croaks)*
ANNIE:	*(Whispering)* It is Sniffley, papa, and his new friend.
JOHN:	This is the cathedral dome.
UNCLE:	I lack words.
JOHN:	The orb of the world.
JEANNE:	Why, John, you're a poet.
JOHN:	Jeanne, here?
JEANNE:	Here. Take my hand. Let us pretend we are children, again, and the sky is as big as it was then. We used to stand with Father and he'd name each constellation for us; funny, I've forgotten them all and yet there they are the same as ever. I could feel myself aloft, as if dancing in the night sky. I'd get dizzy and fall.
ANNIE:	It's so. If you squint. Squint, papa, squint. See, you fly right up there. I'm twirling in the middle of the stars.
UNCLE:	Tip me out of this chair!
JEANNE:	Goodness, no.
UNCLE:	Lay me down, spine to ground.
ANNIE:	Papa, help.
	(ANNIE and JOHN tip UNCLE out of his chair.)
UNCLE:	Thank you, John, Annie child. Now, all able-bodied ones, the same. Eyes up. Spirits aloft.
	(REBECCA and ANNIE lie down. JOHN follows them, then JEANNE. The stars spin overhead; the sounds of insects below echo the music of the spheres.)
REBECCA:	There's Sirius, the Dog star.
ANNIE:	In Canis Major, of course.
UNCLE:	'The grand processional of all the stars of night.'
REBECCA:	Lyra fading out. Aquila growing bright.
ANNIE:	I'm dancing with the Dolphin Delphinus.
REBECCA:	I'm astride Capricornus, the sea-goat.
JOHN:	The sky will endure.
REBECCA:	As long as we see.
ANNIE:	Heaven's song…

UNCLE:	Will be sung. The unfortunate ones, the lost, who struggled and wept whose voices never were heard on earth, they sing to us in the night.
JEANNE:	What a lovely thought.
UNCLE:	Attend; you, too, shall be blessed by those who sparkle and shine, who cry in the dark.

(Music of the spheres. Sniffley and friend croak.)

JOHN:	*(Jumps to his feet)* By god, I feel full of such power. I'll draft a speech that will be unforgettable.
REBECCA:	Do that, John, yes.

(Black out. Night music shifts to morning music of the birds.)
(Early the next morning; John has been up all night; Rebecca enters, surprised to see him, she pulls her thin robe around her nakedness.)
John, I thought surely you had gone to bed. But, please, can I read your speech. I'll start typing as soon as I've made my coffee.

JOHN:	There's coffee on the stove.
REBECCA:	You've worked all night.
JOHN:	This fax made it impossible to work.
REBECCA:	Let me. *(She takes the fax.)* Do they actually dare to say 'upon consideration of the Press Office?'
JOHN:	My climate change chapter has been dropped completely from the agency's annual report!
REBECCA:	Your report was peer reviewed; set in type. How dare they?
JOHN:	The budget slashing was just the start. It is now nothing but total and complete government censorship of my work.
REBECCA:	John, your speech is that much more important because of this. You'll be speaking outside of NASA as a private citizen. You must come out directly, without hedging, and clearly say that the current administration is censoring its own best scientific minds. Then, you *will influence* the election. Things will go against them.
JOHN:	This threw me so. Science is *not* a matter of opinion, or of political affiliation. I am not some wild speculator who somehow got on the government payroll. My work has been verified by scientists around the world.
REBECCA:	That is exactly how you must start. Come, now, let's go into your study. You will talk; I shall write. We'll edit it later, together.
JOHN:	There's worse, Rebecca, worse! The White House has stricken the words 'to know and protect the home planet' from the agency mission statement; they have actually done that. Evidently, the earth does not matter anymore; it is, now, all about getting to Mars.
REBECCA:	Then that will be the title of your speech. 'To Know and Protect the Home Planet.'

JOHN:	It's censorship, plain and clear.
REBECCA:	The censorship will end once you speak out.
JOHN:	I never imagined things would go this far. That climate science could be seen as dangerous! I'm a mild-mannered man, a reasonable, plodding sort of fellow.
REBECCA:	But now you have a chance, a real chance. You are not going to capitulate. I'll be right by your side. You'll get national press.
JOHN:	If only I can speak clearly, decisively enough…
REBECCA:	Think of it, John, the growth of a national will. The people will shake off the gloom, the war-weariness, the despair of these last years. There will be no more of this rancor. What joy we will see once the people join together in our common work: to save and protect the home planet.
JOHN:	Yes, Rebecca, yes. We can fix this. I must work, work.
	(JEANNE enters.)
JEANNE:	Up early, everyone.
REBECCA:	There's coffee, shall I bring some?
	(REBECCA goes.)
JOHN:	Good morning, Jeanne. I hope you slept well.
JEANNE:	Like a child in my own bed. And you?
JOHN:	Who are these people: (Scoffing) 'True Science'?
JEANNE:	Nearly on his deathbed, John, Frank's thoughts were only of me. If something should happen to Frank, he doesn't wish me to be alone.
JOHN:	You wouldn't be alone. This is also your home.
JEANNE:	How I idolized you when we were young. There is nothing I would not have done. Do you remember, I once punched Tommy Claggs in the face because he called you a 'nerd'?
JOHN:	I was mortified.
JEANNE:	Mother was appalled, but father guffawed. And, I still feel that way.
JOHN:	Like punching someone out?
JEANNE:	Loyal to my family, above all else. And, suddenly, I am in a position to look out for you, dear, brilliant brother.
JOHN:	I see.
JEANNE:	What are we arguing about, really? Defend your ideas by all means. No one disagrees with your right to your own thoughts…
JOHN:	This paper is bullshit, Jeanne, simply put.
JEANNE:	Is that the message you would like relayed?
JOHN:	'Natural variability,' 'the sun' do not, cannot explain…
JEANNE:	A reputable, foundation-funded think tank.

JOHN:	Phony science.
JEANNE:	Can you not find something gentlemanly to say, a response that leaves some room for polite discourse?
JOHN:	I can't contradict my own research.
JEANNE:	But you don't know everything.
JOHN:	Of course not.
JEANNE:	Then, you might try to moderate your tone.
JOHN:	You sound like mother when you talk that.
JEANNE:	Mother was usually right.
JOHN:	No doubt.
JEANNE:	Well, then?
JOHN:	I refuse to comment on this willful distortion of fact, this useless rubbish, these base and malicious lies.
JEANNE:	Well, that's very clear. I believed I might actually be doing you a favor.
JOHN:	What sort of favor, actually, would you have been doing me?
JEANNE:	Don't raise your voice. Your position is perfectly clear.
JOHN:	You act as if it's my fault the world is heating up.
JEANNE:	There are many, highly placed, educated and powerful people, who believe that your prognosis, if that's what you call it, is vastly premature, even alarmist, and would cause enormous economic damage.
JOHN:	Did you memorize this? Did your friends in high places tell you what to say?
JEANNE:	I do have my own brain, John. It even functions most of the time. If you don't wish to become a martyr, you should know that now is hardly the time to challenge our energy policies.
JOHN:	We have an election coming up. These 'True Science' phonies might soon be out-of-work.
JEANNE:	I would not be so certain of that.
	(REBECCA *enters, dressed, with two coffee cups.*)
REBECCA:	Here's coffee, Jeanne. Or would you rather come into the kitchen and sit.
JEANNE:	Thank you. No. I must get back to my post.
JOHN:	Quite a brief visit.
JEANNE:	Frank thought some fresh air would do me good.
JOHN:	More like a mission.
JEANNE:	Is that so wrong, an attempt to help my noble brother get along.
REBECCA:	I'll run Jeanne to the train. You can get to work.
JOHN:	I'll excuse myself. (JOHN *exits.*)

No bother, I've called a car. In the old days, Uncle would run us down to the station in the pony cart. Poor, dear, crippled Uncle.

I'll wait with you. We can go out on the porch; the morning air is so sweet.

JEANNE: So, we still have nice mornings; despite John's catastrophic predictions.

REBECCA: But of course, up here.

JEANNE: This house seems to have found a new sense of purpose overnight. What is so pressing?

REBECCA: Why, John's to give a major policy speech.

JEANNE: A speech? John puts people to sleep. Even he used to joke; he got his PhD so easily because his entire committee slept through his defense.

REBECCA: Not with something so important to say.

JEANNE: But John always says the same thing, 'Far below 2 degrees Celsius.' No one quite knows what he means.

REBECCA: This time, John will have the press on his side.

JEANNE: I see. Where and when is the great day?

REBECCA: Before the election, you can be certain of that.

JEANNE: Splendid. Impressive, in fact.

REBECCA: Once John tells the whole truth, people will listen.

JEANNE: Just what is the *whole* truth, Rebecca, dear?

REBECCA: That the science is being fixed around the current administration's energy policy. It is exactly like the invasion of Iraq. Weapons of mass destruction, only, in this case, such weapons do exist. They are greenhouse gasses. This administration wishes to ignore them, and so they are censoring John.

JEANNE: Censoring is quite a strong word. Tell me, Rebecca, what is your birth name?

REBECCA: What do you mean?

JEANNE: Only that you were semi-adopted by Dr. West, and you took his name growing up. Don't look so shocked; John must have mentioned it to me. *(Car horn)* There's the car. Don't bother to see me out.

(JEANNE goes; ANNIE enters.)

ANNIE: Papa! Tell papa I'm going up to the pond. Come with me, Rebecca, do.

REBECCA: I must help John with his work.

ANNIE: Oh, I see.

REBECCA: I'm sorry, Annie. Next time.

ANNIE: I rescued Sniffley just in time. His life on earth was at risk.
(She goes toward the back door, still talking.)
Perhaps, the entire life of the pond. Therefore, I embark, alone, on a rescue mission, now. It is atrazine; Uncle and I have no doubt. Nor does poor Sniffley, I suspect. A poisonous pesticide, already banned by the European Union. But you cannot come. You have more important work.

REBECCA: I am sorry, Annie.

JOHN: *(Off)* Rebecca!

REBECCA: Your father needs every ounce of me.
(The back door slams.)
(Musical interlude. UNCLE *and* ANNIE *are working at the pond. Several days later.)*
Annie, come in, I've made lunch.

ANNIE: I shall eat tomatoes from the garden.
(UNCLE exits.)

REBECCA: I've made soup.

ANNIE: No thank you, Rebecca. I am consuming only raw food. Vegetables, nuts, and fruit which can be picked and the seeds shit, or shat … whatever, wherever, so the source is replenished, the garden grows up again.
(REBECCA comes out of the door.)
(ANNIE is outside, at the pond, intently watching the frogs. Silence, then…)
Sniffley is a gender-challenged frog as I am a gender-challenged girl, or as I prefer birl. There may be a difference, however, Sniffley, born a male, albeit, so-called deformed with a total of six uneven legs, has, also, in the process of becoming an adult frog been feminized, made into a hermaphrodite by the herbicide atrazine that got by groundwater into his pond… and atrazine can do this to 'real men,' lower their testosterone levels, I am told by Uncle, who still feels quite potent himself.

REBECCA: Uncle told you all this?

ANNIE: Uncle and I are engaged in serious research. We are working to ban atrazine in the United States. We believe once American men understand they are being de-balled, there will come an insurrection. And we are working locally; we have made up how-to dig a frog pond flyers and we are going to distribute them in town.

REBECCA: *(Repressing a smile)* This is all quite impressive. Does your father know?

ANNIE:	Papa is far too busy to know anything at all about me. I am a birl by choice, perhaps, also, perhaps, do to other forces. We, Sniffley and I, have a profound cross-species bond.
REBECCA:	These things work themselves out. We are works in progress, each of us. *(She musses* ANNIE's *hair affectionately.)*
ANNIE:	You mustn't play with me, Rebecca.
REBECCA:	Of course, not. I only mean to say, gender identity is fluid throughout our lives. There is no need to label yourself.
ANNIE:	Sniffley had no choice.
REBECCA:	But you, my birl, must be whatever you wish.
ANNIE:	I am thirteen. I am alternately too young and too old for my age. I understand, very well, I am strange.
REBECCA:	I think at thirteen I felt exactly the same. And, I don't think you are in the least strange.
ANNIE:	I think you are beautiful, Rebecca.
REBECCA:	I like you, too, Annie, oh, so very much, I do!
ANNIE:	*(Hurt)* Well, Sniffley had better go for a swim. (ANNIE *leaves.* JOHN *comes out, slamming the door.* REBECCA *laughs.)*
JOHN:	What are you laughing about!
REBECCA:	It is so hard to be young. What a glorious day. *(Silence)*
REBECCA:	Come, let's take the afternoon off. The leaves are changing. The exercise will do your mind a world of good. You can practice the opening of your speech while we walk. And, John, I need to discuss my work; I've got new satellite results that show quite disturbing new trends... *(He turns from her)* John? Are you listening to me?
JOHN:	They've cancelled my speech.
REBECCA:	That can't be. Not after all this.
JOHN:	Never mind. I can stop working so hard. Insane to believe that I might have influenced the election by giving a speech on climate change. How did such a foolish idea take root?
REBECCA:	What excuse did they give?
JOHN:	I've been up since 3 am. My mind's a fog.
REBECCA:	What did they say?
JOHN:	It was hubris, Rebecca; you made me believe.
REBECCA:	It would have mattered, John. Someone else other than me believed that it would.
JOHN:	The 'Council on Freedom' is 'suddenly' undergoing an 'internal review of program initiatives.' They've decided to cancel all public presentations until after the election. Of course, mine was the only major policy speech scheduled.

REBECCA:	And they'd promised you major press coverage. Someone got to them, but who?
JOHN:	What does it matter? Along with that email came the usual dozens: 'climate change scientists should be executed. You, Bjornson, are a traitor.' 'You should drown in your own....' Well, you know the word. And others even less well intentioned.
REBECCA:	Oh, John. You must just let me delete those things. You mustn't go through your own email.
JOHN:	Don't be silly. I'm not a child.
REBECCA:	Hardly. You're a prophet.
JOHN:	Not quite. I'm a mosquito; and they've used DDT.
REBECCA:	Not atrazine, at least.
JOHN:	What?
REBECCA:	John, you are not going to lie down and give up... I've gotten new results. You have Annie's future at stake, the future of everyone's children. You must speak.
JOHN:	Do, let's walk up the mountain. I need to clear my head. *(JOHN and REBECCA walk past UNCLE and ANNIE at the new frog pond; UNCLE has cuttings from plants in a basket in his lap in the wheel chair.)*
UNCLE:	So, we shall surround our pond with rosemary, thyme and eglantine, partridge pea and blue eyed grass, a thicket of sassafras, low-bush blueberry shrubs, the red flower called Cosmos, and most miraculous of all, this scruffy little wildflower, Torrey's mountain mint, endangered the worldwide, imperiled, yet, amazement on my face, here it is, to see, to sniff. Sometimes I do despair, how not? Not with you, my dear, no, not in front of you, I tell myself. Forgive me child. Care of this land was passed to me by your grandfather, a noble soul, like your papa in demeanor, Uncle, he said, they called me Uncle even then, though I had no one, was sublimely unattached, had wandered by and struck by the beauty of the view had stopped to linger here. 'You shall be the steward of my land.' 'As far as the eye can see we shall hold in perpetuity.' 'Should my progeny wish to dwell on this domain, you, Uncle, will see the land comes to no harm. No one shall disrupt the mountain top or mountain stream or bubbling brook.' Your grandfather spoke like that. In those days, nature intervened in all our words; we painted with our tongues, we looked and spoke and kept the land forever in our heads. We walked with beauty inside and out. And now we rescue Sniffley and his like from the mountain pond that somehow has been contaminated with run-off from a source outside of my

watch, invisible to my eyes, and we bend down and marvel at a bit of Torrey's mountain mint that is nearly alone in all the world. We have our miracles, still, small though they are: a sprig of mountain mint. Once we walked the land and we seemed miniscule. Old growth forest above our heads, a cacophony of creatures. We sensed our place in the grand design: to marvel at the large and small, the sky, the mountain and the honey bee, the plant beneath our feet, to step lightly, not to leave a mark of where we'd walked, the grasses would rebound, the forest would remain untouched. We would harvest and replace. We would exit as we'd come, gently, unremarked upon.

ANNIE: Uncle, don't cry. You mustn't Uncle. We must work for Sniffley's sake, and others of his kind, for what we can manage to save. There once was Torrey's mountain mint upon this ground. Life is vanishing, Uncle, whole species are no more. I am not numb. I was born into a world where I can feel the vanishing of things. What else can we do, Uncle, but work to save what is?
(Musical interlude. JOHN *and* REBECCA *enter laughing; they have made love on the hill top.)*

REBECCA: I wonder if Annie will be happy, too.

JOHN: I don't think Annie should know about us.

REBECCA: But, of course she will.
(A volley of shots off.)

REBECCA: *(Laughing)* Fireworks.

JOHN: Shots.
*(*REBECCA *and* JOHN *scramble to finish dressing. Frank enters. He has a rifle and bag full of dead ducks.)*

FRANK: Sorry to burst right in. Who knew?

JOHN: There is no hunting on this land.

FRANK: A little sport, man, for us both. It's so good to be alive.

JOHN: This land is a nature preserve.

FRANK: Oh, I didn't realize that. When I was a boy with my dad, we hunted in order to eat. *(To* REBECCA, *with his hand out, smiling)* I'm Frank.

REBECCA: Rebecca.

FRANK: *(To* JOHN*)* No deer, no pheasants, no food. That's how it was. Lucky man.

REBECCA: We are both lucky, as it turns out.

FRANK: We snuck onto the rich folk's land because we had no choice. It was shoot or starve. There was mom and hungry kids back at the house. We were frightened, you bet. They'd rather shoot one of us than have us bag one of their deer.

JOHN:	We don't patrol this land. But I have a child and I don't want hunting here.
FRANK:	I wouldn't do it again.
JOHN:	I'll appreciate that.
FRANK:	Now, I hunt for fun. Pleasure is hard to give up.
	(JEANNE *enters holding the hunting bag with ducks; she sprawls on the ground.*)
JEANNE:	I have never understood why men love to hunt.
JOHN:	It's quite fine when you eat what you shoot.
FRANK:	Thank you for getting my point-of-view.
JEANNE:	I suppose I've never understood men.
FRANK:	Fishing, too; it was a dirty old river, half-polluted with run-off from the yards, but we needed those fish fries. Now, I fish in the deep sea; full of danger and so damn beautiful.
JOHN:	We heard a shark nearly knocked you out.
FRANK:	Heart attack with a 150-pound Marlin on the line. You know what, I reeled him in. Keeled over after I'd won. Jeanne told you all about it.
JOHN:	She didn't tell us you caught it.
FRANK:	Got that fish. I did.
JOHN:	Congratulations.
FRANK:	Damn right. Lying flat on my back, tubes going in and out, I had a – what do you call it?
JEANNE:	We call it an awakening, Frank.
FRANK:	That's it. I woke up, but it was more than opening my eyes. I woke up inside. *(To* JOHN*)* That ever happened to you?
JOHN:	I'm not sure.
FRANK:	You'd sure know if it did. *(Quiet, self-reflective)* I came from nothing, poor people, hard-working folks. Eight of us crammed into four rooms. We were lucky if our shoes didn't pinch, if the furnace worked, if the roof didn't leak. When my father was killed in the yards, I quit school to take his place. *(Pause)* Jeanne loves me despite all of this.
JEANNE:	I love you *because* of it, Frank.
FRANK:	No one gave me a hand. I worked my way up. Everything I have, I've earned. Then, all of sudden, I'm fishing and dying at the same time but I don't let go of that line. I wake up. I'm alive. It's like being reborn. So damn lucky I feel. I wake up determined to live. From now on, whatever I want, I'll have.
JEANNE:	Not quite everything, dear.
FRANK:	Sure, sure; girls are permanently off the table, the desk, out of the private bathroom, too.

JEANNE:	Frank!
FRANK:	She's made me an honest man. And here I am alive on this gorgeous day. Triple bypass, good as new. I love science. Man on the moon and me, strong as a twenty-year-old. Soon, on to Mars. There's water up there. You know you actually get younger when they clear that plaque out, drain those pipes.
JOHN:	Good for you.
JEANNE:	We feel fortunate; we do.
FRANK:	Lucky to live in this great nation with the best medical care in the world. A 250-pound Marlin on the line and a heart that's not worth a damn. But I reeled him in. A miracle that's what that was. Living proof!
JEANNE:	You still need to eat; let's go back to the house, I'll whip something up.
REBECCA:	Duck?
JEANNE:	I only eat organic food.
REBECCA:	Then, I wouldn't eat those.
FRANK:	Best to toss them, unless you've got a dog.
REBECCA:	No dog.
FRANK:	We should get a dog. Dogs keep the blood pressure down. Pointer, how about that, or a hound?
JEANNE:	That's so sad. Whatever happened?
REBECCA:	Pesticides in the rain, or run-off from higher up. Uncle and Annie are on the case.
JEANNE:	Really? Is nowhere safe?
REBECCA:	Atrazine has this bad habit of seeping into everything. In Europe, it has been outlawed.
JEANNE:	Good. I love French pâté.
REBECCA:	And its effects are somewhat unsettling. It feminizes males; they actually start to produce eggs. They grow breasts.
JEANNE:	Why, it's a feminist herbicide. Maybe I will cook the duck, especially for Frank.
FRANK:	What are you talking about; you want me with breasts?
JEANNE:	I want you soft and malleable, my darling; every woman does. We pretend to admire your macho ways, but in our hearts, we want wives.
FRANK:	Your sister's a gem. Brains, looks, and she chooses someone like me.
JOHN:	Who can explain women?
FRANK:	Not me. I'm a simple fellow, without a Ph.D. Changeable as the weather, women are.

JOHN:	(*Looks at* REBECCA) I think I know more about the climate than I do about women, actually.
REBECCA:	But, John, that's just it. Something catastrophic is going on. Already, right now, we have lost 2 million square kilometers of ice.
JOHN:	You're certain Rebecca? You've proof?
REBECCA:	I've been trying to tell you all day what this morning's satellite pictures show. I never imagined a melt like this.
JOHN:	I'd better take a look. We had better get back to work. (REBECCA *and* JOHN *leave.*)
FRANK:	Did you understand any of that?
JEANNE:	The ice is melting and John is in love with that young woman.
FRANK:	Good for John.
JEANNE:	I saw how you looked at her, Frank.
FRANK:	A man can look.
JEANNE:	She's my brother's, whatever she is, she's his.
FRANK:	The girl's been around; (*nuzzling* JEANNE) I can smell it every time. (*She lightly smacks him.*)
JEANNE:	Behave yourself.
FRANK:	I'd grow breasts for you, but you like me randy, you do. (*They kiss.*) (*Musical interlude. Later on, in the house* JOHN *is in his office, out-of-sight.* JEANNE *crosses from the garden, with her phone; she enters the house and speaks to him through the office door.*)
JEANNE:	Let me help you, John. I am your sister, after all.
JOHN:	There is nothing further to be done.
JEANNE:	But, I've done something already. If you'll stop acting so morose, I will tell you.
JOHN:	I'm tired, that's all. Worn out.
JEANNE:	And I can't possibly have anything to offer.
JOHN:	(*He enters the living room*) I didn't say that.
JEANNE:	No, you would never be so rude. You simply ignore me.
JOHN:	I'm sorry, Jeanne. I didn't mean… Rebecca's ice melt statistics are truly alarming.
JEANNE:	Oh, stop, silly boy. You take it all so personally. Listen for one instant to someone other than yourself because I have, in fact, solved your problem quite magnificently. We are no longer bemoaning the loss of an after-lunch talk in front of an insular, liberal think-tank. We are now talking about a national prime-time debate.
JOHN:	A what?
JEANNE:	Indeed; it is all arranged. All I need is your consent. I'll put you in touch with Roger Morley's people immediately.

JOHN:	Morley?
JEANNE:	Morley, yes.
JOHN:	Roger Morley from National Week? He's great.
JEANNE:	That's it.
JOHN:	You've spoken to him?
JEANNE:	In fact, I have. I have spoken directly with Roger.
JOHN:	I've been on Morley's program before.
JEANNE:	I realize that. Roger said he enjoyed having you as a guest. He absolutely won't let anyone return he doesn't like. So, there you are. *A fête accompli.* I've booked you on this Sunday's National Week. You shall have 36 minutes to make your case.
JOHN:	36 minutes…
JEANNE:	It's a lifetime.
JOHN:	My talk is 57 minutes.
JEANNE:	Throw it out. You can't sit there and read like a boozy professor; you have to speak from your heart. *(Pause)* John, do you realize how important this is?
JOHN:	Why are you helping me?
JEANNE:	It is three weeks before the election. Do you have any idea how many important people are clamoring for that spot?
JOHN:	Precisely why I asked.
JEANNE:	You are smart.
JOHN:	Smart?
JEANNE:	Oh, you are brilliant, brilliant, brilliant of course, as father always said; but you've also become a bit savvy.
JOHN:	You are married to a political operative, Jeanne.
JEANNE:	Operative is such a smarmy word.
JOHN:	Forgive me, I didn't mean…
JEANNE:	I'm a publicist in my own right. Why else would Roger Morley have paid any attention to me?
JOHN:	Why do you want to put me on his show?
JEANNE:	Give me credit for some independence, will you. You are my twin. If I use my contacts to help you out, that's how the world works.
JOHN:	Come, Jeanne, be honest. If I tell the truth, President Bush is likely to lose.
JEANNE:	*(She laughs)* Forgive me, dear brother; I had no idea you were that powerful.
JOHN:	I'm not. But the truth is that powerful; and the truth must be heard.
JEANNE:	But, of course, I absolutely agree. Do you want to confirm with Morley or not?
JOHN:	Kindly answer my question, first. Why are you doing this?

JEANNE:	For you, John, and for our democracy, too. Put all the information on the table; the people will make up their minds.
JOHN:	Well, that's very thoughtful of you, Jeanne. Impressive, in fact.
JEANNE:	Thank you. I do not believe in censorship of any sort. Neither does Frank. We are one hundred percent for free speech.
JOHN:	It just didn't make sense, at first. Now, of course, it does. I am grateful. I am; truly, Jeanne; this is very fine of you. I shall call Morley at once.
JEANNE:	Morley's people, but it's cleaner if I speak directly to the great man myself, on your behalf. It makes you seem more important.
JOHN:	Yes, fine. Well, I suppose I'd better begin editing my remarks. Wherever is Rebecca?
JEANNE:	I'm warning you, John, do not read from prepared remarks. Do not rely on jargon. I can prep you, if you wish. You have absolutely got to sound spontaneous, charming and fresh.
JOHN:	I'm not a celebrity; I'm a climatologist.
JEANNE:	Look, do something right now, for me. Tell me to my face why you wanted to give that speech, why you jumped at the chance to be on Morley's show. You have twenty-seconds. Go!
JOHN:	*(With simple force and sincerity)* Because the very climate conducive to life on earth, the climate we've been lucky enough to live in undisturbed for the past 10,000 years, while civilization evolved, that climate is a thing of a past. And we are almost certainly the cause. Man-made, anthropomorphic climate change is almost certainly likely to destroy the planet on which we live.
JEANNE:	Bravo. Simply take out 'almost certainly' and strike 'almost certainly likely' and you are perfect. I love the tremble in your voice.
JOHN:	Science is never 100%. I must leave some small room for doubt. We are 95% certain, of course.
JEANNE:	Quite. It is much better; John, and then I will never say this ever again, it would be much better for you if you were not to leave any room, any room at all, for the slightest doubt.
JOHN:	Well, you may well be right, but almost certain is almost certain, is it not? I cannot speak with utter certainty, no scientist can. I wish I had your skill.
JEANNE:	Mine, my lord; there is something of mine that you covet.
JOHN:	Come, come, Jeanne; you are much more personable than I.
JEANNE:	And yet, you seem so certain of this, this crisis of yours you wish to share.

JOHN:	I am certain enormous damage is being done, as certain as anyone can be.
JEANNE:	Absolutely sure?
JOHN:	I am, yes, absolutely.
JEANNE:	Then say so, loud and clear.
JOHN:	Well, then, I'd best get to work.
	(JOHN *exits toward his office;* JEANNE *walks outside and meets* FRANK *coming across the garden.*)
FRANK:	He's agreed?
JEANNE:	He jumped at the chance. He's grateful, in fact. I'm so pleased, dear; truly I was touched. I told him he must be very forceful, extremely clear.
FRANK:	It will be a great show. Lindsey and Mortimer are also on board.
JEANNE:	Lindsey and Mortimer, whatever for?
FRANK:	It's National Week. It's fantastic exposure for John.
JEANNE:	He thinks he has the entire show to himself.
FRANK:	Morley doesn't take sides.
JEANNE:	But you said it would be good for me to do something just for John.
FRANK:	You think he could have gotten on Morley without you?
JEANNE:	John becomes tongue-tied the moment he feels challenged in any way. Father always over-protected John.
FRANK:	Well, now, he's grown-up.
JEANNE:	I did use the word 'debate.' I'm quite certain I said that.
FRANK:	Good enough.
JEANNE:	It's just that Lindsey and Mortimer...
FRANK:	John can take care of himself.
JEANNE:	I hope so. Really, I do.
	(*Black-out. Music changes to television sounds.* REBECCA, UNCLE *and* ANNIE *sit in front of the television; it is the end of the Morley show.*)
REBECCA:	Energy and energy policy! What happened to climate change?
UNCLE:	Turn it off; spare me.
ANNIE:	Why didn't papa fix it? Why wasn't papa brave?
REBECCA:	Lindsey is a meteorologist, not a climate scientist. And why Mortimer?
ANNIE:	Who cares?
REBECCA:	He's a fossil fuel lobbyist.
ANNIE:	Papa should have said so.
UNCLE:	'Negative forcings,' 'positive feed-back loops' Bah! Things are out of control.
	(*Television voices*)

MORLEY:	Dr. Lindsey will have the last word.
LINDSEY:	Thank you, Roger. It is my privilege, indeed. Let us put this climate-change hoax to rest once and for all. Let us remember the earth and its eco-systems are robust, resilient and self-regulating. Nothing human beings have done or can ever do can or will upset the balance of God's green earth, which is so much more powerful than any of us. It is heresy to believe otherwise. Are we to actually think we are more powerful than God?
	(REBECCA *turns the television off.*)
UNCLE:	We do God's work; if we dare. Does God have hands? No, he has us.
ANNIE:	Papa was so boring, like a teacher.
REBECCA:	All right. They taped this afternoon; he'll be home very soon. We must put on a brave face.
ANNIE:	But he didn't say what he feels. Uncle would have.
REBECCA:	He's worked so hard. He had so much riding on this.
UNCLE:	I hear cries for help. The fish in the sea, the birds on the wing, the frogs, are gasping for breath. We are God's ears.
ANNIE:	All Papa does is listen to Rebecca. All Papa and Rebecca talk is gobble-goop. Uncle says what others feel. We know what is going on. That Morley guy could have talked to Uncle and me.
REBECCA:	What would you have said?
ANNIE:	I'll tell you what, the earth is crying, dying. The earth cannot take care of herself. Papa should have said the pond near the waterfall on the hill on our land is polluted and no one knows why this is, but it is so. He should have said my mother died from a fast-growing cancer that killed her when I was only eight years old. Why was that? He should have said his daughter is intersex. Her clitoris is as large as a small penis and it gets as hard when she looks at her father's lover. Why is that? She is still only thirteen and she doesn't know who she is or what she has to live for. Everyone thinks she is so peculiar. No one loves her but Sniffley, and he's a frog with six legs who cannot hop straight and Sniffley is making eggs.
UNCLE:	Annie, listen to what you say. You and Sniffley are free, to break boundaries, to be. You and Sniffley are hope.
ANNIE:	Papa should have said the whole entire world is coming unhinged. He should have slammed the door and left.
	(ANNIE *exits, slamming the door.*)
UNCLE:	We transform. We molt. No moment is ever too late. That *is* what he should have said.
REBECCA:	What have I done?
	(*Outside*)

	Annie? Where are you? I can't see.
	Go away.
REBECCA:	No, dear, truly, it is not as bad as you make it out.
ANNIE:	It's not? Papa is going to be in a rage.
REBECCA:	Yes, I suppose he is. But it wasn't his fault.
ANNIE:	It is never *his* fault, is it?
	(UNCLE, *standing up, exits the house.*)
UNCLE:	I am walking, I tell you. I've regained use of my legs. A miracle it is.
ANNIE:	You are, Uncle, you are.
UNCLE:	When we least expect it, we become new. I'm proof.
REBECCA:	Uncle, sit down before you fall.
UNCLE:	Standing upright. On my own two feet! I imagined it so. It became true. Now, I can get back to work. Not a moment too soon. Great plans can be put into effect. We are saved. Solar panels on the roof, wind turbines on the hill, waves in the sea will power the world.
	(*Sound of a car approaching; stopping, car door slamming.* JOHN *walks past them.*)
REBECCA:	John…
	(*He enters the house, the door slams. She follows him.*)
JOHN:	It's my fault.
REBECCA:	It's not.
JOHN:	Jeanne warned me to be 'certain.' 'Absolutely certain.'
REBECCA:	She ought to have warned you about Lindsey and Mortimer…
JOHN:	Perhaps she didn't know.
REBECCA:	Please. It's impossible to be that naïve.
JOHN:	You are saying my twin sister set me up.
REBECCA:	I'm saying she withheld information from you. Lindsey and Mortimer, for instance. If you'd known… Yes, she set you up.
JOHN:	I was terrible.
REBECCA:	You were measured, careful. You had the facts.
JOHN:	The facts are impossible for ordinary people to understand.
REBECCA:	And the lies are so very easy to digest. God controls the weather, doesn't He?
JOHN:	I was so startled I didn't know how to respond.
REBECCA:	'Are you crazy?' might have been a start.
JOHN:	I didn't even speak about the Arctic Ice Melt. I shall never forgive myself.
REBECCA:	You mustn't blame yourself so.
JOHN:	No? I've worked for months, years, my whole life. The words ran altogether in my head. It was a jumble, a roar. I could not speak.

Then all of a sudden Lindsey seemed right. That was the most terrible part. I actually sat there and thought, why ever can I not agree with him!

REBECCA: It is late, John. You should sleep.

JOHN: Mortimer called me 'dangerous to humankind.' He said I am 'against the poor.' For my own 'malicious agenda' I would drive 'millions of people into poverty.'

REBECCA: Don't...

JOHN: I hit a deer with the car.

REBECCA: Oh, John.

JOHN: The thing flew right at me; I thought it would come through the windshield. Instead there was a horrible crack, like a heart splitting in half. I saw the terror in her eyes.

REBECCA: John, please, sit down. I'll make you something warm.

JOHN: She looked at me, I tell you, as if she knew me as her executioner. I ought not to have been rolled over like an animal. I could not get out of their way. They were zeroing in right at me with their impossible cant: world poverty. Poverty is flood, drought, when you can't breathe the air, when you can no longer grow crops; when you have to abandon your land. But I couldn't speak. The thing fell to the road with the most terrible thud. Her eyes were open the entire time. I didn't even take my foot off the gas. She's lying on the ground bleeding out.

REBECCA: John, you've got to calm down. You've had a terrible disappointment, then a horrible shock. You must sit.

JOHN: Where's the gun?

REBECCA: What are you doing?

JOHN: Don't follow me, Rebecca.

(REBECCA *tries to hold onto him; he wrests himself free and grabs the rifle.*)

REBECCA: John.

JOHN: I'm warning you. Leave me be.

(*Outside in the dark.*)

REBECCA: John! Uncle, Annie, where are you?

UNCLE: I'm taking steps.

ANNIE: It is, Uncle, a miracle.

UNCLE: We must believe in miracles, my girl. Because it must happen, it does. You will transform a thousand times. You can be whatever you wish. Sun, wind and waves will provide. Tomorrow, we'll work. Take my hands. Dance.

(UNCLE *and* ANNIE *do a little jig; Sniffley croaks.*)

233

(Further up the road, car headlights; the car comes to halt. JEANNE *gets out.)*

JEANNE:	John, whatever are you doing out here on the road?
JOHN:	Whoever you are, don't come any closer.
JEANNE:	It's me, Jeanne. Put that gun down.
JOHN:	Don't you ever again tell me what to do.
JEANNE:	Don't shoot. I came up here to explain.
JOHN:	Stand back.

(A shot.)

JEANNE:	John!

(The morning light begins to dawn.)

John, are you all right?

JOHN:	Of course, I'm all right. Why are you here?
JEANNE:	Once I know you are all right, I will go.
JOHN:	What did you do to me tonight?
JEANNE:	Put the rifle down. We can talk.
JOHN:	Damn the gun. The rifle, whatever you call it. I came here to put a poor beast out of misery. Now get the hell off of this land.
JEANNE:	It is also my land, John.
JOHN:	It's not yours because you don't give a rat's ass about it. You don't care a fecal pellet about anything but your damned profits and that lout of a husband of yours.
JEANNE:	I will not stand here and be spoken to like that, like gutter trash…
JOHN:	Good.
JEANNE:	Because I am on your side. I got you on Morley's show. Believe me, I tried my best. I'm sorry, John; truly, I am. I drove here in the middle of the night just to say that.
JOHN:	Sorry? For what? For setting me up?
JEANNE:	I would never set you up. I coached you, in fact.
JOHN:	You lied.
JEANNE:	I promise you, I did not know.
JOHN:	Foolish of you, Jeanne. Stupid, you have always been.
JEANNE:	You dare say that to me?
JOHN:	Foolish, yes. That is what stupid means.
JEANNE:	*(Hurt)* I see. Not everyone always thinks as you do, John, and if you are to become paranoid whenever someone expresses an opinion that is not yours, that makes it extremely difficult to live in this world.
JOHN:	Fuck off, Jeanne. Go.

(He points the gun at her and she backs away.)

JOHN:

(REBECCA *enters and stands. Gently, she holds out |*
walks towards her and gives her the gun.)
It's not loaded. I used the last bullet; put it through |
eyes rolled but she looked at me. The god taking her out. She didn't
utter a sound. They are watching us. Mute. They don't shout. I
myself feel numb. I cannot make myself heard. Truth. Facts. The
future. None of it matters. So, tonight I killed my first deer. We are
criminals, every one.

Act II

*(Since the last act, the environmental situation has continued to worsen; no meaningful public
action has been taken. It is now the summer of 2012 and it is as if time and no time has passed.
The living room.* REBECCA *is urgent, while* JOHN *seems distracted, disinterested. He is reading
a journal.)*

REBECCA:	How I wish I could have seen it, John, before the fact.
JOHN:	Sure.
REBECCA:	With clarity, certainty, yes.
JOHN:	Then what?
REBECCA:	Why, then, I would have known. I would not have been so flummoxed, so absolutely blind-sided, stunned.
JOHN:	You would have been prepared?
REBECCA:	I would have understood. I'm having a very hard time understanding, now…
JOHN:	You're not the only one.
REBECCA:	None of us got it; that's what astonishes me. No one was prepared for this summer of 2012. The unprecedented, precipitous dive. More than half of the ice in the Arctic is gone. *(Pause)* It's a death spiral, John.
JOHN:	Well, well.
REBECCA:	It's not a death spiral, then?
JOHN:	Trends end.
REBECCA:	It's been holding steady these past years. It could all stabilize again.
JOHN:	I suppose.
REBECCA:	Still, we ought to have seen it coming. We ought to have been able to know…
JOHN:	For eons change happened slowly.

REBECCA:	I am speaking of something else: I am speaking of willful blindness.
JOHN:	*(Turns back to whatever he is reading)* Oh, well…
REBECCA:	What if we didn't want to know? Could not face it, ourselves, and so we closed our eyes. Our predictions were off because the truth terrified us.
JOHN:	Perhaps…
REBECCA:	I'm saying our fear made us blind. I'm saying, we actually *did not want* to know.
	(UNCLE *crosses the garden, carrying a rope and wearing work gloves, on his way up the hill.)*
JOHN:	It's of no matter, now.
REBECCA:	We simply could not bear it. *(Pause)* But it's our business. It's our job to see, to know, to warn, and avoid. We should have sounded the alarm. I should have. Me.
JOHN:	*(Sarcastically)* 'Should'?
REBECCA:	If only I had been able to see. Because that is what I want most of all, that is what really thrills me, the thought that someday I will be able to see into the future. That our models will be perfect enough and, now, to think that I may have lost my nerve and willfully blinded myself…
	(Silence; JOHN *returns to his reading.)*
	John? Talk to me.
	(He ignores her. The phone rings on the table next to him. REBECCA *leaps for the phone standing between* JOHN's *legs, picks it up.)*
	Hello. Hello?
	(She hangs the phone up.)
JOHN:	Who was that?
REBECCA:	I don't know.
	(The phone rings. JOHN *picks it up.)*
JOHN:	Hello. *(Silence)* He hung up.
REBECCA:	He?
JOHN:	Whomever.
REBECCA:	No one, really.
	(The phone rings, again. This time REBECCA *leaps for it. She picks it up and holds the receiver so that* JOHN *can also hear.)*
REBECCA:	Who is this? Who!?
	(Silence. Click)
REBECCA:	Hung up. He.
JOHN:	Who?
REBECCA:	I told you, I don't know.
JOHN:	Why are you trembling so?

REBECCA:	Perhaps it was a wrong number.
JOHN:	Why are you looking away?
REBECCA:	A mistake, that's all.
JOHN:	Fine. *(Pause)* I'll go to my study.
REBECCA:	Don't go. It was just a crank call.
JOHN:	I simply wonder why you seem so upset.
REBECCA:	Because, because... because you were not engaging with me before the phone call. You were answering me in monosyllables. I was trying to talk to you.
JOHN:	Yes, yes, blind eyes.
REBECCA:	The wish, the desire to be able to know things ahead of time and the feeling, the fear that I actually didn't want to know the truth about this ice melt.
JOHN:	There's the flaw.
REBECCA:	Yes, that is what I am saying: wanting and at the same time not being able to know.
JOHN:	It's human nature.
REBECCA:	It's dangerous.
JOHN:	Perhaps. But human nature no longer matters all that much.
REBECCA:	How can you say such a thing?
JOHN:	Obsolete.
REBECCA:	But, we have nothing else. Why do human beings exist, if not to tell the story of the universe? You've said that often enough.
JOHN:	I was hubristic.
REBECCA:	You were wise.
JOHN:	We must stop this, Rebecca.
REBECCA:	Yes, let's.
JOHN:	We must stop putting ourselves at the center of the universe, as if what we knew mattered, as if we could figure things out. Oh, I realize how impossible that is for ego-driven creatures like us. What difference can we possibly make? You or I, to what happens here? Yet we persist in believing once we know the truth we can control results. When, in fact, our intelligence has been the ruin of us. Human beings are responsible for global warming. Our ingenuity has brought us here. But, Rebecca, I hesitate even to say this out loud. This is the conclusion I've reached: events have flipped out of our control, no, not just control, natural events are now far beyond our ability to know. That's what your catastrophic ice melt is telling us, along with the tornadoes, hurricanes, droughts, fires and the sea-level rise. The causes and effects we thought we understood, the clever models we built, have become obsolete. We have reached the

tipping point. Now. This summer of 2012. Whether we wish to know the truth or not is of absolutely no significance any more. Intelligence might have worked in our favor ten or twenty years ago, when we first understood. Willful blindness might have been harmful last year. But what happens next will be completely outside the realm of human understanding. We can no longer predict because all of the systems we have studied so carefully over the years, all our graphs and the charts, our satellites, the models, observations, the theories no longer reflect anything but a world that has vanished on our watch. The systems we came to rely upon no longer exist. The human brain can no longer comprehend because human kind is no longer at the center of anything except the chaos human kind has caused.

REBECCA: Oh, John, no.

JOHN: I am sorry, Rebecca.

REBECCA: What do we do?

JOHN: What can we do but keep trying to describe our demise. That's the final irony, I suppose.

REBECCA: The voice on the phone; I do not know who it was, he said, it was a he, he said, 'mind your decimal point on page 5.' I swear to you that's what he said.

JOHN: That's all?

REBECCA: He also said 'fraud.'

JOHN: There were proofs.

REBECCA: Of course, there were proofs. I initialed them myself. I assumed, of course, I was sloppy, of course, there is no excuse. I just did not check each decimal point.

JOHN: Does this one decimal point disprove your work?

REBECCA: My mistake, or the tampering, it could have been that, the change, however it was made, is not actually significant to the conclusion I've made.

JOHN: Nothing to bother with, then. Simply write a letter to the editor correcting your error.

REBECCA: But that equation, that very one, with the decimal back in its proper place, is crucial for the argument I make in my new paper, the one I just put on your desk. And the argument I am making is crucial to you.

JOHN: All of a sudden you are getting crank calls.

REBECCA: Threatening calls, 'fraud,' in a threatening voice, as if you, John, could be said to be relying upon fraudulent work.

JOHN: *(He begins to fiddle with the phone)* How the hell do you do this? There is a way to see who called, who knows. Annie! Annie, please.

REBECCA:	Let's not get Annie involved.
	(UNCLE *comes down the hill.*)
JOHN:	Involved. She'll know which button to hit. Annie!
REBECCA:	She's with Sniffley; suddenly he's sick.
	(FRANK *enters with his gun; he walks close to* UNCLE *on his way to the house.*)
FRANK:	Oh, I thought, surely, you two'd be off in bed.
JOHN:	I no longer allow guns inside this house.
FRANK:	Well, I don't want to leave it outside. Who knows who might wander past?
JOHN:	I don't allow hunting on this land.
FRANK:	I'm going after duck in the morning.
JOHN:	There are no more duck.
FRANK:	The duck hunt here has always been great.
JOHN:	They no longer migrate this way.
FRANK:	Where have they gone?
JOHN:	I'm a climate scientist, not a naturalist. It has something to do with the weather, I would suppose.
FRANK:	There must be something to shoot.
JOHN:	Don't be so sure about that.
FRANK:	There always is.
JOHN:	Always is no longer forever, if you get my point.
FRANK:	You are a cheerful one. This land you call yours so often is held in trust. It belongs to you and to my wife.
JOHN:	It was left as a land trust, first to us, then to our heirs, finally, in perpetuity to the state.
FRANK:	That is almost exactly right.
JOHN:	Exactly. Rebecca, it's suddenly all coming clear in my head.
REBECCA:	What, John?
JOHN:	The connection, the reason why.
FRANK:	You were not even in the country.
JOHN:	The equation you left on my desk is crucial, yes…
FRANK:	Jeanne was here by herself, all alone with her father.
JOHN:	I was studying abroad. I must excuse myself.
	(*He exits.*)
FRANK:	Well, well, alone.
REBECCA:	Please, be careful with that gun.
	(JEANNE *enters speaking on her phone.*)
JEANNE:	… that is why the ad must say; we will be ever so careful to do everything safely, and to restore any land we might harm to its original pristine state. Got it? Right. Good. Done.

FRANK:	How much?
JEANNE:	$12 million to start.
FRANK:	Not bad.
REBECCA:	For what?
JEANNE:	Hello, Rebecca, dear. Why for clean energy ads. You and John will surely agree. Good stewardship is certainly an important part of energy independence. Simply put, we should clean up our mess. Isn't that just what women have always done?
REBECCA:	I thought you have servants at home.
JEANNE:	Well, I'm a working girl.
REBECCA:	Me, too.
JEANNE:	And just like you, I, too, am involved in Arctic sea ice.
REBECCA:	These $12 million dollars in ads of yours are not about Arctic ice melt.
JEANNE:	They are about the amazing possibilities for unlocking Arctic oil that have suddenly opened up.
REBECCA:	You stand here in this house and say this to me?
JEANNE:	My father's house, yes. But, no one disagrees with you, Rebecca, dear. Industry can and will be good stewards. As we exploit all possible sources of domestic oil, clean coal and natural gas, we pledge to be environmentally responsible. 'I'm an energy voter' is our slogan. Good?
FRANK:	Brilliant.
REBECCA:	Just what does it mean?
JEANNE:	You know, of course. Everything.
REBECCA:	In the Arctic you can't clean up oil spills; no airports, roads, no way in.
FRANK:	It's time for a little reality check. We fought a nine-year war in Iraq. We got squat. We're damn lucky the Arctic is opening up.
JEANNE:	It feels like the hand of Providence. God is melting that ice.
FRANK:	Energy independence. That's the goal. Drill everywhere we can here at home. Get that pipeline built for the tar sands oil. Millions of jobs.
REBECCA:	I cannot listen to this.
FRANK:	Oh, yes, you will.
JEANNE:	We have something we need to tell you, Rebecca.
REBECCA:	I've heard quite enough, thank you.
FRANK:	A list. Depending how far we need to go.
JEANNE:	There is something John does not know.
REBECCA:	If it's John's business, then John…
FRANK:	Sit down, Rebecca.

JEANNE:	Yes, why don't you.
FRANK:	We have a few things to say, just to you.
	(REBECCA *sits in* JOHN's *chair; they stand in front of her.*)
FRANK:	First off, about this place. Go ahead, Jeanne.
JEANNE:	I think you have heard, Rebecca that my father was ill for quite some time. Those were difficult years, and all that time, John hardly ever appeared. Of course, Father, as always had been the case, was extremely proud. He demanded nothing of John. And all this time, Father was weakening. He could do virtually nothing for himself. I don't wish to go into detail… but I was young and very much alone.
REBECCA:	I'm sorry. I didn't know.
JEANNE:	Of course, not. Who would have told you? But, I loved Father terribly, and, all of a sudden, something miraculous happened. Father began to appreciate my mind.
REBECCA:	That's very nice.
JEANNE:	It was, yes. I felt vindicated, at last. And when Father passed I went by myself out into the world and I dare say I've earned the respect…
FRANK:	You sure have.
JEANNE:	Thank you, dear. I love you, my angel, I do.
REBECCA:	This is what you wanted me to know?
JEANNE:	Just one more thing: before Father died he said he wished to make me a gift, as a mark of his gratitude, he said; as a mark of his trust Father rewrote his will. He left the northwest section of this land to me alone.
REBECCA:	John doesn't know about this?
FRANK:	We thought you should be the one tell him. He's so quick to fly off the handle.
JEANNE:	John has always had the most fearsome temper. I think that is, also, why Father felt I had to have something for myself.
REBECCA:	But, how could John not know. If it is in the will, as you say?
JEANNE:	Oh, John paid very little attention in those days. The division of the property simply didn't enter into anyone's mind.
REBECCA:	Why should it now?
FRANK:	That northwest corner is pretty interesting, as it turns out.
REBECCA:	How so?
JEANNE:	Really, Rebecca, the only point I am trying to make is that Father left the northwest section to me; the rest of the land is jointly held.
REBECCA:	Are you planning to sell it off?
FRANK:	Not on your life.
	(REBECCA *stands.*)

REBECCA:	Nevertheless, I think John had better take a very close look at that will.
JEANNE:	I've told you the absolute truth.
REBECCA:	Your father had some sort of dementia at the end.
JEANNE:	Father was always in his right mind.
REBECCA:	I cannot believe John never knew. I cannot believe your father would have deceived...
JEANNE:	It happened just as I've said.
FRANK:	And there's not a damn thing John can do about any of it.
REBECCA:	I wouldn't be so sure. Wills have been tampered with...
JEANNE:	How dare you?
REBECCA:	John is a legal heir.
JEANNE:	As am I.
REBECCA:	I know for a fact, the last time John saw his father he did not recognize his only son.
JEANNE:	He asked me every day, painfully, when John would come!
FRANK:	Be quiet, Jeanne. Rebecca just thinks this conspiratorial way. You see, we know about your work with Dr. West, and now there's this thing with the decimal point.
REBECCA:	It was you on the phone!
FRANK:	Hardly. I don't make my own phone calls.
REBECCA:	Who, then, some hired goon?
JEANNE:	But, dear, your decimal point is out of place.
REBECCA:	But why would you care about that?
FRANK:	In the interest of True Science, of course. Tell me something, Rebecca, what was your father's name?
REBECCA:	What does that matter?
JEANNE:	Your mother and Dr. West were never legally married, yet you and she took his name. When your mother died, you continued to live with Dr. West – as a dutiful daughter, of course, although, Dr. West was not your father...
FRANK:	'I used John's *Nature* trick,' just what is that? (UNCLE, *carrying a ladder, crosses the garden on his way up the hill.*)
JEANNE:	Answer the question, Rebecca.
REBECCA:	It's a figure of speech.
FRANK:	'Trick,' meaning what?
REBECCA:	A neat idea.
FRANK:	By trickery.
REBECCA:	No, a way of figuring, a way of, something that works well and quickly...
FRANK:	Lies. Forgery.

REBECCA:	Not so.
FRANK:	'I used John's *Nature* trick to show the death spiral.' In your paper in which a crucial decimal point is now under dispute. Just what does that mean?
REBECCA:	I've no idea.
JEANNE:	But, the words come from emails you sent.
REBECCA:	I never used those words in a sentence.
FRANK:	They sound as if you pulled a fast one, exaggerated your results to prove whatever you want. Do you normally just move things around? Or, only when it's convenient? When John needs you to?
REBECCA:	You've taken my words out of context.
JEANNE:	But, dear, your decimal point is in the wrong place.
FRANK:	And you share those phony numbers you got by tricks with your scientific friends...
REBECCA:	Not phony, no. We share our results with our colleagues; it is common practice.
FRANK:	'John's *Nature* trick' those are your words on an email from you we have in our possession.
JEANNE:	And, now, most unfortunately, of course, John is also implicated.
REBECCA:	'Trick' is a figure of speech. How did you read my emails? What is going on?
JEANNE:	National security, I suppose.
FRANK:	Folks are upset, all this outrageous talk about what do you hoaxsters call it, a 'death spiral' up in the Arctic, when all that is happening is some ice is melting and a few good shipping routes are opening up because of that.
JEANNE:	And just when we need it most, the Arctic oil is becoming available, good things for the United States, for the economy and for our allies.
FRANK:	But you and your sort want to put the kibosh on that.
REBECCA:	My email has been hacked; my decimal point has been moved...
FRANK:	I think the real sticky part is this forgery, the 'trick' you played with your 'death spiral' results for John's sake.
REBECCA:	My figures are correct. 'Trick the results' is an expression we use.
FRANK:	Because there is also that business about the problem with Dr. West's research.
JEANNE:	The very fact that you were willing once to cover up for Dr. West might have made you that much more attractive to John.
REBECCA:	Nonsense. We have no secrets between us. I told John that Dr. West once exaggerated his results and I confronted him.
JEANNE:	But you did nothing.

REBECCA:	There was nothing I could do; I was young, without even a bachelor's degree.
FRANK:	There's just one thing John doesn't know.
JEANNE:	Come, Frank, there is no need for that.
FRANK:	You can trust us. Dr. West wasn't your biological father, after all. He was like a father though, enough so that you covered up for him when he changed his results. And if you slept with him a few times, maybe more, in the years after your mother died, that's no reason to ruin your life. Technically speaking, it was not incest; you weren't related.
REBECCA:	How dare you say such things…
JEANNE:	Of course, we realize, no one ever quite knows the truth. Global warming is so very complex, as is one's personal life.
FRANK:	Just so you know your place.
JEANNE:	I recommend reticence. And, of course, we don't want you to compromise John.
REBECCA:	I would never compromise John…
JEANNE:	We are very much more fortunate than we thought; there are enormous natural gas deposits underground on this very land.
REBECCA:	No. John would never allow such a thing; nor would Uncle. (UNCLE *comes back down the hill. He pauses to observe the frog pond, listening to the conversation inside the house.*)
FRANK:	You just don't get it. John has nothing to say. Uncle's a servant.
REBECCA:	There will be no fracking here.
FRANK:	There sure will.
REBECCA:	Why would you do such a thing? Don't you have enough money?
FRANK:	Who ever has enough?
JEANNE:	Hush, dear. It's not just the money; of course, the money will be nice. Frank and I support a number of worthwhile charities and cultural events. But, the real reason is that we are in the energy business. I am a public relations consultant to the industry. If I were *not* to allow environmentally sound natural gas drilling on my own land, what sort of message would that send?
FRANK:	We've got to drill, baby, drill.
REBECCA:	That shall never happen. Never.
FRANK:	Oh, yes, it will.
REBECCA:	You wish to discredit John through these slanders about me so he won't fight the will.
FRANK:	Very smart. Because you did cover up for Dr. West after you'd slept with him.
REBECCA:	Please, stop.

JEANNE:	Come, come, Rebecca. Scientists don't run the world.
FRANK:	She's right. You and John should shut up. You should stop exaggerating things.
JOHN:	*(Off) Rebecca!*
FRANK:	Right on cue.
REBECCA:	*(Distraught)* Don't John, please, I can't talk to you, now.
JEANNE:	We'll leave you two to work things out.
	(They exit.)
JOHN:	*(Enters)* But this paper of yours is perfect. Tell your stalker to go to hell next time he calls. This new work of yours is precisely what I need. I've called a press conference; we'll announce our results together. Rebecca, you will speak as my equal, my colleague.
REBECCA:	I am frightened John.
JOHN:	Don't be. You, Rebecca, have found the missing link between the Arctic ice melt and the current extreme weather events.
REBECCA:	Yes, it is quite clear, isn't it John.
JOHN:	So, Rebecca, because of you, we do know the future. As the ice melts the Jet Stream elongates; weather patterns get stuck. The temperate regions of the globe, the industrialized world, the great polluters, are now being affected. Sea-level rise, storms and storm surge, drought, mud-slides, tornadoes, torrential rains and the rest; the damage alone will cost billions… every island nation, the entire Eastern seaboard, all the world's major coastal cities…
REBECCA:	Yes, John, but I cannot have any part of this.
JOHN:	What are you saying? If this Arctic ice melt goes unchecked, the oceans will continue to heat the air, and the permafrost *will* melt. Our health, homes and food supplies are at stake. Across the globe. Nowhere is safe. Mass extinctions, massive refugee populations. There's your death spiral, that's your tipping point! Methane gas is far more lethal than carbon dioxide. You will do the interviews with me. Your name will be first. You've done it, Rebecca. Now, at last, the public will demand action. There is nothing left for rational people to do.
REBECCA:	But we are not rational beings, John.
JOHN:	That is no excuse for not being able *to think*.
REBECCA:	I can't think anymore.
JOHN:	Then, listen. The political solution, my dear, is brilliantly simple; we put a price on carbon fuel.
	(REBECCA pulls away from him. The door slams. ANNIE enters, older, sad; holding a small box.)

ANNIE:	Amphibian means two lives: come from water to the land. Now Sniffley goes to a third. What is that, I wonder?
REBECCA:	Annie, I am so, so sorry.
ANNIE:	No, you're not. Papa didn't even know.
JOHN:	Yes, I did. I am very sorry, my dear.
ANNIE:	Sniffley lived far past his allotted time, in my care. His children and their children remain. Sniffley's line. The pond is populous. And what is most remarkable in these times, most of the tads are healthy; some, of course, are not. Still, Uncle and I control the small eco-sphere like demi-gods. *(She cries.)* He was my favorite guy, or girl. His six legs and his gonads made him forever special.
REBECCA:	A birl.
ANNIE:	Yes. Sniffley was the most like me. Sometimes, it happens like that, two creatures stare across species, there is no common language, there cannot be, yet, you know, Sniffley knew, I knew, he knew, he and I were kindred spirits. As long as Sniffley lived, I was never alone.
JOHN:	Annie, my dear, dear…
ANNIE:	I am going to prepare to bury Sniffley, now. I think I shall make a pyre. I think since he lived in water and air, he shall go out in fire.
REBECCA:	May we come?
ANNIE:	Yes, if you wish. I believe that would be appropriate, Sniffley was…
REBECCA:	Part of the family.
	(ANNIE exits, the door slams.)
REBECCA:	In all these years, you've never fixed that door. How do you expect people to wake up to climate change?
JOHN:	What has come over you, at the moment of triumph, when finally we can speak with one voice? As my colleague. No. You, Rebecca, as lead researcher. A title I've never ceded before. We, two, never again will stand alone.
REBECCA:	Use the work, John, yes; that would please me very much.
JOHN:	After the press conference, we shall get married. Something simple, no fuss. It will be better for Annie, and for us.
REBECCA:	Stop. After Sniffley's funeral, I think, oh, John, I don't really know what I should do.
JOHN:	You're frightened of your own success. I understand. But, it's I who am able to give courage to you. We are not lemmings; we won't leap off the cliff. Suddenly I know. We can fix this.
REBECCA:	It's too late, John.
JOHN:	Never. It cannot be. I told you, I figured it out. We put a *price on carbon*…

REBECCA:	We?
JOHN:	We, the people, we tell the government to. We charge emitters at the source, at the mine shaft, the well or port of entry for the damage they do, fossil fuels finally cost their true price. Here's the best part: we redistribute that money equally to each person in the country. We bypass party politics; the cost of fossil fuels rises sky-high. Renewables of all sorts come within reach. The people vote with their pocket books.
REBECCA:	It's a good idea, John.
JOHN:	Simple, clear, it's really a…
REBECCA:	But ideas don't matter anymore.
JOHN:	Nonsense.
REBECCA:	I'm going for a walk.
JOHN:	Yes, dear, of course; take some time by yourself. I was so full of joy, suddenly, Rebecca, while I was reading your paper. Dire as your predictions are; it was joy that I felt. All of a sudden, the pieces fell into place, like a beautiful cosmic design. *(He goes to embrace her but she pulls away.)*
REBECCA:	John, you must let me go. *(REBECCA exits; the door slams.)*
JOHN:	*(Calls after her)* And I am going to fix that door. Uncle! *(The door slams; UNCLE is dressed like a frontiersman in the skins of the deer JOHN killed.)*
UNCLE:	You've heard of Sniffley's demise?
JOHN:	I have. Will you kindly, finally, fix that door?
UNCLE:	That door cannot be fixed. It has slammed since your father's time.
JOHN:	You will fix it, now. And take off that ridiculous outfit. Haven't you any other clothes?
UNCLE:	I wear the skins of the deer you killed. I stitched them for years.
JOHN:	You look absurd.
UNCLE:	Some use must be made of waste. We neglected to eat her meat. Screws and a new spring; I shall add them to my list.
JOHN:	Thank you very much.
UNCLE:	However, let me provide you with fair warning, I fix what needs fixing first. I'm standing perpendicular to the good earth for but a flash, not to be wasted on mundane tasks. Sniffley's loss serves to remind us how fleeting is life; though Sniffley lived long and well. He left a pond populated by his descendants; he had friends across species. He served by devouring his fair share of insects.
JOHN:	Uncle, please.

UNCLE:	Solar, wind and wave: these alone endure forever and ever, sufficient to our needs and those who come after. As soon as Sniffley has been mourned, I shall return to my last great work up on the hill. Yes, great work, I tell you, John. I shall not be moved. I saw surveyors up there, with Frank, in hard hats.
JOHN:	Doing what?
UNCLE:	But it's of no matter. I, John, am constructing a wind farm on the northwest corner. Not only this small domain, but the whole town below shall be able to exist on nature's endless bounty alone. A beacon to all. The solar panels on the house caused my past lameness, the wind turbines on the hill will be the source of my death. But the wind shall blow for eons and eons. Eternity will be here, on earth, where it belongs. *(He exits. Frank enters.)*
FRANK:	Well, well, whatever is wrong with Rebecca?
JOHN:	She's taking a walk.
FRANK:	She's a beauty. Best to give her her head; like a fine mare. Loosen up.
JOHN:	Thank you for the advice.
FRANK:	There's no need for this.
JOHN:	What?
FRANK:	Hostility, burning, right underneath that oh-so-proper front. Like I'm a peasant and you're some sort of Oxford don. Hatred, I'd even go that far. You're an angry man. A sore looser, too.
JOHN:	To the contrary; I believe we are finally poised on the verge of winning, just at the last, fatal moment. I'm feeling quite optimistic for a change.
FRANK:	So, she didn't tell you, anything?
JOHN:	I told her, her paper is brilliant. She's a bit shaken by all of it.
FRANK:	Oh, there's more to it than that.
JOHN:	Indeed, there is.
FRANK:	There's a lot about Rebecca you don't know.
JOHN:	I know she's a damn fine scientist whose results are about to have major impact. It's not too much to say Rebecca's observations of the widening waves of the Jet Stream will help save the world.
FRANK:	I never understand one word. *(JEANNE enters.)*
JEANNE:	'Head Climate Change Alarmist's Lover Lies about Results.'
JOHN:	What are you talking about?
FRANK:	Sounds good to me.

248

JEANNE:	The headline to *my* press release. I read yours, John; announcement of your upcoming press conference about what do you call it: 'Catastrophic Ice Melt Linked to Extreme Weather.'
JOHN:	Rebecca has never lied in her life.
FRANK:	You don't know everything.
JOHN:	I know that much.
JEANNE:	Maybe so, but we do know enough to impugn your credibility, as soon as your press conference is held, that is, if you actually wish to proceed.
JOHN:	Stop your nonsense, Jeanne. We are onto something big.
JEANNE:	Always, with you, John, always so. Everything you ever touched has been ever so much more important than anything else. Why, it's a miracle the earth still exists.
JOHN:	Rebecca predicts the Arctic will be ice-free by the summer of 2040!
JEANNE:	There is more we could say about Rebecca; we simply chose to let that part about Dr. West go.
JOHN:	You can't bully me. I see the way, now. You won't shut me up.
JEANNE:	But, it is not at all personal. We happen to disagree. Your alarmist predictions just don't resonate with most people, John. Most people, John, worry about jobs. And don't try to throw me out of *your* house. I'm going outside to make some phone calls. (JEANNE *exits.*)
JOHN:	Tell me, why do you do it?
FRANK:	Do what?
JOHN:	For money? For greed? It doesn't matter; we are going to charge for the damage done by fossil fuel.
FRANK:	Come, come, no one disagrees with you, any more. Most people know global warming is happening, and that most probably human beings are at least partly to blame. The Arctic ice as your ice woman points out is melting. I'm on your side, John.
JOHN:	My side! My god. I thought it was the stink of the compost heap, but it's you, standing shoulder to shoulder with me.
FRANK:	We both understand the world is changing, changing in unprecedented ways, to use some of your fancy language; for you it looks like catastrophe. For me it's a chance, challenge, innovation. I'm an entrepreneur. We can move food producing areas around, if we have to.
JOHN:	Are you mad? Listen to what you are saying. You are going to move the entire Midwest farther north? Where? To Greenland? To grow corn?

FRANK:	We can seed clouds. Dump iron shavings into the ocean. Do other stuff, too. Geo-engineering is a brand new field…
JOHN:	Geo-engineering is magical thinking…
FRANK:	Enormous profits to be made. We exploit and fix, that's what we do. Because, there's a wealth of energy right under the home land; right under the sea, and we can get it, now, for the first time in human history, just when we need it the most for production, for growth, for millions of good paying jobs. Natural gas is abundant.
JOHN:	Unburned natural gas leaking into the atmosphere is twenty-three times better at trapping heat than CO_2.
FRANK:	That so?
JOHN:	Fracking could have worse effects than burning coal. Tar sands is the dirtiest oil there is. There is no good fossil fuel. It's got to be left in the earth.
FRANK:	Well, well. That's news to me.
JOHN:	You'll understand once you and your kind have to pay the true cost of the damage you do.
FRANK:	Come, come, we all realize fossil fuel reserves are limited; they won't last forever, nothing does. By the time we've burned the last barrel of oil, used that last piece of clean coal, gotten that natural gas out of the ground, and we will do these things, it is not in human nature to stop, when have we ever turned back, when the fossil fuel age is finally over, by then, we will have learned how to fuel ourselves on something else. Till then, I, for one, am going to enjoy every last burst…
JOHN:	You're a lunk head; there are tens of thousands of lunk heads like you, with enormous financial power, greedy bullies, who willfully distort the facts, but there are millions more people waking up. We can fix this and we will. Your energy stock will be rendered worthless; there will be no more free ride for destroying the earth.
FRANK:	Well said. That will never happen, but I admire your passion.
JOHN:	As long as I live I will defy the lies, the destructive desires of people like you.
FRANK:	I'm going out to shoot something. What will you do?
JOHN:	Prepare a funeral oration for a frog. Go kill. Just, please, don't slam the door.

(JOHN *exits.* FRANK, *too, but with no door slam.*)

(ANNIE *enters ringing a ritual bell;* UNCLE *carries in Sniffley's body in a hand-made box.* JOHN *joins the funeral procession; they arrive at a clearing in the woods.* UNCLE *places the small box on the ground.*

Then REBECCA *joins the group, coming from her walk.* ANNIE *removes her hat and stares at her father until he does the same.)*

ANNIE: Sniffley came when I called. Sniffley ate from my hand. Sniffley liked oatmeal cookies into which instead of raisins I would bake some flies. Sniffley listened. This is a quality of soul most rare in humans. Sniffley looked out at the universe with a clear gaze. He wanted nothing more than to be. This is what I learned from Sniffley: I was seen and I was heard. I was. I am. Sniffley was. He/she/me/birl/Sniffley-boy-girl, the world is far more precious for you lived. Those who knew Sniffley, I would now like each to say a few words.

(Silence)

JOHN: What struck me most about Sniffley, despite his deformity, which meant that every time he jumped he nearly fell on his face, was how utterly dignified he was.

REBECCA: I shall miss his frog song, morning and night; I shall miss his croaks.

UNCLE: I shall be brief. I have said it before and I shall say it again: where is Sniffley, now? In that slim slice of air that surrounds the earth, our atmosphere, no thicker from space than tissue paper. We are breathing him in. Sniffley is now of us; we are of him. So, it goes, in death we unite. We are no more alone. We become. Enough. Being is.

(During ANNIE's *song,* FRANK *enters and stands outside the group, observing.)*

ANNIE: I should now like to close with a song:
(Sings)
Sniffley was
And the world was, too
The most decent frog
Most beautiful place
We knew
Sniffley rose
And the world rose, too
Out of H$_2$O. Ocean
River, lake, pond, womb
Give form
Sniffley asked
For nothing at all
He cocked his head
Listened, Dreamt, felt, caught bugs

	Thought some
	Sniffley was
	A hop, a croak, a fall,
	Nothing of him does remain
	Life surrounding
	(The last line is repeated twice more, with JOHN, UNCLE *and* REBECCA *joining in.)*
ALL:	Life surrounding
	Life surrounding
UNCLE:	We shall retire to the funeral pyre.
	*(*JOHN *hugs* ANNIE *and they follow* UNCLE *off.* FRANK *stands in front of* REBECCA.*)*
FRANK:	Well, well.
REBECCA:	Well, well?
FRANK:	I mean a funeral for a flippin frog. You know what, I almost cried.
REBECCA:	Me, too.
FRANK:	'Sniffley was.' It was nicer than mine will be.
REBECCA:	Mine, too.
FRANK:	So, why can't we get along?
REBECCA:	You ask me that?
FRANK:	I do.
REBECCA:	Let me count the ways…
FRANK:	Look, a lot of this is just business; we can put business aside.
REBECCA:	You're out to ruin my career and John's, through me.
FRANK:	We're human first.
REBECCA:	Not for long.
FRANK:	You're young. You'll be fine.
REBECCA:	How human will you and I be when we're fighting for water to drink, food to eat; when the refugees from the rising oceans appear here, desperate, wanting our shelter, willing to stop at nothing?
FRANK:	That's a grim prognosis all right.
REBECCA:	What do you *think* is going to happen?
FRANK:	You are a passionate woman all right, you attract passionate men.
REBECCA:	You should stop this nonsense. You want to ruin me; now you come on to me. That is a truly insane feedback loop.
FRANK:	You like danger. Danger appeals to you.
REBECCA:	Money and power, is that all you care about?
FRANK:	What else is there? *(He grabs her arm, sexually, roughly)* Should I care about you, Rebecca?
REBECCA:	You do care about me, though, don't you Frank?
	(He lets her go.)

FRANK:	You're a little minx, all right. I'm standing in line, right behind Annie who is right behind her father, when you are done with them. There's time.
REBECCA:	Tell me something, please, what do you say to future generations?
FRANK:	I'll be dead and gone.
REBECCA:	Put with all your lucre into your grave like some Pharaoh.
FRANK:	That's right. After I'm dead, I'll be dead. That's all there is to that.
REBECCA:	It's a failure of imagination on your part.
FRANK:	That's the trouble with people like you, over-active imaginations and scare tactics.
REBECCA:	Are we really so very strange? You and I, I mean, 'people like you' we both say as if we were looking at another species. What has happened to the human race? Have we split in half? Are there now people like you and people like me, and have we nothing anymore holding us together except animosity, a sort of burning mutual hatred that replaces fellow-feeling. How did it come to this, Frank?
	(Silence)
FRANK:	People like you make me want to fuck you, Rebecca. I'd like to fuck you until you lie limp, your neck loose, head thrown back as if you were dead, covered in sweat. If I can't fuck you in private, if you are some sort of feminist bitch with work to do, standards and all the rest, then, I will fuck you big time, on the big screen, for the thrill of seeing you squirm. I want to fuck you because you are standing in my way. I want to take you down. And I will. You can watch with that stunned look on your face because your kind, 'people like you' have no defense against us.
REBECCA:	We have truth.
FRANK:	Truth! What is that?
REBECCA:	John and I will hold a major press conference.
FRANK:	I just wouldn't do that, if I were you.
	(REBECCA *goes toward the house and* FRANK *goes toward the hill.*)
	(JEANNE *exits the house.*)
JEANNE:	Are you leaving, dear?
REBECCA:	No.
JEANNE:	Dear me. Why would you want to destroy John?
REBECCA:	I would never harm John.
JEANNE:	Well, then, I think, perhaps, you might actually wish to absent yourself. Adding in all the trouble with Dr. West, forging his research and *the rest*, it is really…

REBECCA:	And if I do go?
JEANNE:	Then, no one will ever know. You have my word. I will tear up my press release. John is my brother, after all. Father demanded loyalty from us, to family. John will even be able to give his press conference; I'll be mum. All you have to do is leave this house. We'll put this rancor behind us once and for all.
	(REBECCA *walks by her into the house.*)
	(*Sound of drumming.* ANNIE *sits alone on the hill, drumming.* FRANK *approaches.*)
FRANK:	Hey, kiddo.
ANNIE:	Hey.
FRANK:	What you doing up here?
ANNIE:	Watching.
FRANK:	Watching what?
ANNIE:	Out
FRANK:	Out?
ANNIE:	Stars come out.
FRANK:	Good place to watch.
ANNIE:	Best.
FRANK:	You all by yourself? Alone, in this beautiful place?
ANNIE:	Yep. (*She looks around*) All Alone. No one else.
FRANK:	That was some funeral.
	(*Silence*)
FRANK:	I never thought much before about frogs.
ANNIE:	I guess.
FRANK:	You made that little guy seem real.
ANNIE:	He was.
FRANK:	I didn't know you have such a great voice.
ANNIE:	Thanks.
FRANK:	I mean it, and the words, well, you've got talent.
ANNIE:	Are you a scout from that TV show?
FRANK:	(*Laughs*) I wish. I'd sign you right up.
ANNIE:	What do you do, Uncle Frank?
FRANK:	Oh, lots of stuff.
ANNIE:	Like what?
FRANK:	Like, basically, I consult.
ANNIE:	Consult?
FRANK:	Yeah, I, well, someone has a problem; they feel they are being misunderstood. I help them figure out how to explain, clearly and simply, what they are actually doing.
ANNIE:	Did you come up here to consult?

FRANK:	Not exactly. I work with companies, mainly. Look, there, there's the dipper; it just came out behind the clouds.
ANNIE:	Yep.
FRANK:	You know the sky?
ANNIE:	Somewhat.
FRANK:	Show me. *(He moves closer to her.)*
ANNIE:	*(She looks around, again)* It's different in every season. Night by night. There's the bear.
FRANK:	Where?
ANNIE:	There. *(She points)* See. Big paws.
FRANK:	Hmmm. Yep. Yes, I see.
ANNIE:	Sometimes you can see the Pleiades from here.
FRANK:	The what?
ANNIE:	They were sisters; they hid among the stars to get away from the hunter.
FRANK:	No kidding.
ANNIE:	Nope. They turned into doves. They're up there somewhere, twinkling.
FRANK:	Hey, the bear is gone.
ANNIE:	Clouds coming in.
FRANK:	You're very pretty; you know that.
ANNIE:	I'm not.
FRANK:	You are. Fresh. Like this land. Untouched. You are beautiful just like this place.
ANNIE:	I don't care.
FRANK:	What do you care about?
ANNIE:	I care about this hill.
FRANK:	I care about it, too. You're sitting on top of a fortune, you and your Auntie Jeanne.
ANNIE:	You want the money, too.
FRANK:	Of course I do. And you know what: I want you to have what I have, too. I want you to have whatever you want. What do you want, Annie, more than anything else in the whole world? *(Silence)* I'll tell you what: you want to be free to do whatever you want. You want to be treated like a grown-up, like the beautiful woman you are. *(He takes her face in his hands and then he kisses her.)*
ANNIE:	*(She pulls away)* Yuk.
FRANK:	It's a secret, Annie, between us. You're too pretty, that's all, like this place.
ANNIE:	You're disgusting.

FRANK:	No I'm not. I want what I want. Everyone does. I'm hard, Annie. Do you know what that means when a man gets hard?
ANNIE:	I hate you.
FRANK:	Oh, no, you don't. Give me your hand, I'll show you.
ANNIE:	Get off me. *(She kicks him.)*
FRANK:	Go, ahead, fight. I like that.
	(There is a huge sound, like an explosion.)
	What the fuck?
	(The early red light of dawn. FRANK *moves away from* ANNIE. ANNIE *wipes her hands on her pants and she spits on the ground. In the distance there appears the shadow of a wind turbine turning, lit by the moon, and its hum. Music of the wind.)*
UNCLE:	Stand back from that child. *(*UNCLE *has a bow and arrow.)*
ANNIE:	It works. Uncle, it works!
UNCLE:	She's as precious to me as earth herself. There will be no fracking on this land. The wind turbine sits on top of the gas.
ANNIE:	The land can't act in its own defense, so I fought you off.
UNCLE:	You believe yourself beyond restraints that bind us to the earth. *(*UNCLE *pulls an arrow from the quiver.)*
FRANK:	Will you shut up. *(*UNCLE *takes aim)* Put that thing down. *(*UNCLE *shoots the arrow.)*
UNCLE:	I missed. I can't believe I missed.
ANNIE:	It's all right, Uncle.
FRANK:	You're nuts. You're both nuts. He tried to kill me. You took over private property. You'll be charged. We'll tear that fucking windmill down.
ANNIE:	No you won't.
UNCLE:	I missed. What a chance. How could I miss?
FRANK:	You're trespassing, eco-terrorists.
UNCLE:	Frothing fossil fuel fanatic!
FRANK:	The drills are coming up here tomorrow. You've got no choice but to swallow it. You're going to have to swallow it all.
UNCLE:	Give me one more chance.
	*(*UNCLE *reloads and shoots the arrow;* JOHN *appears, out of breath.)*
	Missed, again. I cannot believe it.
JOHN:	My father was out of his mind. Jeanne held his hand and moved the pen.
FRANK:	There were two witnesses. Uncle was one.
JOHN:	*(To* UNCLE*)* Was Father competent when he resigned his will?
UNCLE:	Your father called me to stand by his bed. I was his friend.

256

JOHN:	Did Father know what he was doing? It's a simple question.
UNCLE:	Who knows if anyone knows what they do ever. Look at him…
JOHN:	You mean to say you stood right there while the will was changed? Answer me.
UNCLE:	… without a thought…
JOHN:	Was my father in his right mind?
UNCLE:	… he takes away the future from the young.
JOHN:	*(In a rage)* There will be no drilling on this land if I have to live up here forever.
ANNIE:	*(Softly)* Papa.
JOHN:	*(Too loud)* What! What is it now!?
ANNIE:	Never mind.
JOHN:	*(Softer)* What, Annie, what?
ANNIE:	No, never mind. Really.
JOHN:	Tell me, Annie. What were you going to say?
ANNIE:	You wouldn't care. I've got to go wash my mouth out.
	(ANNIE runs away.)
FRANK:	This man tried to kill me. You saw that for yourself.
UNCLE:	The greatest regret of my whole life. Twice, I missed.
JOHN:	You *(to FRANK)* are no longer welcome in my house. I'll be phoning a lawyer. There will be no drilling here; the will is under contest.
FRANK:	I think that's a mistake; you see we have a legal team comparable to none. It will cost you millions to fight.
UNCLE:	Our land, our child, he assaults them each; innocence he hates.
FRANK:	Uncle is crazed. He can't see past his nose.
JOHN:	Wash her mouth out. Are you some kind of a monster?
	(JOHN goes for him, pushing him. FRANK puts up his hands to stop JOHN.)
FRANK:	Calm down. Why would I do such a thing? Why jeopardize myself? I'm neither insane, nor self-destructive. I admit I'm fond of Annie. She's such a strange little thing. I would never harm a hair on her odd, befuddled head. Uncle's half-blind; you know that.
JOHN:	*(To UNCLE)* Did you see him clearly?
UNCLE:	Not completely.
JOHN:	What the hell does that mean?
UNCLE:	My sight is dimming or I wouldn't have missed him.
FRANK:	I'm leaving. The drills will be up here by ten.
	(REBECCA is standing outside the door; ANNIE rushes past. Door slams.)

REBECCA:	Annie, come back.
ANNIE:	For what?
REBECCA:	I'm leaving, Annie. I must go away from here. Come back for just a minute. Let me say goodbye. *(Silence; then a voice.)*
ANNIE:	Where are you going?
REBECCA:	I don't know myself. *(ANNIE comes outside.)*
ANNIE:	Take me with you.
REBECCA:	Annie, dearest, I can't.
ANNIE:	You can if you want.
REBECCA:	I've got to just vanish, like you never knew me. That would be best, if anyone asks. I was never here, at all. I never worked with your father.
ANNIE:	What does it matter? I can jump off the bridge. We can jump together.
REBECCA:	Annie, dear, what's happened? Is it Sniffley?
ANNIE:	Sniffley died but he lived life… I feel sick…
REBECCA:	Sit down. You must tell me.
ANNIE:	You're not going to go?
REBECCA:	Not right this minute, not if you need me, no. *(They sit with their arms around each other.)* *(JOHN arrives.)*
JOHN:	Did Frank hurt you, Annie?
REBECCA:	Not that. Annie? Yes. He tried with me, and then, oh, Annie. I am so, so sorry. You did nothing wrong. It wasn't your fault.
JOHN:	Annie, tell me what he did.
ANNIE:	He thinks everything belongs to him. I kicked him. Spat at him, too. Uncle's wind turbine works. Fracking is what I care about. Not that other word. We won't let them frack.
JOHN:	No, we won't. I'll sue the bastard. Let's just sit together for a while. We'll figure things out.
REBECCA:	They'll crush us with their lies. They'll crush you.
JOHN:	They've done their worst. Here we are.
REBECCA:	Then, we must do the press conference, John.
JOHN:	The press conference is just the start. I'll go on a national speaking tour. Hell, I'll chain myself to the White House fence. I'll yell until people wake up. You can chain yourself to me. I'll resign my post. I'll sue the government if I have to. That's the only rational thing left to do. We've truth on our side.
ANNIE:	Life, also, papa. Life is with us.

Epilogue

(The air is pea green, heavy and dense; a few coughs are heard. Slowly, a yellow light comes up, as if a piercing sunlight is struggling to cut through the fetid atmosphere, bringing with it greater heat. JOHN, ANNIE, REBECCA, *sit together on the hill top. Behind them is* UNCLE's *wind turbine, but the blades are not moving. Deathly still.)*

REBECCA:	Pass the water.
JOHN:	There is no more water.
REBECCA:	Uncle dug us a well.
ANNIE:	The turbine's stopped working.
JOHN:	There is no more wind.
REBECCA:	It's so hot.
JOHN:	The ocean water seeped in.
	(Silence)
ANNIE:	The salinity of the ocean water is very great.
	(Silence)
REBECCA:	The air is so thick.
JOHN:	Just sit.
REBECCA:	This is what Venus is like.
JOHN:	Not quite.
	(Silence)
JEANNE:	*(Off)* John.
	*(*JEANNE *appears, crawling.)*
JOHN:	Jeanne.
JEANNE:	I don't want to die alone.
JOHN:	Of course not.
REBECCA:	Where is Frank?
JEANNE:	Massive heart attack.
REBECCA:	Lucky Frank.
JEANNE:	I no longer loved him.
	(Silence)
JEANNE:	Where is Uncle?
REBECCA:	Uncle died serene. He left us a working well and a wind turbine …
	(Silence)
ANNIE:	Papa!
JOHN:	Yes, Annie, what?
ANNIE:	I want to wake up. Will you wake me up, please, papa, like you used to do, remember, shaking my shoulders, holding me, saying, 'Annie, wake up. You've been having a bad dream. That's all it is.

Wake up, now? I think everyone should wake up, Papa, now. Let's wake up, please. Wake up and tell me what you see.

(*Music of nature slowly begins.*)

REBECCA:	I see trees.
JOHN:	I see deer, and frogs.
ANNIE:	Sniffley's line. I hear birds.
JEANNE:	The ocean is teaming with fish.
REBECCA:	Ice.
ANNIE:	Wind. I feel wind.

(*The wind turbine begins to turn. The multifold sounds of the music of nature begin once again to intensify.*)

REBECCA: Stars.

(UNCLE *appears. Stars come out.*)

UNCLE: Attend. I have given you everything. You, too, shall be blessed by those who sparkle and shine, by those who cry in the dark.

END

Imagining the Present Future: Thoughts on *Extreme Whether*

Alexander M. Schlutz

At the heart of Karen Malpede's play *Extreme Whether* lies an act of mourning: the funeral for the six-legged frog Sniffley. Its ritual assertion of an ecological community that extends beyond the boundaries of the human speaks to the deepest concerns of the play, and it is no accident that an image of Sniffley, the entire globe enveloped in his vocal pouch, adorns the play's promotional material for its first run at the Theater for the New City in New York's East Village in 2014. The run was timed to coincide with the historic People's Climate March in New York City that fall, making a strong statement for the theater's role in building a vibrant and creative environmental movement. Given *Extreme Whether*'s main story line, one might offer windmills and solar panels; desperate scientists, seeing their research, models and predictions actively undermined by industry lobbyists; or Uncle, the play's vigorous defender of the land and an ethos of stewardship and nature-preservation as *Extreme Whether*'s most obvious representatives. Instead, the non-normative amphibian Sniffley, who has trouble with locomotion but sings with a beautiful voice for anyone who cares to listen, makes for the most powerfully symbolic character of the play. In the promotional image created by Luba Lukova, Sniffley, poised to leap and about to sing a new globe into being, looks anything but dead.

Sniffley shares a strong cross-species bond with Annie, the inquisitive teenage daughter of the climate scientist John. Annie is a self-proclaimed 'birl,' whose insights and fluid gender identity defy any rigid social constructions of the 'natural' just as much as does the non-human outsider Sniffley. When differently-abled Sniffley and Annie communicate, evolution takes another step, and man-made, socially-enforced distinctions disappear to reveal a connection that is both stranger and more wonderful than those we are usually allowed to perform on the various stages of our everyday lives. As the audience attends the funeral for Sniffley together with Annie and her family in the ritual space-time of the theater, we can recollect the bond between humans and non-human species as one that informs our identities in the world beyond the theater as well. We'd do particularly well to remember this connection, because Sniffley's mutation, if Uncle's and Annie's scientific observations are correct, is the effect of atrazine, one of the world's most widely used pesticides, commonly found in rain-, tap- and groundwater, making the frog's changed genome the effect of human-induced changes in the environment. An endocrine disruptor that can turn male frogs into females at concentrations as low as 2.5 parts per billion, atrazine is unlikely to be beneficial for humans, either, as we share 50% of our DNA with frogs. Meanwhile, Sniffley's death is by no means an isolated phenomenon: globally, 43% of amphibian species, frogs foremost among them, are currently threatened by extinction, part of the ongoing, sixth, mass-species extinction in the globe's geological history, a crisis for which the human species is centrally responsible. Habitat loss, pollution, spread of disease and invasive predator species through global trade and travel, over-exploitation and the exotic pet trade all play a role in the drastic decline of amphibians. All these factors are exacerbated by the effects of anthropogenic climate change and rising global temperatures, rapid environmental changes that far outpace the evolutionary time-spans required for species adaptation. 'Naturally,' as more and more links in the network of global biodiversity disappear, while human activity transforms the planet beyond recognition, our place in that web becomes increasingly precarious as well. The strong connection between Sniffley and Annie is by no means a fanciful theatrical ploy, but rather a fact of life in the twenty-first century.

Sniffley and Annie's story is for that reason not the sub-plot it might appear to be, but is rather emblematic of the core ecological principle of interconnectedness. As such, it is indissolubly linked to the story of John, the senior climate scientist, Rebecca, the climatologist specializing in Arctic ice, and their (family) conflict with John's twin sister Jeanne, the public relations specialist, and her predatory husband Frank, the industry lobbyist. In art as in the biosphere, all stories in their myriad differences are related and mutually influence their intertwining plots, narratives we keep separate at our peril.

Sniffley's amphibian song with its notes that blur the distinction between the spheres we call nature and culture is for that reason *also* the song of our changing climate. CO_2 and atrazine are both pollutants, products of human activity released into the environment on a vast scale without much thought about the consequences. As John and Rebecca try to combine their scientific research to make the case for drastic changes in human behavior in order to secure the future of the human as well as non-human species on the planet, Jeanne and Frank, concerned about industry profits, work to call the scientifically established causal connections and their ethical as well as social and economic consequences into question. They can manufacture the 'extreme whether' that gives the play its title because causality itself, just like the future, is never empirically present – to make it a force that might change our behavior requires acts of imagination even more than scientific data. Like the totality of the biosphere, Sniffley, though clearly present to the characters on stage, is invisible to the audience and must be envisioned in an imaginative act that may then also produce an understanding of the interconnectedness of the ecological web of which we form part.

In this way, like the globe in Sniffley's vocal pouch, the small contains the infinitely large, just as seemingly inconsequential individual human decisions can cumulatively change the face of the planet. Anthropogenic climate change and the way human activity, particularly the relentless carbon emissions of a modern, industrial civilization powered by oil, gas and coal, is rapidly warming the planet constitutes without a doubt the biggest crisis in human history, and the biggest, multi-voiced story that currently needs telling. It is one to which we urgently needed to attend as a global society decades ago, when alarming scientific research about inevitable climate change due to carbon pollution was first released. Thanks to in-depth investigative reporting by *Inside-Climate News*, first published in the fall of 2015, we now know that one of Exxon's own senior scientists warned the corporation's leadership of fossil fuels' role in climate change and their potential danger for humanity as early as 1977, long before the global public started to become aware of the problem, and more than a decade before James Hansen, the NASA scientist on whom the character of John is partially modeled, delivered his now famous climate-change report to congress in 1988. While Exxon assembled a well-funded team of scientists that would study the issue for a decade, the corporation ultimately valued its own profits higher than the planet's future and discontinued its research efforts by the end of the 1980s, to launch instead the concerted public disinformation campaign over climate science, the nefarious workings of which *Extreme Whether* puts on stage. Higher stakes and richer material for drama could hardly be imagined.

The wake-up call of Malpede's play, even though it features climate scientists who suffer the fate of Cassandra, is of course no longer a prophecy by any stretch, but is sounded rather in the face of a climate catastrophe that is already our present. The ongoing drought in California and its raging wildfires, the scorching heat across the Southwest and the devastating, thousand-year floods in West Virginia are only some of the most recent climate-change-induced weather events in the United States alone as of this writing. June 2016 has been the fourteenth consecutive hottest month on record, and half-way through the year it is already clear that 2016 will easily surpass the previous temperature record set by 2015. The confirmation of catastrophic sea ice-melt in the Arctic that shakes Rebecca and John to their core in Act II, set in 2012, has been followed since by the even more distressing scientific news of the impending disintegration of the vast West Antarctic Ice Sheet, assuming continued high carbon emissions. In that scenario, predictions for global sea-level rise by 2100 are now at a possible 20 feet, a sure death-knell for the world's coastal cities, and twice as high as predicted only three years ago. Real-life developments constantly prove even seemingly 'alarmist' scientific predictions to have been too conservative, and we are moving closer to the play's disconcerting epilogue than we might like to believe. In a chilling example of climate-adaptation, mass-graves were preemptively dug in Pakistan at the end of May 2016, ahead of a looming heat wave, to avoid repetition of a traumatic 2015, when graves could not be dug quickly enough for the bodies of the 1300 people that died in the heatwave of that year. Extreme whether, the manufacturing of doubt where none should be held, and extreme weather, the inevitable consequence of inaction in the face of anthropogenic climate change, are one and the same thing, as the pun of Malpede's title makes clear. The true tragedy is indeed the fact that a play like *Extreme Whether* is necessary at all.

The policy suggestions the play explicitly and implicitly puts forward – a carbon tax, a concerted push toward clean, renewable energy, the protection of eco-systems around the world from the destructive practices of extractive industries – are far from radical and would in a sane world have long been implemented. In a world like ours, the one we see reflected in *Extreme Whether*, however, taking steps toward them requires no less than a miracle. Uncle, the symbolic representative of a spirit of nature conservation, a traditional land ethic and of a concept of nature as ecological community rather than as resource to be exploited, begins the play in a wheelchair. When John fails to make his case for climate action in a rigged televised debate during the run-up to the 2004 election, Uncle miraculously regains the use of his legs, to work tirelessly for a clean-energy revolution on the family-owned land for the rest of the play. Such a symbolic 'uprising' of a grassroots environmental spirit, paralyzed, one might say, since Ronald Reagan had the solar panels installed by Jimmy Carter removed from the roof of the White House in 1980, aligns *Extreme Whether* with activist positions like that of Naomi Klein. In her 2014 book on climate change, *This Changes Everything: Capitalism and the Climate*, Klein takes her cue from a paper by geophysicist Brad Werner, 'Is Earth fucked? Dynamical futility of global environmental management and possibilities for sustainability via direct action activism,' where Werner identifies civic resistance as our only remaining hope to prevent utter catastrophe (Klein 2014: 449–50). Klein counts on the combined people power of grassroots movements across the globe, already arising in the 'sacrifice zones' where the hidden costs of modern life are not so hidden, to wrestle power away from the fossil fuel industry and to transform global civilization just in time before the clock strikes midnight. In this context, Uncle's regaining the use of his legs is also a meta-narrative moment in the play: since scientists like John have not been able to effectively communicate the urgency of the current environmental situation to the general public, due among other things to the rhetorical limitations of scientific discourse and the ill-suited formats of the mainstream media for informed discussion, the theater and the communities it can shape in the encounter of performance becomes an important forum to spark the communal, imaginative transformations we so desperately need. To take on that role, *Extreme Whether* suggests politically and socially conscious theater will need to get up from its wheelchair and learn to walk again.

We should not hope for too much, however, even from a miracle. The effect of 25 years of business as usual, open denial of climate reality and failed international climate negotiations means that we have already lost the planet we once knew. The climatic 'sweet spot' of more or less stable global temperatures for the past ten thousand years that made the development of human civilization and its technological progress possible in the first place is now a thing of the past, a fundamental change in the truest sense of the word, brought about by our, sometimes real, sometimes willful blindness to the effects of our own collective actions. Consequently, the concepts of nature conservation and preservation and the ethics of stewardship, derived from a Christian concept of the human species as the caretakers of a planet entrusted to us by a creator deity, much as they work to counteract an unrestrained exploitation of natural resources, are no longer sufficient to guide us through the present future we have already created. The beautiful, flower-encircled pond that Uncle and Annie create like a miniature nature preserve, where endangered species can find a place to survive, and the pristine family estate onto which the play's Prologue opens up, where nature just as much as childhood memories can be preserved in a refuge from the destructive influences of modernity, are crucial imaginative spaces that remind us of our deepest needs, but they are not places to which we can return. Set in motion by past actions we cannot undo, climate change already forces plant and animal species to migrate out of areas set aside for their conservation, and invasive species jump any protective boundaries we might erect around such asylums, while contaminated rain-, surface- and groundwater, together with genetically modified organisms on the move, will inevitably make their way to any conceivable retreat. There can be no doubt that a new-found humility, a retrieval of ecological thought in which '[w]e sensed our place in the grand design: to marvel at the large and small, the sky, the mountain and the honey bee, the plant beneath our feet' as Uncle recalls it in his lyrical speech by the pond in Act I, will be essential to our survival. We can, however, no longer hope to 'step lightly, not to leave a mark of where we'd walked,' since the planet now bears humanity's un-erasable footprint everywhere, from the atmosphere down to the plastic-saturated plankton in the world's oceans, the chemical make-up of our soil and rivers and the animals and plants that live in and on them, as well as the very DNA of the plant and animal species we have consciously modified according to our own designs. Even Uncle's wisdom will not be enough to guide us through our uncharted and to a large extent unchartable future, a future that will belong to his younger companion Annie.

Hope may paradoxically lie in the play's deepest moment of despair, when, at the beginning of Act II, John seems ready to give up on the modern scientific project and its powers of prediction altogether 'because all of the systems we have studied so carefully over the years, all our graphs and the charts, our satellites, the models, observations, the theories no longer reflect anything but a world that has vanished on our watch.' 'We must stop putting ourselves at the center of the universe, as if what we knew mattered, as if we could figure things out,' John concludes, and brings the project of western modernity, begun in earnest with the scientific revolution in seventeenth-century Europe, effectively full circle by voicing precisely the ancient skeptical position that the modern, scientific project was meant to overcome. Maybe it is time to unlearn a few things, even as we continue to draw on our collective ingenuity to bring about a global sustainability revolution that may yet keep utter and complete future climate catastrophe at bay. Crucially, that process of unlearning will entail revisiting and remaking our ideas of community and of home, of the beautiful and the natural, so they become capacious and flexible enough to embrace the hybrid, the new, the changed and the unpredictable. We also share in common with frogs and amphibians our capacity for metamorphosis, and we will need to embrace that essential human capacity whole-heartedly as we move forward in a less and less stable world. 'We transform. We molt. No moment is ever too late,' Uncle asserts and suggests that this is the message John should have shared with his television audience. To truly drive that point home, however, John would have required a theatrical stage, where such transformations can be made palpable and rendered present in the miraculous community between actors and audience. For this reason, Sniffley's funeral and its promise of rebirth forms the beating heart of the play.

We participate in it both to mourn the loss of a world we cannot retrieve and to imagine an affective ecological community in which we can preserve our home and humanity precisely because we give up on the idea that the form it will take must be a reflection of our limited understanding. With enough imaginative energy at our disposal, we may yet evolve as a species and change enough to embrace the beauty in Sniffley's hybrid song and to hear in it the promise of the globe's future.

Reference

Klein, N. (2014), *This Changes Everything: Capitalism vs The Climate*, NY: Simon & Schuster.

Afterword: A Feminist Theater

Cindy Rosenthal

I will never forget the visceral impact of *The Beekeeper's Daughter* when I saw it for the first time in February 1995. I was nine-months pregnant with my second daughter, Adin, and I went into labor the next morning. Returning now to the play, which I saw in a new production directed by Karen Malpede in May 2016, *The Beekeeper's Daughter* strikes me as a particularly apt launching pad for this important and timely anthology of plays – gutsy, tangled, sensual and lyrical. Quintessential of Malpede's theater art, *The Beekeeper's Daughter* reflects the intense cataclysms, the delicate harmonies, the grotesque atrocities and the desperate hopes and dreams of the last decade of the twentieth century and the first decade of the twenty-first.

Malpede wrote these plays during what some scholars and critics describe as a period of 'postfeminism,' where *'feminist futures*?' – to cite the title of Elaine Aston's and Geraldine Harris's anthology (2007) – are in question. There is no question, however, given the contemporary rape culture and the devastating global refugee crisis that rages on as I write in 2017, that women – privileged or not – continue to be targeted with horrific outcomes. Malpede's work provides a lively critique of the world we live in; her plays are representative of a feminist theater we need now, more than ever.

Each of the four plays in this volume interlaces blood and guts and miracles and wonder associated with the pain and fear of birth, of miscarriages – combined with the shock and awe and grief that accompanies monumental loss and death. Malpede peoples the worlds of her plays with a diverse spectrum of humanity that lives and dies in vibrantly etched, magical-realist landscapes. Expectations are exploded and barriers based on constructs of and assumptions about gender, geography, culture, age, religion and education are dissolved, broken, erased. We come face to face with wounded bodies and psyches at war that strive to survive and build lives together in the tumult of modern-day war zones.

In *The Beekeeper's Daughter* three women struggle with post-traumatic stress disorder brought on by very different traumatic experiences. Ultimately, they transform and heal each other, a witchy trio on an unnamed Adriatic island. The beekeeper, aptly named Sybil Blaze, is tortured by visions of the death of her daughter; her niece, Rachel Deming-Blaze, an American human-rights worker, is enraged by her mother's suicide and resents her father – both were renowned poets who had an open and tumultuous marriage. Rachel brings with her to the island Admira Ismic, a brutalized, pregnant Bosnian Muslim refugee. The women serve (against their wills?) as the muses for Rachel's father, Robert Blaze, and his current lover, Jamie Knox, a young American male critic/Dionysian-figure, also in residence on the island.

The seeds of high drama – bordering on melodrama – are planted in the (at first) clandestine coupling of the daughter with her father's lover. This is but one instance of women 'acting out' in the play. Following Lynda Hart and Peggy Phelan in their interrogations of feminist performances (1993), Malpede's dramaturgy allows for shifts in the play's temporal and spatial frames. With these shifts, the women's narratives in the play cut away from 'reality,' resisting and disrupting the patriarchal order/system – and so it goes, on the island. Ultimately, what looks like the beekeeper's 'madness' is translated 'into divinity' (Hart 1993: 2). Dionysian rituals and revels morph and Malpede's spectators witness the communion of two of the wounded women when an intimate, non-realistic space is created for the beekeeper and the refugee to share their difficult stories.

In 1994, I published an essay about the world premiere of Malpede's *Kassandra*, a theatrical re-visioning of Christa Wolf's powerful novel (1983), which centered on the prophetess of Greek mythology. Since that time I've recognized Cassandra-like figures in many of Malpede's plays – the beekeeper is one, foretelling of love, birth and tragedy – on and off the island.

The indelible, irrepressible language of *Prophecy* is explicitly explored by Malpede in her play of that title, the second in this volume. Consuming sexual desires are aroused and war-wounds re-opened in scenes that break out of their mundane settings – a Manhattan apartment, a college rehearsal room. Suddenly and movingly, the play moves into the terrain of Greek tragedy as Malpede weaves verse from *Antigone* into her play, essayed by undergraduate actors who struggle to master Sophocles' difficult, beautiful language with near-violent results. Scenes in the rehearsal room are followed by scenes from the marriage of Sarah Golden, the acting teacher and her husband, Alan, who directs an international relief organization. Their marital crisis is of Biblical proportions – remember Sarah, the infertile wife of Abraham? And Alan, like Abraham, wants a child. Scenes in the apartment are interrupted by scenes between Alan and his lover, Hala Jabar, a Lebanese-Palestinian rights worker with whom he has a daughter. The daughter, Mariam, arrives from Beirut, and may or may not be a terrorist. 'The Greeks are too much' warns the smarmy Dean Muffler at the college. Not true for Malpede, who suggests a *parados*-type setting used in classical theater for the contemporary scenes with snappy dialogue that she sets in 2006. These are spliced together with numerous flashbacks, including those of Sarah and a young lover from the Vietnam War era, who happens to strongly resemble Sarah's most gifted student, Jeremy Thrasher, an Iraq War veteran (the same actor plays both these roles). Other double casting Malpede prescribes throws spatial and temporal cohesion into further question – these realms continually fracture and re-knit in *Prophecy*. The play ends with the suicide of the young veteran – a plot twist mirroring a persistent, tragic reality for veterans today, multiplied by many thousands each year. A recent study (July 7, 2016) reveals that 20 US veterans commit suicide every day. Malpede weaves together verses of her own with a choral lament for 'Man' from Sophocles' *Antigone*, a moving testimony and tribute, spoken by the Latina girlfriend of the veteran at the end of *Prophecy*.

Another Life is a tragic fantasy about twenty-first-century torture and terrorism. Malpede's starting point for the play is September 11, 2001, in the modernist downtown loft-living room of a 'mogul,' as Malpede describes him. Indeed, it would be hard to imagine an anthology like Malpede's without a '9/11 play.' The nightmare scenario of that blue-skied Tuesday morning initially unfolds through the mind's eye of the mogul, Handel. Handel pours forth his coming of age story – and it's not a pretty or an easy one. This epic monologue, a kind of 'aria,' is the springboard for George Bartenieff's tour-de-force performance as an icy-evil, global capitalist, sexual deviate, devil incarnate – Dick Cheney and yes, Donald Trump come to mind. This is not realism, magical realism nor melodrama. Malpede is not building a bridge between the real and the political via the poetical. In *Another Life* Malpede establishes, via Handel, a new and different level of detachment in a character. Handel's opening monologue bears a strong resemblance to Beckett's work, reflecting the isolation at the heart of Beckett's novels (*Molloy, Malone Dies*) and some of his more fragmentary prose works (*Worstward Ho*). Although Handel lacks the sweetness and the clownishness and the vaudevillian quality of Didi and Gogo in *Waiting for Godot* and the occasional warmth and wit in the repartee between Clov and Hamm in *Endgame* – this is definitely a character embroiled in a sadistic and masochistic endgame. The harsh grotesquerie of the torturers and the extreme powerlessness of the tortured in this play veer into Theater of the Absurd. With *Another Life* Malpede takes spectators on a truly harrowing roller-coaster ride – experimenting with a theatrical style that sometimes evokes postmodernism in a play stuffed with extremely difficult content. The issues at the heart of the play continue to be sickeningly relevant; abuse and torture continue in US prisons and globally. As of late summer 2016, even with fifteen newly released prisoners, there are still 61 detainees at Guantanamo, some of whom have been held without charges of a crime or a trial for over a decade.

George Bartenieff, Malpede's life partner and the co-founder and co-artistic director of Theater Three Collaborative serves as a powerful muse and creative force field for Malpede; he performed in productions of all the works in this volume. Malpede's female characters are power-houses of strength and complexity, one and all, but Bartenieff's performances in the plays propel the stories forward with distinctive grit and grace; the lyrical poetry meshed with the incisive political edge of Malpede's plays is often at the center of his nuanced character work. Bartenieff – a true national treasure – has a resume filled with over six decades (!) of achievements on mainstream stages and screens as well as on the fringes of the avant-garde; trademarks of his acting work are soulful passion, gentle humor, sharp intelligence and tragic depth.

In some ways, *Extreme Whether* is as much a love letter to Bartenieff as it is a fable and a cautionary tale and a manifesto about the imminent dangers and catastrophic fallout of climate change. Bartenieff's character is infinitely lovable and quirky, a kind of spicy, wise and wizened leprechaun, the best friend of and most devoted advocate for an intersex teenager named Annie, who cares passionately about the environment and specifically for a pet frog. *Extreme Whether* reflects the spirit and agenda of Jill Dolan's manifesto on

'Feminist performance and utopia' (2007): 'I still need to believe it's possible to change the world' declares Dolan (212). In the last-ditch efforts of Rebecca, the female climatologist in *Extreme Whether*, who fights the hard fight for truth against corporate and governmental greed and corruption, in the all-species-rights fervor of the teenager and the old man, there is continued hope – and there is love. This, the final work in Malpede's anthology of plays, speaks volumes about her commitment to continue to experiment artistically and her ongoing passion for environmental political work. She and Bartenieff have created a productive, collective laboratory that melds deep research on climate change with community building. Through symposia, workshops and talk-backs they've facilitated in conjunction with *Extreme Whether*, natural and social scientists, humanitarians and artists, teachers and young people have come together in multiple venues and contexts – in performance spaces, on the street at mass protests and at academic and political conferences to 'speak with insight about their work and its social and political context' as Dolan puts it (2007: 216). And the plays, especially *Extreme Whether*, seem to reflect the beliefs of the theologians Dolan cites – Martin Buber, 'who sees utopian possibility in "fantasy pictures" that infiltrate the real as a "wish" for the future of human community,' and Abraham Joshua Heschel, who advocates for seeing 'through the lens of "radical amazement."' In Dolin's words: 'We must describe what it feels like to experience the potential for transformation during those magical moments in the theatre' (2007: 215–16).

Malpede's plays give us a lot to think and argue about – the women at the center are lovers, fighters and transgressors. They talk back; they are very brave, wicked-smart and on a mission. They endure.

Attention must be paid to Malpede's stories – rich with voices and bodies in action – humans joining forces in efforts to save the planet, creating, experimenting, collaborating. What better humans to learn from, to listen to and to watch as we move forward into the third decade of the twenty-first century!

References

Aston, Elaine and Harris, Geraldine (2007), 'Feminist futures and the possibilities of "we"', in E. Aston and G. Harris (eds), *Feminist Futures? Theatre, Performance, Theory*, London: Palgrave Macmillan, pp. 1–16.

Dolan, Jill (2007), 'Feminist performance and utopia', in E. Aston and S. E. Case (eds), *Staging International Feminisms*, London: Palgrave Macmillan, pp. 212–21.

BBC (2016), 'Guantanamo Bay: US in largest detainee transfer under Obama', BBC.com, 16 August, http://www.bbc.com/news/world-us-canada-37090851. Accessed 19 August 2016.

Hart, Lynda (1993), 'Introduction', in L. Hart and P. Phelan (eds), *Acting Out: Feminist Performances*, Ann Arbor: University of Michigan Press, pp. 1–12.

Philipps, Dave (2016), 'Suicide rate among veterans has risen sharply since 2001', *The New York Times*, 7 July, https://mobile.nytimes.com/2016/07/08/us/suicide-rate-among-veterans-has-risen-sharply-since-2001.html. Accessed 19 August 2016.

Notes on Contributors

Marvin Carlson is the Sidney E. Cohn Professor of Theatre, Comparative Literature and Middle Eastern Studies at the Graduate Center of the City University of New York. He has received an honorary doctorate from the University of Athens, the ATHE Career Achievement Award, the ASTR Distinguished Scholarship Award, the George Jean Nathan Award for Dramatic Criticism and the Calloway Prize for writing in theater. He is the author of 23 books, the most recent of which is *Shattering Hamlet's Mirror* (University of Michigan Press, 2016).

Christen Clifford is a feminist performance artist, curator, mother, professor and writer. She lectures about performance art, rape culture and contemporary feminisms at The New School. Her work has been written about in *Art in America, The New York Times* and the *Huffington Post*. She lives in Queens and online @cd_clifford.

Rebecca Gordon teaches in the philosophy department and at the Leo T. McCarthy Center for Public Service and the Common Good at the University of San Francisco. Her books include *Mainstreaming Torture: Ethical Approaches in the Post-9/11 United States* (Oxford University Press, 2014), *American Nuremberg: The Officials Who Should Stand Trial for Post 9/11 War Crimes* (Hot Books, 2016) and *Letters From Nicaragua* (Spinsters Ink, 1986). Prior to her academic life, Rebecca spent a few decades working in a variety of national and international movements for peace and justice: for women's liberation and LGBT rights; in solidarity with the struggles of poor people in Central America; the anti-apartheid movement in the United States and South Africa; and movements opposing US wars in Iraq and Afghanistan.

Karen Malpede is a playwright and co-founder of Theater Three Collaborative. She is author of *A Monster Has Stolen the Sun and Other Plays* (Marlboro Press, 1987), editor of *Acts of War: Iraq & Afghanistan in Seven Plays* (Northwestern University Press, 2011) and three books of theater history. Her plays, fiction and essays have appeared in numerous anthologies, *The Kenyon Review, TriQuarterly, Confrontations, Torture Magazine* and elsewhere. She teaches theater and environmental justice at John Jay College, City University of New York.

Najla Said is an author, actress, playwright and activist. She is author of the memoir *Looking for Palestine: Growing Up Confused in an Arab-American Family* (Riverhead Books, 2014) and the one-woman play *Palestine*.

Alexander M. Schlutz is associate professor of English at John Jay College and the CUNY Graduate Center. He works mainly on British and German Romanticism and the relationship between literature and ecology. He is associate editor of the journal *Essays in Romanticism* and coordinates John Jay's Sustainability and Environmental Justice program.

Cindy Rosenthal is professor of drama and dance at Hofstra University, and a performer and director. She has authored essays in *TDR, Theatre Survey, Women: A Cultural Review* and the *New York Times* as well as a monograph, *Ellen Stewart Presents: Fifty Years of La MaMa Experimental Theatre*. She recently co-edited *The Sixties, Center Stage* with James Harding (University of Michigan Press, 2017) and *The Modern American Drama: Playwriting in the US: 2000–2009* with Julia Listengarten.

Part V

Part V

Production Photographs

Beatriz Tiche Schiller and Ari Mintz

Figure 1: Di Zhu as Admira Ismic in the June 2016 production. Still from video by Kurt Brumgarde.

Figure 2: P.J. Brennan as Jamie Knox and George Bartenieff as Robert Blaze in the 2016 production of *The Beekeeper's Daughter* © Beatriz Schiller.

Figure 3: Robert (George Bartenieff) with the baby, 2016. © Beatriz Schiller.

Figure 4: Najla Said as Rachel and Evangeline Johns as Sybil, 2016. © Beatriz Schiller.

Figure 5: P.J. Brennan as Jamie Knox, 2016. © Beatriz Schiller.

Figure 6: Lee Nagrin as the Beekeeper, Sybille Blaze, and Christen Clifford as Admira Ismic, 1995 production of *The Beekeeper's Daughter*. © Beatriz Schiller.

Prophecy, 2010

Figure 7: Kathleen Chalfant as Sarah, Najla Said as Miranda Cruz and Brendan Donaldson as Jeremy, 2010. © Ari Mintz.

Figure 8: George Bartenieff as Alan Golden and Kathleen Chalfant as Sarah Golden, 2010. © Ari Mintz.

Figure 9: Brendan Donaldson as Jeremy Thrasher, Kathleen Chalfant as Sarah Golden, George Bartenieff as Alan Golden, Najla Said as Mariam Jabar, 2010. © Ari Mintz.

Figure 10: Najla Said as Mariam Jabar and George Bartenieff as her father, Alan Golden. © Ari Mintz.

Figure 11: Peter Francis James as Dean Charles Muffler and Kathleen Chalfant as Sarah Golden. © Ari Mintz.

286

Figure 12: Brendan Donaldson as Jeremy Thrasher and Najla Said as Mariam Jabar. © Ari Mintz.

Another Life, 2013

Figure 13: George Bartenieff as Handel and Christen Clifford as Tess. © Beatriz Schiller.

Figure 14: George Bartenieff as Handel and Di Zhu as his daughter, Lucia. © Beatriz Schiller.

Figure 15: Christen Clifford as Tess and Abbas Noori Abbood as Abdul. © Beatriz Schiller.

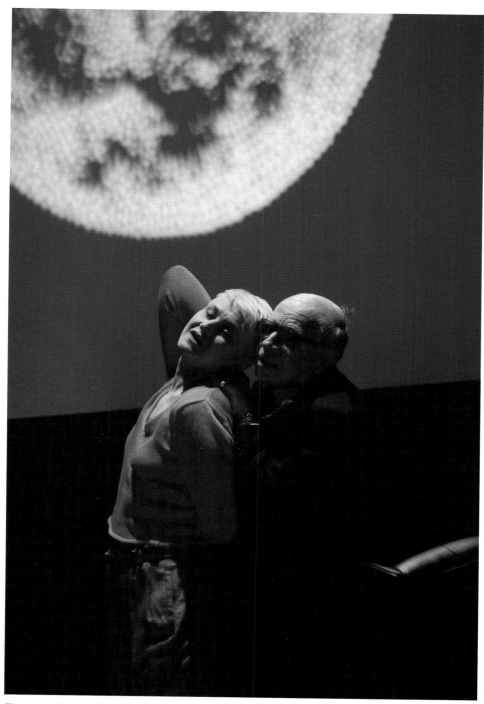

Figure 16: Christen Clifford as Tess and George Bartenieff as Handel. © Beatriz Schiller.

Figure 17: Abbas Noori Abbood as Abdul, George Bartenieff as Handel © Beatriz Schiller.

Figure 18: Di Zhu as Lucia, Abraham Makaney as Geoff's ghost and Alex Tavis as David Abbas. © Beatriz Schiller.

Figure 19: Di Zhu as Lucia, Alex Tavis as Frank
© Beatriz Schiller.

Figure 20: Di Zhu as Lucia and Alex Tavis as
David Abbas. © Beatriz Schiller.

Figure 21: Abbass Noori Abbood as Abdul, Christen Clifford as Tess, George Bartenieff as Handel © Beatriz Schiller.

Figure 22: Di Zhu as Lucia, testifying before Congress. © Beatriz Schiller.

Figure 23: George Bartenieff as Uncle and Kathleen Purcell as Annie. © Beatriz Schiller.

Figure 24: George Bartenieff as Uncle, Di Zhu as Rebecca, Ellen Fiske as Jeanne, Jeff McCarthy as John, and Kathleen Purcell as Annie. © Beatriz Schiller.

Figure 25: George Bartenieff, Uncle, Kathleen Purcell, Annie. © Beatriz Schiller.

Figure 26: Alex Tavis as Frank, Kathleen Purcell as Annie and George Bartenieff as Uncle. © Beatriz Schiller.

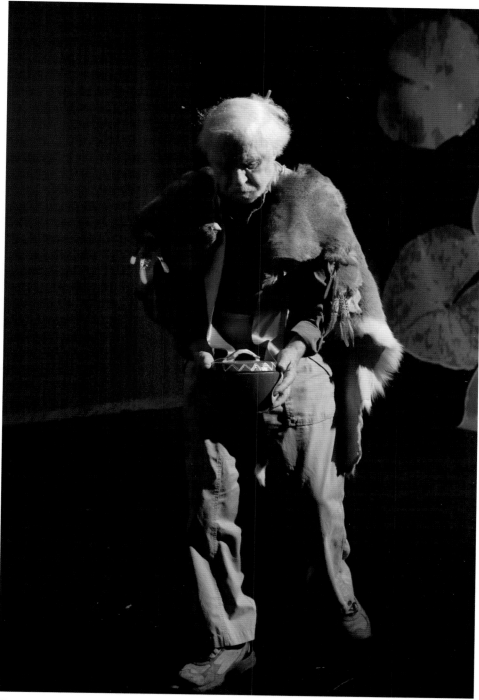

Figure 27: George Bartenieff as Uncle, carrying Sniffley's coffin after the frog's funeral. © Beatriz Schiller.

Figure 28: Di Zhu as Rebecca, Kathleen Purcell as Annie and Jeff McCarthy as John. © Beatriz Schiller.

Figure 29: Epilogue: Di Zhu as Rebecca, Jeff McCarthy as John, Kathleen Purcell as Annie, Ellen Fiske as Jeanne and George Bartenieff as Uncle. © Beatriz Schiller.